CW01283091

THE TREMELOES

Even The Bad Times Are Good!

PETER CHECKSFIELD

Copyright © 2023 Peter Checksfield
All rights reserved.

The editorial arrangement, analysis, and professional commentary are subject to this copyright notice. No portion of this book may be copied, retransmitted, reposted, duplicated, or otherwise used without the express written approval of the author, except by reviewers who may quote brief excerpts in connection with a review. All images are used in accordance with Fair Use copyright laws.

FOR ALAN & DAVE

CONTENTS

Page 1   - Introduction
Page 2   - THE TREMILOS [1958-1961]
Page 10   - BRIAN POOLE AND THE TREMELOES [1962-1966]
Page 72   - BRIAN POOLE - SOLO
Page 90   - THE TREMELOES [1966 - 1976]
Page 206 - DAVE, RICK, ALAN, CHIP - SOLO
Page 229 - THE TREMELOES [1978 - 2023]
Page 292 - The Tremeloes member's timeline
Page 298 - TV & Film Appearances
Page 313 - BBC Radio Performances
Page 317 - UK Discography
Page 322 - Song Index
Page 329 - Bibliography & Websites
Page 332 - About the author

INTRODUCTION & ACKNOWLEDGEMENTS

As one of the most historically important and musically thrilling bands of the '60s and '70s, the prospect of writing a book on The Tremeloes was an exciting one. It was also a daunting one, with many sources online, in magazines and on sleeve notes both inaccurate and contradictory. Fortunately, help has been on hand. My sincere thanks and gratitude go to former Tremeloes Rick Westwood, Brian Poole, Aaron Woolley, John Berry and Philip Wright, as well as Jeff Christie, William 'Junior' Campbell, Alan Lovell and Tony Hazzard. I never had the opportunity to ask Len 'Chip' Hawkes any questions directly, but he did answer a few queries via Carol Hawkes online, so a big thank you to them too. Thanks also to Joe Gillingham for the CDs!

As well as the above sources, I'd like to thank the following people, for the photos, memorabilia and information: Bert Van Breda, Bren Goodwin, Jack Marsh, Rebecca Xibalba, Dawn Thompson, Noreen Rolph, Paul Trondl, Linda Knight, John Truman, Frank Connor, Scott Awcock, Tony Rees, Chris Bergner, Alan Dunbar, Hans Dieter, Haydn Jones, Geoff Coles, Chris Cornwell, Adam Smith, Valerie Slater, Ashley Wood, William McGregor, Michael Vogel, Grant Purcell, Kev Hunter, Hans Dieter Fickeisen, Jim McAlwane, Chris Cornwell, Trevor Cajiao and John Beecher. An extra thank you to Dick Stoll, whose knowledge and diligence has been second to none.

I've used numerous sources, both online and in print for archive interviews. These are listed near the back of the book, but my thanks to all the original interviewers and interviewees. If I've overlooked crediting any sources for anything used in this book, do not hesitate to contact me so that I can rectify it for future print-runs.

All opinions / reviews are my own, and may not always reflect the views of the musicians involved!

Last, and definitely not least, I couldn't have written this without the love, patience and support of my better half Heather.

Peter Checksfield (November 2023)

www.peterchecksfield.com

PART 1:

THE TREMILOS

(1958 - 1961)

It all started with Buddy Holly. More specifically, Buddy Holly and The Crickets' UK Tour in March 1958. Mike Pender of The Searchers cites the performance at Liverpool Philharmonic Hall on the 17th as the birth date of the whole Mersey Beat scene, while Mick Jagger eagerly watched the show at Woolwich Granada on the 14th, taking particular note of a song called 'Not Fade Away'. And so it was for the future Tremeloes, at a nearby show on the 13th March.

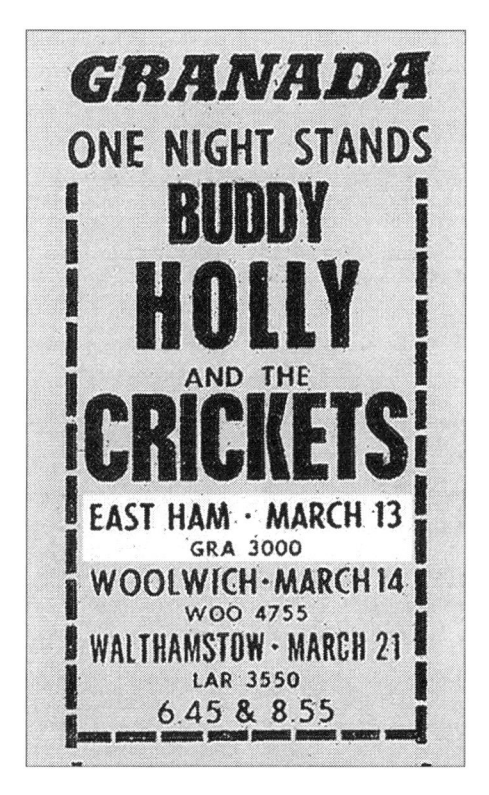

GRANADA
ONE NIGHT STANDS
BUDDY HOLLY AND THE CRICKETS
EAST HAM · MARCH 13
GRA 3000
WOOLWICH · MARCH 14
WOO 4755
WALTHAMSTOW · MARCH 21
LAR 3550
6.45 & 8.55

Brian Poole: "Yes, we saw them at East Ham Granada in '58. We went by bus and while waiting for it, Alan Blakley said to me, 'We have decided. You are going to be front man in the band!'. 'What shall we call it?' I said, and we all laughed."

They lived in Dagenham, Essex, about 15 miles from London. Brian [Brian Edwin Poole, b. 2nd November 1941] and Alan [Alan David Blakley, b. 7th April 1942], as well as the group's other co-founder Alan Howard [Alan Henry Howard, b. 17th October 1941], had met at school.

Brian: "Alan Blakley and Alan Howard had arrived at our school, Park Modern Secondary, from another Barking school to sit their O levels. Rugby was the school game, and we had two lessons per week of it. When I used to ask Alan Blakley how we first met, he would always explain 'It wasn't much of a meeting really - just my nose on the end of your elbow and then nothing for a few seconds'. Alan and I were to become best friends and were very close until he sadly died in 1996, leaving me with the memories of our dreams and aspirations from our teens till now."

Already passionate about music, one night they stumbled upon the person who inspired a whole generation to play their first painful chords on a guitar.

Alan Howard, Alan Blakley, Brian Poole, Dave Munden, Graham Scott.
(© Brian Poole)

Brian: "Portable radios were all the rage and you could listen to Bill Haley, early Buddy Holly and many others on stations like Radio Luxembourg. One night after watching 'Sputnik' go across the sky for the first time Alan and I went by bus to a place called the 'Cellar Jazz Club' in Ilford Essex. Being underage, we were not allowed into the club, but once the show had started we would 'bunk in' and hide under the stairs where we would watch the Monty Sunshine Band, the Chris Barber Band and many other traditional jazz bands. On one occasion we watched as, during the band's break, Lonnie Donegan the banjo player, and a couple of musicians played the music known as Skiffle. Of course we went straight home and decided to acquire guitars by hook or by crook. Maybe we could play this great music we were hearing both live and on Luxembourg with just guitars and a tea chest bass."

Their first attempts at both acquiring and playing guitars were less than successful...

Brian: "Alan Blakley decided we should try and make guitars in our school woodwork class but this was spectacularly unsuccessful and gave us many a laugh over the years. Feeling sorry for us, our dads decided to buy us our first guitars. We had little idea of chords, so if we couldn't get the noise we wanted we would retune the strings to suit our needs."

Still, they persevered, with Brian and the two Alans getting together with a couple of other local lads along the way, Dave Munden [David Charles Munden, b. 2nd December 1943] and Graham Scott [b. 1940].

(© Brian Poole)

Dave: "I kind of started right from the very beginning with Brian Poole and Alan Blakley, one of my old friends, because we all come from Dagenham in Essex and I was always keen and liked singing, and I was in the school-choir. I loved the Everly Brothers and Buddy Holly and I used to meet up with Brian Poole and Alan Blakley at local parties. They both had blonde acoustic guitars and they used to sing and I thought of pulling all the birds… I used to join in singing with them at parties you know. Alan Blakley came round to my house one day and said 'Do you want to come round Dave, we are having a practice?'I said 'Yeah, OK', and so I went round there and started. Alan had a drum kit (which belonged to his brother Mike), and taught me how to time keep on the drums, so I sat down and tried to keep time. I was singing along with them anyway. And we kind of started up along with a guy called Graham Scott on the lead guitar, from the local area, same area, and so we started getting a few little gigs in youth clubs and so forth."

And the band's name?

Brian: "There were some bands that had already started playing live in Essex, such as Mike Berry and the Outlaws and Johnny Kidd and the Pirates. We watched and learned adding drums to our line up. So with Alan Howard, Alan Blakley, Dave Munden and Graham Scott (another school friend) we had started a band, a conglomeration of Lonnie, Johnny Kidd, Buddy and Bill, called The Tremilos. Yes, it was spelt like that!"

Dave: "We didn't actually have a name then. We got our name actually from; you plugged into one of the amplifiers and it gave you the vibrato sound on the guitars. It was what we called a tremelo unit. And that's where we got the name of the band from."

And this, for the next few years, was the first proper line-up of 'The Tremilos': **Brian Poole** (lead vocals & occasional guitar), **Alan Blakley** (vocals & rhythm guitar), **Alan Howard** (bass), **Graham Scott** (lead guitar), **Dave Munden** (vocals & drums).

Brian: "We worked hard at our singing and we could harmonise our three parts to anything. At Christmas, we used to say 'You name the carol!', and we could sing it in three-part harmony."

Building a reputation as an entertaining and hard-working band, The Tremilos quickly progressed to playing for American servicemen at airbases.

Dave: "We prided ourselves in the way we performed songs by Buddy Holly and The Crickets, and we were really thrilled one evening when one of the American airmen said that he had seen Buddy Holly and The Crickets play live and that we sounded just like them. It made our day to hear that."

They also gained a residency further afield, forcing them to choose whether or not to turn professional.

Brian: "I was waiting for the 'A' level results that would determine whether or not I'd be able to go to the University of Leeds. Suddenly, the group were offered a 21-week season at the Calypso Ballroom at Butlin's in Ayr. My dad said I should do whatever would make me happy, so it was an easy decision to go to Butlin's with The Tremilos, playing four hours a night."

That same year, 1961, they also gained a highly prestigious regular spot on BBC radio's 'Saturday Club' - even before they released any records.

Brian: "Two girls from Southend wrote into the programme, asking if we could appear. We also sent in a tape, and the show's producer, Jimmy Grant, remembered that he'd seen us play somewhere, maybe when we'd auditioned for Butlin's at the Astor

Club."

The Tremilos came to Decca in an unexpected way - albeit, working as independents, and initially only as a vocal trio of Brian Poole, Alan Blakley and Dave Munden.

Brian: "My optician, John Cremin, was a big fan of ours. John got in touch with another of his clients, Mike Smith, a Decca A&R man who lived in Ilford. Mike came to see us, told me to get rid of the glasses, and gave us a studio test."

As well as giving them ample opportunity to learn the recording process, they got to sing on records by some of the big stars of the day.

Brian: "Tommy Steele, Jimmy Savile on 'Ahab The Arab', Gary US Bonds, Johnny Burnette, Lyn Cornell, who was an ex-Vernons girl... and if you listen to the Vernons Girls' cover of 'The Locomotion', it sounds like blokes singing behind the lead vocal. Well, that was us too! We also backed auditionees who came in, either us, or it was The Kestrels, with Roger Greenaway, Roger Cook and Tony Burrows. Even when we were famous, we were helping out on sessions for Jack Good and Shel Talmy, because it paid really well."

They even went on the road with a few of them.

Brian: "We had the choice, which we were pleased with, to go on a tour with Clyde McPhatter, Gary US Bonds and Johnny Burnette. We bought new suits for this, only to be told by the promoter that we would only be back stage! We still hadn't recorded anything ourselves, but were getting very popular live."

Much has been written about Brian Poole and The Tremeloes' Decca audition, and the fact that they were signed instead of The Beatles. However, it wasn't quite as memorable for the group themselves.

Brian: "This was sometime in 1961, not, as it says in lots of books, New Year's Day, when The Beatles did their audition for Decca. I think we had been in Decca before, so this doesn't stick in my memory much. We played all our Rock and Roll songs plus some vocal harmony songs, don't know which ones, but mostly loud and fast. Lots of bands came to these auditions, and we and The Beatles were only two of them, but it essentially came down to us or them. And I've got to say, The Beatles did a very bad audition. If I had been Decca, I would have chosen us as well!"

Dave: "I don't know why we got the audition and they didn't. Maybe we were a bit well-rehearsed and perhaps they came down from Liverpool looking a bit scruffy. We looked like nice boys and all that, so I guess they must've liked us and we got the deal."

Nevertheless, the band became both friends and fans of The Beatles.

Dave: "We played three times with them 'live'. For me, they were the best group. There'll never be anybody that comes up to them. They just had a certain magic. They weren't maybe the best players in the world, individually, but they gelled fantastically. They were something really different then. I think they taught a lot of bands a lot about music. They were brilliant."

Finally getting signed as a full group, there was one final thing to do: Change the name from The Tremilos (sometimes The Tremelos) to Brian Poole and The Tremeloes - a spelling that started with a Decca miss-pressing but somehow stayed.

Dave: "The record company thought it was a good idea. So, that's what happened. That's what it became. We didn't really worry too much about it."

PART 2:

BRIAN POOLE AND THE TREMELOES

(1962 - 1966)

April 1962: SINGLE [Decca F 11455]

TWIST LITTLE SISTER (Beveridge / Oakman)
LOST LOVE (Leonard / Darvell)

Brian: "The first one of our own was 'Twist Little Sister' in April 1962, written by Johnny Beveridge and Peter Oakman of Joe Brown's Bruvvers. There were two previous singles that never came out. 'Twist Little Sister' got a lot of airplay, particularly from Jimmy Savile and on the BBC's 'Saturday Club', but it took three more singles to get us into the British charts."

Still with a line-up of Brian Poole, Alan Blakley, Alan Howard, Dave Munden and Graham Scott, **'Twist Little Sister'** is a catchy enough Pop-Rocker with a pounding drum intro, but the thin-sounding guitar and dance-orientated lyrics make it very much of its time. Still, it was enough to get them on the country's top music TV show 'Thank Your Lucky Stars' - and this was at a time when The Beatles were still without a contract! It also inspired at least two Spanish covers, Mike Ríos Con Los Relámpagos' 'Twist Del Mundo' in 1962 and Los Sonor's 'El Twist Del Mundo' the following year. The B-side, **'Lost Love'**, is a mid-tempo Pop song, similar to the kind of thing that Cliff Richard often specialised in during this period.

September 1962: SINGLE [Decca F 11515]

BLUE (Favilla / Renis / Altman / Mogol)
THAT AIN'T RIGHT (Hirst)

Co-written and originally recorded by Italian singer Tony Renis, '**Blue**' is an excellent Rock-A-Ballad, something one can easily imagine Elvis Presley performing in a movie such as 'Blue Hawaii'. It is enhanced by some low register Hank Marvin-styled guitar, as well as some subtle organ almost buried in the mix - played by Graham Scott and Alan Blakley, respectively - no session players were needed for Brian Poole and The Tremeloes' records, a probable reason they got signed.

Brian: "Decca liked the fact that we didn't need session men - we *were* session men!"

The song features the band wearing their Buddy Holly and The Crickets influences on their sleeves, complete with 'Peggy Sue'-inspired drumming. Indeed, Brian's vocal sounds not unlike Holly-influenced Bobby Vee (a 1963 Italian single incidentally instead featured 'A Very Good Year For Girls' as the flip-side). This turned out to be the final single with this line-up.

Graham: "I think I left The Tremeloes at the end of 1962, and I played lead guitar on 'Twist Little Sister'/'Lost Love' and 'Blue'/'That Ain't Right'."

Dave: "During this period our lead guitarist became unhappy with playing with The Tremeloes. We had seen another lead guitarist in a local band who we thought was really good, his name was Rick Westwood [aka 'Ricky West', Richard Charles Westwood, b. 7th May 1943]. Alan Blakley decided that we wanted Rick to play in our band, so in his own inimitable way Alan persuaded Rick to join and Graham Scott joined the band that Rick had left. We definitely got the best part of the deal!"

Rick Westwood: "After a few years with (my first band) 'Joe and The Teens' I was then asked to join a band named 'Tony Rivers and The Castaways'. I was with that band for just a few months when I was asked by The Tremeloes to join them. The Tremeloes were the most famous band in our area and it was great to be asked. I went on my motorbike to the first rehearsal at Alan Blakley's house. On the way back home I was stopped because I was speeding but I did not care because I was so excited about joining a famous band!"

Joe and The Teens, circa 1959.

Rick: "Members are from the left: Mervyn Greenaway, Rick Westwood, Joe Wheal, John Haylock and Mick Clarke. We never had a bass player in those days but after watching Mike Berry and The Outlaws with Chas Hodges on bass, Mick bought a bass.

January 1963: SINGLE [Decca F 11567]

A VERY GOOD YEAR FOR GIRLS (Tobias / Ballard)
MEET ME WHERE WE USED TO MEET (Powers / Wayne / Jordan)

Rick: "I was not in the band when they recorded 'Blue' or 'That Ain't Right' but it must have been very shortly after. I was on 'A Very Good Year For Girls' and 'Meet Me Where We Used To Meet'."

And so was born the line-up that would make them famous - the band who played on every Brian Poole and The Tremeloes hit record:

Brian Poole (lead vocals), **Alan Blakley** (vocals, rhythm guitar & keyboards), **Alan Howard** (bass), **Dave Munden** (vocals & drums), **Rick Westwood** (vocals & lead guitar).

First recorded by Vic Dana in 1962 and later covered by Johnny Tillotson, '**A Very Good Year For Girls**' is a rather slight Pop song, despite an imaginative arrangement complete with a bass guitar intro. With its syncopated drumming and organ solo, the dramatic '**Meet Me Where We Used To Meet**' is vastly superior - indeed, it was considered strong enough to include on Brian Poole and The Tremeloes' 2nd album - 'Twist and Shout' - some eight months later.

March 1963: SINGLE [Decca F 11616]

Italian picture sleeve

KEEP ON DANCING (Poole / Blakeley / Smith)
RUN BACK HOME (Mitchell / Jeeves)

Written by Brian and Alan B. along with producer Mike Smith, '**Keep On Dancing**', with its fast guitar licks, piano and "Ooh gaga" backing vocals, made a commercial-sounding A-side, albeit one that perhaps sounded a little dated compared to the Beat sounds then emerging from Liverpool. As well as a return appearance on 'Thank Your Lucky Stars', the song was performed in the Columbia Pictures movie 'Just For Fun', alongside such luminaries as Bobby Vee, The Crickets, Freddy Cannon, The Tornados and The Springfields - making them arguably the first British Beat group to appear in a movie (an early incarnation of the Dave Clark Five were in a couple of low budget movies in 1961, but as they were just an anonymous back-up group to a couple of crooners, they don't really count!). The B-side '**Run Back Home**' is an interesting R&B-tinged Pop-Rocker that sounds more aligned to the Mersey groups, and perhaps would've made a better A-side (in the USA, 'Blue' was issued as the B-side instead).

Appearing in 'Just For Fun', and the soundtrack album of the same name.

'Just For Fun' movie poster.

May 1963: ALBUM [Ace Of Clubs ACL 1146]
BIG BIG HITS OF '62

Album cover:

DON'T EVER CHANGE • ROSES ARE RED • SPEEDY GONZALES • STRANGER ON THE SHORE • THINGS • BREAKING UP IS HARD TO DO • SHEILA • HALFWAY TO PARADISE • RETURN TO SENDER • LET'S TWIST AGAIN • LOCO-MOTION • HEY BABY • LET'S DANCE • DANCE WITH THE GUITAR MAN • DREAM BABY • TWISTING THE NIGHT AWAY • I CAN'T STOP LOVING YOU • SWISS MAID • IT MIGHT AS WELL RAIN UNTIL SEPTEMBER • GINNY COME LATELY • SHERRY • DEVIL WOMAN

BIG BIG HITS OF '62
*** THE 22 TOP TUNES OF 1962 ***

MEDLEY #1: SPEEDY GONZALES (Kaye / Hill / Lee) - **(DANCE WITH THE) GUITAR MAN** (Hazlewood / Eddy) - **SHEILA** (Roe) - **LET'S DANCE** (Lee)
MEDLEY #2: TWISTIN' THE NIGHT AWAY (Cooke) - **THINGS** (Darin) - **RETURN TO SENDER** (Blackwell / Scott)
MEDLEY #3: GINNY COME LATELY (Udell / Geld) - **STRANGER ON THE SHORE** (Bilk / Mellin) - **DREAM BABY (HOW LONG MUST I DREAM)** (Walker) - **THE SWISS MAID** (Miller)
MEDLEY #4: HEY BABY (Channel / Cobb) - **SHERRY** (Gaudio) - **IT MIGHT AS WELL RAIN UNTIL SEPTEMBER** (Goffin / King) - **I CAN'T STOP LOVING YOU** (Gibson)
MEDLEY #5: DON'T EVER CHANGE (Goffin / King) - **LET'S TWIST AGAIN** (Da Vinci / Apell / Mann) - **LOCO-MOTION** (King / Goffin)
MEDLEY #6: BREAKING UP IS HARD TO DO (Sedaka / Greenfield) - **DEVIL WOMAN** (Robbins) - **ROSES ARE RED (MY LOVE)** (Evans / Byron) - **HALFWAY TO PARADISE** (Goffin / King)

Despite not yet having a hit of their own, the group were commissioned to cut an album for Decca's budget subsidiary label Ace of Clubs. Recorded around December 1962 and featuring half a dozen medleys of the previous year's hit records, it was one of the first albums of its kind (pre-dating 'Stars on 45' by almost two decades), and is a great insight into the band's wide repertoire and versatility. The album remained affectionately remembered by all involved, even half a century later.

Dave: "The first album we ever recorded in 1963, which was called 'Big Big Hits of '62', was a mixture of all the biggest hits from 1962. It was released on a very small label called Ace of Clubs. It wasn't a hit, but I liked it."

'**Speedy Gonzales**' kicks things off, first recorded by David Dante in February 1961 but a hit for Pat Boone in May 1962, and it is immediately apparent just how good the band already are at this point in their career. This quickly segues into Duane Eddy and The Rebelettes' '**(Dance With The) Guitar Man**', showcasing both Rick's guitar playing and some wonderful harmonies, then all too quickly it's into Tommy Roe's Buddy Holly-inspired classic '**Sheila**', with Chris Montez's '**Let's Dance**' closing things, complete with the well-known organ part.

Rick: "I was on all of 'Big Big Hits of 62', enjoyed working out all the segues between songs. As a note, the 1st album I ever bought was Duane Eddy's 'Especially For You'."

Sam Cooke's **'Twistin' The Night Away'** is particularly noteworthy for Alan Howard's solid bass playing and an album highlight, followed by Bobby Darin's **'Things'**, and finishing with Elvis Presley's unbeatable **'Return To Sender'**.

Brian Hyland's lovely ballad **'Ginny Come Lately'**, is followed by another highlight, with a Shadows-like cover of Acker Bilk's instrumental **'Stranger On The Shore'**, while Roy Orbison's **'Dream Baby (How Long Must I Dream)'** makes one wish it was in complete form, as does Del Shannon's **'The Swiss Maid'** (a song first recorded by the song's composer Roger Miller as 'Fair Swiss Maiden' in October 1961), with some prominent organ and impressive yodelling.

The harmonica on Bruce Channel's **'Hey Baby'** when played by Delbert McClinton (someone who Brian, Alan and Dave had recorded with) was a major inspiration to John Lennon, but here it is substituted for an organ, while **'Sherry'** was the first but wouldn't be the last time the group covered The 4 Seasons. Carole King's **'It Might As Well Rain Until September'** is one of the album's weaker tracks, compensated by a fine version of Ray Charles' (via Don Gibson) **'I Can't Stop Loving You'**.

The Crickets' **'Don't Ever Change'** was also recorded by The Beatles for BBC radio - which makes it a good opportunity to compare the two groups: The Beatles put more of their own stamp on it, but The Tremeloes recapture the sound and spirit of the original with greater accuracy. What a shame it's just an excerpt though! Chubby Checker's **'Let's Twist Again'** must've filled dance floors when performed in the clubs of London and Essex, while Little Eva's **'The Loco-Motion'** was also a UK hit by The Vernons Girls - a record that featured Brian, Dave and Alan B. on backing vocals.

The final medley kicks off with Neil Sedaka's **'Breaking Up Is Hard To Do'**, complete with handclaps, and is followed by a beautiful excerpt of Marty Robbins' **'Devil Woman'**, a Country & Western song (with the emphasis on Western) that it is difficult to imagine many other Beat groups getting to grips with. Bobby Vinton's **'Roses Are Red (My Love)'** is an album filler, but Tony Orlando's/Billy Fury's **'Halfway To Paradise'** makes a fine closer.

A project of this kind was never going to have the same impact in later years as The Beatles' and The Rolling Stones' debuts, but 'Big Big Hits of '62' remains a highly worthwhile album, and is just as ground-breaking in its way.

June 1963: SINGLE [Decca F 11694]

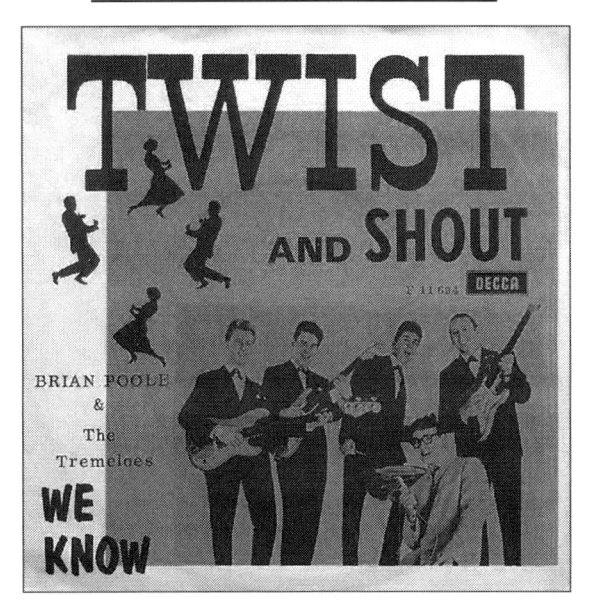

Danish picture sleeve

TWIST AND SHOUT (Russell / Medley)
WE KNOW (Hidden)

By June 1963, Liverpool had revolutionised the previously London-dominated British music scene, with a Hit Parade dominated by The Beatles, Gerry and The Pacemakers and Billy J. Kramer, and they would soon be joined by The Searchers, The Fourmost, The Mersey Beats, Cilla Black and The Swinging Blue Jeans. Brian Poole and The Tremeloes have the distinction of being the very first Beat group from the south to give these groups any real competition, long before the less experienced The Dave Clark Five, The Rolling Stones, Manfred Mann, The Kinks, and all the rest. Ironically, the song that did it was one that The Beatles had covered for their debut album 'Please Please Me', released three months earlier - though The Tremeloes very likely heard **'Twist and Shout'** via The Isley Brothers' April 1962 single (which in itself was a cover of an August 1961 release by The Top Notes) - the same as The Beatles did.

Brian: "We were doing 'Twist and Shout' on stage before we knew anybody else doing it!"

The recording session for their faster but smoother treatment was a productive one.

Brian: "Because we had such a great stage sound, all Fender and Marshall equipment, we took the PA into the studio, mic'd it up, used an up-ended table to isolate the drums, and recorded live. It only took one take for 'Twist and Shout' and only about three for 'Do You Love Me'. A few weeks later, we were at Dartford's Paget Ballroom, and a telegram arrived from Mike Smith: 'Congratulations! 40,000 sold on the first day! This looks like the one!'"

As well as appearing on 'Thank Your Lucky Stars', the song was performed on a brand new TV show - the legendary 'Ready Steady Go!'.

Brian: "We have the distinction of being on the very first 'Ready Steady Go!'. When we played 'Twist and Shout' on the rehearsal the audience was sitting, but they decided to dance on the tables, so after getting rid of the tables, for the first time the producer of the show decided to run cameras through the audience which they had to dodge. This was then adopted by many other shows over the years."

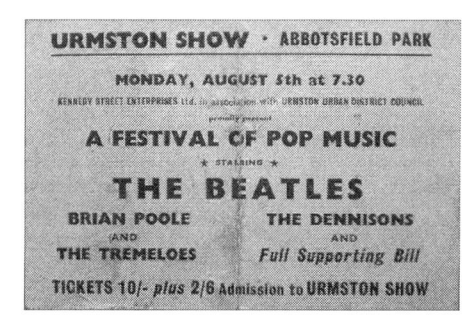

```
URMSTON SHOW · ABBOTSFIELD PARK
MONDAY, AUGUST 5th at 7.30
KENNEDY STREET ENTERPRISES Ltd. in association with URMSTON URBAN DISTRICT COUNCIL
proudly present
A FESTIVAL OF POP MUSIC
★ STARRING ★
THE BEATLES
BRIAN POOLE            THE DENNISONS
     AND                      AND
THE TREMELOES     Full Supporting Bill
TICKETS 10/- plus 2/6 Admission to URMSTON SHOW
```

The B-side, **'We Know'**, actually sounds closer to the Mersey sound than the A-side and is good enough to be a single in its own right. The end result of all this promotion was a No. 4 in the UK, No. 3 in Ireland, No. 4 in New Zealand, No. 10 in Germany and No. 38 in Belgium. A slower, more Beatles-like performance of 'Twist and Shout' from BBC radio in October 1965 is on the 'Live At The BBC 1964-67' CD, released in 2013.

September 1963: SINGLE [Decca F 11739]

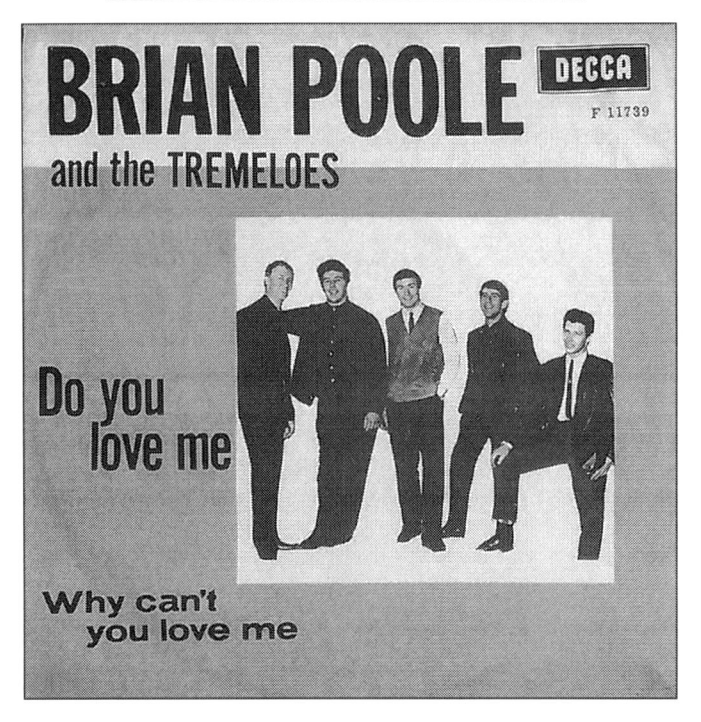

Danish picture sleeve

DO YOU LOVE ME (Gordy, Jr.)
WHY CAN'T YOU LOVE ME (Blakely)

If 'Twist and Shout' gave them initial fame, it was their driving, exciting version of '**Do You Love Me**' that really put The Tremeloes on the Pop map. There are conflicting reports of whether they first heard the song via a single purchased by a band member or on an album sent to them by Norman Petty, but they all agree that they got it from a Contours record rather than any other source.

Brian: "Some people reckon we got the song from hearing Faron's Flamingos' cover version from Liverpool, but that's bollocks. Faron knows that as well as I do, because we worked with them many times, though by then we were pretty well known because we had a regular spot on BBC radio's 'Saturday Club'. Quite a few bands were playing Contours songs and we decided

'Do You Love Me' would most likely be our next single. It was one of our biggest selling singles and is still the song that everybody gets up and moves to, even in theatres. We could not and did not try to emulate The Contours, we just put our slant on the song. When I listen to our original now it seems fast and furious, but that's how the dancing was in those years. Thanks to Berry Gordy, they have been dancing to it ever since 1963, when it sold over 1 million and gave Brian Poole and The Tremeloes longevity."

Promoted on shows like 'Lucky Stars - Summer Spin' and 'Ready Steady Go!', the record replaced The Beatles' 'She Loves You' at No. 1 in the UK charts, also reaching the top spot in Ireland and New Zealand, as well as No. 5 in Norway and No. 19 in Australia. The Dave Clark Five's rival version, released around the same time, stalled at No. 30, and The Hollies would record the song for their debut album the following January. Coincidentally, The Tremeloes were in Liverpool when it topped the charts.

Brian: "That was one of the luckiest three days of my life and the Tremeloes' lives. We used to play in Liverpool along with Gerry and the Pacemakers, a band called the Big Three, The Swinging Blue Jeans, The Merseybeats and bands like that. We were invited up there to play one time for three days and we knew our record was creeping up the charts but we didn't know The Beatles were No 1. The Beatles weren't in Liverpool at the time, but we were. In those days you got a notification if you'd got a telegram and someone said to us that we'd got one and we had to go to the Post Office to pick it up. So we went to get it and it read 'Well done lads, you've just sold over a million and something records'. We never thought we would sell six! Really. That's true, we didn't think we were a big record-selling band. So suddenly we got this telegram and we just jumped with joy. The Post Office was near, or maybe in, Lime Street station. We walked into the station and there were these great big headlines in the Liverpool paper, the Echo I think, saying 'Beatles knocked off top by London band' with a story all about it. We bought about ten papers each! It was a great time. The people of Liverpool, as usual with us, were really fantastic."

Dave: "We were on top of the charts and having a wonderful time. I bought my first car, an MGB sports car. I brought the car home and took my Mum straight out for a drive with the roof down. After playing at a gig we drove up to London to get copies of the Sunday papers just to see the name Brian Poole and The Tremeloes at No.1 in the pop charts. What a feeling."

The self-composed B-side '**Why Can't You Love Me**' has some similarities with the A-side, though the major/minor chord sequence gives it an Isley Brothers Gospel-Soul feel (not for the last time, Alan Blakley's surname was misspelt on the label, this time as 'Blakely'). The song inspired a couple of overseas covers, with Jean-Claude's 'Quand Tu Me Dis Oui' in France in 1964, and The Gisha Brothers' German release in 1965.

September 1963: ALBUM [Decca LK.4550]

TWIST AND SHOUT

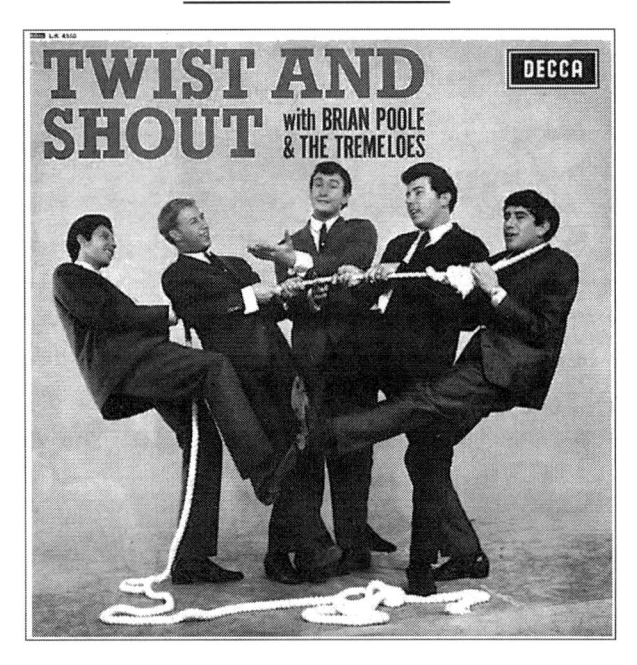

TWIST AND SHOUT (Russell / Medley)
TWENTY MILES (Mann / Lowe)
IF YOU GOTTA MAKE A FOOL OF SOMEBODY (Clark)
YOU DON'T LOVE ME ANY MORE (AND I CAN TELL) (Tady)
MEET ME WHERE WE USED TO MEET (Powers / Jordan / Wayne)
DON'T BE AFRAID LITTLE DARLIN' (Mann / Weil)
WE KNOW (Hidden)
ALLEY-OOP (Frazier)
BABY WORKOUT (Wilson / Tucker)
OVER THE MOUNTAIN, ACROSS THE SEA (Garvin)
TWIST LITTLE SISTER (Beveridge / Oakman)
DA DOO RON RON (Spector / Greenwich / Barry)
RUN BACK HOME (Mitchell / Jeeves)
SOUTH STREET (Mann / Appell)
PEANUTS (Cook)
KEEP ON DANCING (Poole / Blakeley / Smith)

Just four months after their first album, Decca issued a follow-up, this time on their main label rather than a budget subsidiary. Featuring a generous 16 songs, six of them had been previously released on singles: **'Twist and Shout'**, **'Meet Me Where We Used To Meet'**, **'We Know'**, **'Twist Little Sister'**, **'Run Back Home'** and **'Keep On Dancing'**. The other ten were all covers of American songs, from a wide variety of original sources.

For **'Twenty Miles'**, a Chubby Checker B-side from February 1963, The Tremeloes up the tempo a little, also adding marching sounds to their version. Ray Brown and The Whispers would have a big hit in their native Australia using a similar arrangement in 1965.

Rick: "The track needed a 12-string guitar and I never had one. I played the whole track including the solo on Alan's 6-string acoustic guitar then very slightly detuned the guitar and played it again alongside the 1st track giving a 12-string effect. The marching sounds on the track was Mike Smith, the producer, marching along on a huge tray of pebbles which had a mic over it."

James Ray's 1961 single **'If You Gotta Make A Fool Of Somebody'** was covered by Buddy Britten and The Regents, and, more successfully, by Freddie and The Dreamers earlier in 1963. The Tremeloes' cover retains the 3/4 'waltz' timing of previous versions, though with the addition of some fine bluesy guitar licks.

The gentle ballad **'You Don't Love Me Any More (and I Can Tell)'** was previously recorded by Rick Nelson earlier the same year, and the equally mellow **'Don't Be Afraid Little Darlin''** was issued on a February 1963 single by Steve Lawrence. Both sound a little out of step with the Beat sounds heard elsewhere, nice though they are.

A stage favourite, Hollywood Argyles **'Alley-Oop'** from 1960 was already sung in a comedy voice, but here Brian Poole ups the silliness further. The Tremeloes without Brian would record an even more outlandish version in 1968.

'Baby Workout', a February 1963 single for Jackie Wilson that was also covered by The Dovells, is a tough Rhythm 'n' Blues workout, while Johnnie and Joe's 1957 Doo-Wop classic **'Over The Mountain, Across The Sea'** probably owes more to Bobby Vinton's February 1963 single than it does to the original.

Phil Spector's Girl Group classic **'Da Doo Ron Ron (When He Walked Me Home)'**, an April 1963 single for The Crystals, was covered by The Searchers on their debut album, but The Tremeloes' version probably has the edge. Billy J. Kramer with The Dakotas would include it on their debut album before the year was out, as would The Four Pennies the following year.

A single for The Orlons in January 1963, and covered by both Johnny Cymbal and Dee Dee Sharp on albums, The Tremeloes' fun cover of **'South Street'** is another great Girl Group song, proving the group to be as adept at covering the genre as any of their Northern contemporaries.

Up until now, the only voices heard on Brian Poole and The Tremeloes' records were Brian Poole, Alan Blakley and Dave Munden, but **'Peanuts'** features the recording debut of Rick Westwood's falsetto, something that would come more to the fore in the future. The song was originally released by Little Joe and The Thrillers in July 1957, but The Tremeloes' version was probably inspired by The 4 Seasons' October 1962 album track. It was deemed good enough to be a single A-side in Brazil!

A mixed and diverse bag for sure, but 'Twist and Shout' (the album) compares favourably to much of their contemporaries' output at the time, helping cement Brian Poole and The Tremeloes' reputation as a solid, dependable band, capable of tackling a wide variety of genres.

OUT OF MY MIND (Tillotson)
ONE BROKEN HEART FOR SALE (Blackwell / Scott)
LET'S TURKEY TROT (Goffin / King)
MR. BASS MAN (Cymbal)
SANDY (Di Mucci / Brandt)

Shortly before the release of the 'Twist and Shout' album in September 1963, a couple of 12-song 'Test Pressings' were made, featuring two very different track listings:

Decca LL 3314: Twenty Miles / You Don't Love Me Anymore / South Street / Out Of My Mind / Over The Mountain, Across The Sea / Baby

Workout / Peanuts / One Broken Heart For Sale / Let's Turkey Trot / Mr. Bass Man / Don't Be Afraid Little Darlin' / Sandy

Decca LL 3364: Keep On Dancing / Twist and Shout / Do You Love Me / Alley-Oop / Da Doo Ron Ron / Swinging On A Star / South Street / Mr. Bass Man / Don't Be Afraid Little Darlin' / Why Can't You Love Me / Yakety Yak / Candy Man

Of the six songs that hadn't been released on the 'Twist and Shout' album or previous singles, 'Yakety Yak' would surface on an EP in May 1964, but the other five songs were issued exclusively on a Canadian album from 1963 (which actually predates the UK 'Twist and Shout' album), entitled 'Big Hits' (London - HT.503). Here's the full track listing:

Twenty Miles / You Don't Love Me / South Street / Out Of My Mind / Over The Mountain / Baby Workout / Peanuts / One Broken Heart For Sale / Let's Turkey Trot / Mr. Bass Man / Don't Be Afraid Little Darlin' / Sandy

A pure Country song, **'Out Of My Mind'** was a February 1963 single for Johnny Tillotson, and was quickly covered by Johnny Cymbal the following month. Beautifully sung and played, probably the *only* other Beat group who could play straight country music this good in 1963 were Liverpool's Sonny Webb and The Cascades.

Unlike many of his Rock 'n' Roll contemporaries, Elvis Presley's songs were overlooked by most of the top tier Beat groups. The Tremeloes were amongst the few exceptions, and having already tackled 'Return To Sender', they have a stab at **'One Broken Heart For Sale'**, a song that was in Elvis' latest movie 'It Happened at The World's Fair'. Their version is a tad faster but otherwise largely similar, with Brian Poole's Elvis mannerisms subtle enough not to become a parody.

Little Eva's biggest hit was 'The Loco-Motion', a song The Tremeloes had already covered, both on their album debut, and as back up for The Vernons Girls' single, but another fondly remembered hit is January 1963's **'Let's Turkey Trot'**. A song loosely based on The Cleftones' 'Little Girl of Mine' from March 1956, The Tremeloes' fine version substitutes a memorable guitar solo for the saxophone on the Little Eva original. The song was also covered by Liverpool group Ian and The Zodiacs in October 1963.

A Johnny Cymbal hit in January 1963, on his original of '**Mr. Bass Man**', the bass singer was Ronnie Bright of The Valentines, later in The Coasters; for The Tremeloes' fine cover, an Engineer/Producer steps up to the microphone - *probably* Glyn Johns - proving himself a perfect vocal foil to Brian's tenor lead.

Originally recorded by Dion in July 1962, '**Sandy**' is a fast Doo-Wop Pop-Rocker, and once again it is covered in fine style.

November 1963: SINGLE [Decca F 11771]

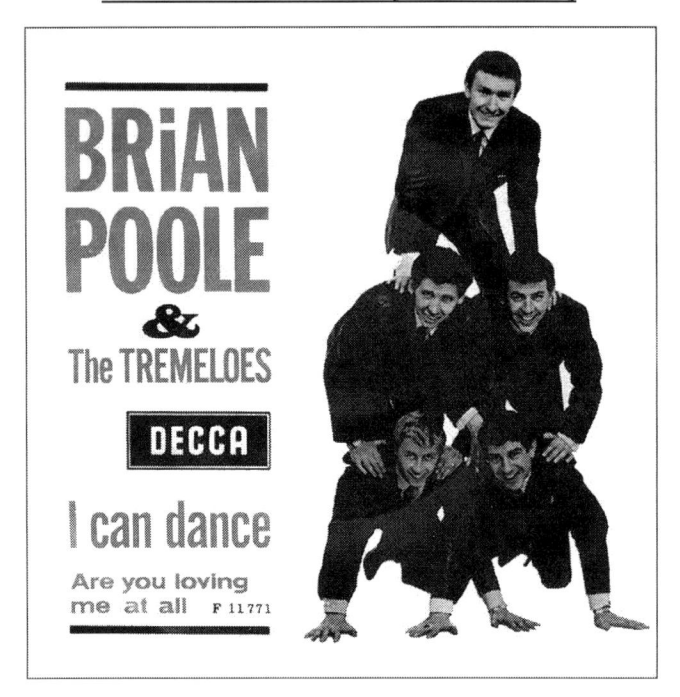

Danish picture sleeve

I CAN DANCE (Jeeves)
ARE YOU LOVING ME AT ALL (Blakeley / West)

After two smash hits, Brian Poole and The Tremeloes had a couple of choices: either come up with another song, in a similar style to the others, or try something completely different: they went for the former. The trouble is, '**I Can Dance**' is a bit *too* similar to 'Do You Love Me', and, despite rockin' even harder, has little real identity of its own. Consequently, despite major promotion on 'Ready Steady Go!', 'Thank Your Lucky Stars', 'Scene at 6.30', 'The Five O'clock Club' and 'Crackerjack', it stalled at No. 31 in the UK charts, doing slightly better at No. 24 in Australia, and failing altogether almost everywhere else. Greece decided to use it as the belated B-side to 'Twist and Shout', which in all honesty, is probably no more than it deserved.

An Alan Blakley and Rick Westwood co-write, '**Are You Loving Me At All**' is a simple but likeable mid-tempo Pop song with some nice guitar licks.

THE TREMELOES - EVEN THE BAD TIMES ARE GOOD!

January 1964: SINGLE [Decca F 11823]

Swedish picture sleeve

CANDY MAN (Ross / Neil)
I WISH I COULD DANCE (Mulhall / Edwards / Benson / Jeeves / Collier)

Originally released by Roy Orbison in July 1961, **'Candy Man'** - American slang for a drug dealer - was suggested as a suitable recording for The Tremeloes by none other than 'The Big O', himself.

Brian: "In 1964 the Tremeloes and me were on tour with the great man, and a few others in the UK. One night a few of us were sitting in the tour coach outside one of the theatres, when Orby played us a song accompanying himself on guitar. His rendition of 'Candy Man' was slower and more bluesy but he suddenly said 'Hey you can make this a dancer', and speeded it up. When we came to record 'Candy Man' it had changed from being a bluesy song, to being a fast dance song. In fact the 'Candy Man' was now a pussycat, a sweetie giver."

Rick: "It was stated that Jimmy Page played lead guitar on 'Candy Man', but he didn't. I'm sure he would've done a better job than me but I got away with it."

However, The Tremeloes were determined to give it that little something extra.

Brian: "We already had Orby's influence on 'Candy Man' but when we came to recording the drums there was a slight problem. We wanted a really dry snare drum sound, which was quite hard to get when you only had one or two tracks to record all the instruments on. Norman Petty had told us about the way a match-box was used on one or two Cricket songs, so we tried this. Dave Munden our drummer taped the match box to his knee, using one stick, a mic was carefully placed, and Bobs yer uncle - 'Candy Man' was born. To this day people still remember being hit on the head by us throwing sweets at our gigs in the '60's."

A No. 6 in the UK, No. 8 in Ireland and No. 18 in Australia, the song was performed on 'Thank Your Lucky Stars', 'Ready Steady Go!', 'Hi There! It's Rolf Harris', and a brand new show, BBC's 'Top Of The Pops'.

Brian: "They tended to use the same piece of film if your record was in the charts for a few weeks. I had a letter from someone who said that I had worn the same jacket for all this time and could he have it, because he wanted to put it in an old car of his and keep his chickens on it! Nice eh. By the way it was donated to the Victoria and Albert Museum many years ago. But a good laugh anyway."

In the USA, 'Candy Man' was coupled with 'I Can Dance', while Beat groups The Hollies (1964), Casey Jones and The Governors (1965) and Denny Seyton and The Sabres (1965) all covered it in a similar style to Brian Poole and The Tremeloes' hit.

Another song on the theme of dancing, the mid-paced rocker '**I Wish I Could Dance**' is actually more memorable than the previous *A-side* 'I Can Dance', and if it weren't for the albeit stronger 'Candy Man', it would've made a good A-side in its own right.

As well as Jimmy Page, another legendary '60s guitarist has wrongly been credited for playing on the group's records.

Rick: "The guitarist, Big Jim Sullivan stated that he played on all Brian Poole and The Tremeloes and all The Tremeloes hits… But he never did, not one. I would've loved Big Jim to have played because he was a top session guitarist along with Jimmy Page, but he didn't play on anything at all."

Prior to 1964, success in America seemed just that little bit out of reach for British artists. There were exceptions, including Lonnie Donegan with 'Rock Island Line' in 1956, Laurie London with 'He's Got the Whole World in His Hands' in 1958, The Tornados with 'Telstar' in 1962 and Frank Ifield's 'I Remember You' in 1963 - but these were largely one-hit-wonders. British Beat groups, including Brian Poole and The Tremeloes, made massive inroads around the world in 1963, but success in the USA continued to elude them; This all changed in the February of 1964, when The Beatles made three appearances on 'The Ed Sullivan Show', opening the flood gates for The Dave Clark Five, Gerry and The Pacemakers, Herman's Hermits, The Rolling Stones, Peter and Gordon, The Zombies and The Animals, who all followed in their wake. Yet, American success somehow passed Brian Poole and The Tremeloes by.

Brian: "I believe that our managers could see everyone else going off to America and thinking 'There's a big market in the rest of the world'. So we did the rest of the world, something like four world tours before 1967. We did some touring in America and had some modest chart success, but nothing massive. But we were huge in all of Europe, Australia, even Asia. We didn't have a choice, 18-20 year olds and everything was new. Decca and Walshie (Peter Walsh) arranged everything and we spent many years after that touring in all these countries. Even into my seventies, I still went to all these great places. So, definitely didn't miss the USA, went later anyway."

Dave: "What happened was, when we started having our success, we had a number one with 'Do You Love Me' in England with Brian Poole and The Tremeloes. I think this was in 1963. This was on Decca Records. We wanted to get it released in the States. The Dave Clark Five also recorded it, but they got into the bottom part of the English charts with it. We wanted it released in America and we were told by the record company 'There's no point in releasing it because The Contours have already had a hit with it, two or three years previously.' So, they wouldn't release it. After that, Dave Clark released stuff in America and was a huge success. We felt we missed out on that really."

Meanwhile, Brian Poole and The Tremeloes continued to concentrate on the rest of the world, and, as well as the tours, recording sessions, radio promotion and TV appearances, they found time to appear in another *four* movies, adding to their 1963 debut in 'Just For Fun'.

'Swinging UK' and 'UK Swings Again' were both B-feature 'shorts', filmed in colour, and taped on the same day, with 'Do You Love Me' mimed in the former and 'Someone, Someone' in the latter.

The other two movies are far more obscure: 'Africa Shakes' (which had the working title 'Shakin' Up Africa') was filmed in South Africa in the spring of 1964, and although largely unseen since, it was shown at a Johannesburg film festival as recently as 2016. At time of writing, this author has been unable to confirm which songs are performed in the movie, though 'Come On In' is pretty certain, and Rick Westwood later recalled them at least *taping* the additional songs 'Don't Cry', 'Do You Love Me' and 'Someone, Someone'.

Even more obscure is 'A Touch Of Blarney'. Filmed in Ireland towards the end of 1964, the only known surviving copy is in Brian Poole's collection, and the only available photographic evidence are some snap shots taken by fan Alan Stapleton that are on Brian Poole's official website. 'Don't Cry' was a likely inclusion, but whether any other songs were featured is long forgotten.

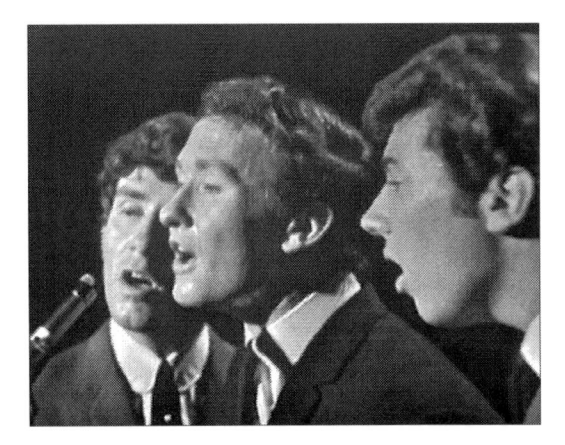

Live on 'The Liverpool Sound' TV Special, Melbourne, 1964.

THE TREMELOES - EVEN THE BAD TIMES ARE GOOD!

Brian Poole and The Tremeloes at the movies: 'Swinging UK' & 'UK Swings Again' (top), 'Africa Shakes' (middle), 'A Touch Of Blarney' (bottom).

41

May 1964: SINGLE [Decca F 11893]

Danish picture sleeve

SOMEONE, SOMEONE (Petty / Greines)
TILL THE END OF TIME (Blakeley / Poole)

After four charting singles with up-tempo material, it was time for a change of pace. They chose a largely unknown post-Holly Crickets B-side from 1959, '**Someone, Someone**'. The Tremeloes however, learnt the song from a demo, sent by Buddy Holly's producer and manager Norman Petty, whom they had met on Buddy Holly's UK tour back in 1958.

Brian: "Norman Petty said he'd stay in touch and send us some songs. He kept to his word, and one of the batches that arrived included a demo of 'Someone, Someone', with just him and his wife Vi performing it. We learned the song and put it into our set long before we recorded it."

When Norman learnt that Brian Poole and The Tremeloes planned to record it, he flew over to the UK to attend the session.

Brian: "Decca Studios at Broadhurst Gardens Hampstead were booked by Peter Walsh, and we were told to go to his offices just off of Covent Garden a couple of days before. When we arrived we were introduced to none other than Norman Petty and old friend Roy Orbison who we had toured with earlier. Norman knew of our antics in the studio, in fact, (Producer) Mike Smith of Decca sometimes used to laughingly walk out of our sessions and come back only if we promised to take it more seriously.

When the session got underway, Norman Petty insisted that this song 'Someone, Someone' had to be sung softly and with feeling. Now, we had been on tour for ages all over the world, so soft singing had kind of rasped out a little. Norman got on the piano and he and The Tremeloes succeeded in using 1 of the 2 tracks putting down a really fine backing track with vocal harmonies by Petty, Blakley, Munden and me. We found Norman to be very serious especially about 'Someone, Someone', but when he suggested to me that I lie down in the recording booth to sing the top line, the rest of The Tremeloes could hardly keep straight faces and suddenly everybody even Norman were laughing loudly. So there I was on my back, feet up, on a chair, ready to sing probably one of the best songs we had ever been graced with. Was this a good idea?

Well Al Blakley the leader of The Tremeloes and my best friend, suddenly appeared in the booth window, both thumbs up and a gigantic smile on his face. He stayed there, and in one take (it had to be because that's all I had), I completed the song. When I heard it I was very satisfied and after completing another song, 'After Awhile', we pulled Mr. Petty from the piano to the local pub, only to find he was teetotal. He sat with us throughout though and asked that we treat 'Someone, Someone' as a special track. It was released later on Decca, and just as he had said it was the song that made people realise we were not just a dance band. It has always been a song about which people will come up to me and say 'This song brought us together or kept us together through the hard times, when we were away from each other'."

Heavily promoted on 'Ready Steady Go!', 'Top Of The Pops', 'Thank Your Lucky Stars', 'Scene at 6.30', 'Open House', 'The Five O'Clock Club', 'A

Swingin' Time', 'Top Beat' and 'The Tich and Quackers Show', as well as cinema short 'UK Swings Again', the record got to No. 2 in the UK and Ireland, No. 5 in Norway and New Zealand, No. 17 in Australia, and even breached the USA Hot 100 at No. 97. A 'Saturday Club' performance is on the 'Live At The BBC 1964-67' set.

The Crickets sound is continued on the self-composed B-side **'Till The End Of Time'**, complete with 'Peggy Sue'-styled drumming and a Rick Westwood guitar solo that closely emulates The Crickets' style. Some other countries featured alternative B-sides, including 'Come On In' in South Africa, 'Why Can't You Love Me' in Greece and 'Meet Me Where We Used To Meet' in the USA.

May 1964: EP [Decca DFE 8566]

BRIAN POOLE AND THE TREMELOES

TWENTY MILES (Mann / Lowe)
COME ON IN (Conrad / Dee)
SWINGING ON A STAR (Van Heusen / Burke)
YAKETY YAK (Leiber / Stoller)

As well as the singles and the albums, Brian Poole and The Tremeloes issued two EPs in the UK - both featuring exclusive material. On this first EP, '**Twenty Miles**' had already been issued on the 'Twist and Shout' album. '**Come On In**' is another 'Twist and Shout'/'Do You Love Me' type song with dance-orientated lyrics, and is notable for appearing in the 'Africa Shakes' movie.

A Bing Crosby song from 1944 that was also revived by Dion and The Belmonts in 1960, The Tremeloes' version of '**Swinging On A Star**' is clearly based on Big Dee Irwin's 1963 hit, which featured an un-credited

Little Eva. Effectively a duet between Brian and Dave, it was a popular live number, and a highlight of the brilliant 1964 'The Liverpool Sound' Australian TV special, which surfaced on DVD in 2020. The song was released as a single A-side in The Netherlands, where it was backed by 'Come On In', and in Sweden, backed by 'Yakety Yak'.

The Coasters were a hugely popular source of material for British Beat groups, with just about everyone *except* The Tremeloes covering 'Poison Ivy' or 'Searchin''. Their cover of **'Yakety Yak'** is notable for Rick Westwood's fabulous Rock 'n' Roll guitar solo.

WALK RIGHT IN (Cannon / Woods)
[BBC Radio - Not released until 2013]
BABY BLUE (Vincent / Jones)
[BBC Radio - Not released until 2013]

Having secured a regular spot on 'Saturday Club' in 1961 before they even had a recording contract, Brian Poole and The Tremeloes probably made more appearances on BBC radio than *any* other Beat group. Sadly though, the earliest *surviving* session is from July 1964, with much of the remainder from 1965-1966, at a time when they'd passed their peak commercially.

Originally recorded by Cannon's Jug Stompers in 1930, **'Walk Right In'** was a big hit when revived by The Rooftop Singers in November 1962, and was also covered by The Kestrels the following year. The Tremeloes' 'Saturday Club' performance features superb 3-part harmonies from Brian, Alan and Dave.

'Baby Blue' is a tough Bluesy rocker, originally released by Gene Vincent and His Blue Caps in April 1958. It takes a brave man to cover it, but The Tremeloes pull it off admirably. Both songs can be found on 2013's 'Live At The BBC 1964-67' collection.

August 1964: SINGLE [Decca F 11951]

Italian picture sleeve

TWELVE STEPS TO LOVE (Kevin / Hart / Carson / Marascalco)
DON'T CRY (Blakely / Poole / Munden / Westwood / Howard)

First released by The Elektras as *'Ten* Steps To Love' in November 1961, Brian Poole and The Tremeloes eschew the slow intro, add two extra steps, and go for a full throttle Rock 'n' Roll treatment. It's an exciting record, but one that would've been more suited to 1961 than the latter half of 1964 - and despite promotion on 'Ready Steady Go!', 'Lucky Stars - Summer Spin', 'The Five O'Clock Club', 'Open House', 'The Beat Room' and 'Top Beat' - **Twelve Steps To Love**' peaked at just No. 32 in the UK, No. 84 in Australia, and failed completely just about everywhere else. A performance from BBC radio can be found on 'Live At The BBC 1964-67'.

'**Don't Cry**' is a gentle Buddy Holly-styled ballad with a syncopated drum beat, and has the distinction of being the only song credited to all five members of Brian Poole and The Tremeloes. Performed in the long-lost 'A Touch of Blarney' movie, the song was covered in Spain by Los Beta Quartet as 'No Llores Más' for a 1965 EP.

THE TREMELOES - EVEN THE BAD TIMES ARE GOOD!

November 1964: SINGLE [Decca F 12037]

Danish picture sleeve (note the alternate B-side)

THREE BELLS (Gilles / Reisfeld)
TELL ME HOW YOU CARE (Blakeley / Poole)

Changing tact again, **'Three Bells'** is a song first recorded in French by Edith Piaf and Les Compagnons De La Chanson as 'Les Trois Cloches' in 1946, and translated into English for The Melody Maids in 1948. However, despite Brian remembering Edith Piaf giving him a copy of the song in a Paris restaurant, it is closer in style to The Browns' 1959 US chart-topper. The song had been part of The Tremeloes' live set for some time, and with its very simple backing and three-part harmonies, it is beautifully played. Promoted on 'Ready Steady Go!', 'Thank Your Lucky Stars', 'Top Of The Pops', 'Pop Spot', 'Discs-A-Gogo', 'The Five O'Clock Club' and 'Crackerjack', it got the group back into the top twenty at No. 17 in the UK charts, as well as No. 29 in Australia. Two versions from BBC radio are on 2013's 'Live At The BBC 1964-67' set.

A contemporary-sounding mid-tempo song with acoustic guitar picking and organ, **'Tell Me How You Care'** features double-tracked Beatle-esque vocals by Brian, without any harmonies. The Danish release featured 'I Could Make You Love Me' (issued in the UK on their next album) as the B-side instead.

Despite a decline in record sales, the band retained their reputation as a top live draw, with an entertaining stage act, a wide repertoire, and a great sound.

Brian: "We were quite popular live and because of my great friend Jim Marshall had a big and clear sound. He took us from Fender to Marshall, even using his first ever PA system. We'd worked with the likes of Johnny Burnette, Bob Luman, Norman Petty and many others, and we were able to cover pretty much anything and everything. We had a repertoire of about a hundred more songs than most other bands of the era."

GO OVER BIG with MARSHALL

THE LATEST AND GREATEST IN AMPLIFICATION

as used by BRIAN POOLE & THE TREMELOES

* CLIFF BENNETT & THE REBEL ROUSERS
* THE NEXT FIVE
* PETERS FACES
* THE NASHVILLE TEENS
* THE YARDBIRDS
* TONY RIVERS AND THE CASTAWAYS
* THE CHEROKEES
* JIMMY ROYAL AND THE HAWKS
* EDEN KANE
* THE T-BONES
* THE HIGH NUMBERS
* THE SECOND THOUGHTS

BASS & LEAD UNIT Pressurised speaker cabinet containing 4 x 12 in. heavy duty ROLA Celestion speakers with a power output of 60 watts. — 75 gns.
Separate 50 watt amplifier unit with 4 inputs. — 60 gns.
21 ft. speaker lead, optional extra 21/-.

LEAD UNIT. Similar in design and specification to the Bass and Lead unit, but the amplifier is built to give more treble. Speaker unit 75 gns. Amplifier unit 60 gns.

P.A. UNIT. Twin column speaker units each containing 2 x 12 in. heavy duty ROLA Celestion speakers with a combined power output of 80 watts. Per Pair. 80 gns.
Separate 50 watt amplifier with 4 inputs. — 60 gns.
21 ft. speaker leads, optional extra, per pair 42/-.

FINISH. The complete range is finished impressively in black PVC with Gilt trim.

Rose-Morris SPONSORED INSTRUMENTS **SEE YOUR DEALER**

Rick: "When Jim started his amplifier factory we were the first band to go there. We used to leave our Fender amps with him so his technical boys could copy the circuitry and try to get the same sound. During the months we were going there I designed a sloping speaker cabinet. Jim didn't like this design, he preferred the straight cabinet. He said to me, 'I can't see that it will sell, but I tell you what Rick - we'll make a side-line with these cabinets and I'll send you a few quid for each one we sell'. Jim used my drawings of the cabinet and started the side-line. After many years and many millions of sales of the cabinet that I designed, I never saw a penny. There was no contract between me and Jim, just a gentleman's agreement. The biggest disappointment of my life."

February 1965: EP [Decca DFE 8610]

TIME IS ON MY SIDE

TIME IS ON MY SIDE (Meade / Norman)
SHO' MISS YOU BABY (Cooke / Lyons)
IT'S ALL RIGHT (Mayfield)
YOU DON'T OWN ME (Madara / White)

The second of two Brian Poole and The Tremeloes EPs to feature exclusive recordings, '**Time Is On My Side**' was first released as a semi-instrumental by Kai Winding with Vocal Group in November 1963, and with full lyrics by Irma Thomas in May 1964, but it will be forever associated with The Rolling Stones' September 1964 release. The Tremeloes' version - like everything on this EP, a regular in their stage act - is a little less raw, but with better harmonies, a prominent organ and busy drums. The Moody Blues issued a cover of the song the same month as The Tremeloes, and a performance from BBC radio's 'Delaney's Delight' is on 'Live At The BBC 1964-67'.

By 1965, the Mersey style groups were largely fading from view, to be superseded by rawer Rhythm 'n' Blues-inspired bands such as The Rolling Stones, The Animals, The Kinks, Manfred Mann and Them. '**Sho'**

Miss You Baby', an obscure Johnnie Morisette song from 1962, proves that Brian Poole and The Tremeloes could play in that genre as well as the best of 'em, with growled vocals, wailing harmonica and tough, fuzzy guitar. A 'Saturday Club' performance without harmonica can be found on 'Live At The BBC 1964-67'.

A much-covered Soul standard, **'It's All Right'** was first released by The Impressions in September 1963 and recorded by Cliff Bennett and The Rebel Rousers (1965), Ian and The Zodiacs (1965), The Zombies (BBC 1965, not released until 1985) and The Swinging Blues Jeans (1967, not released until 2008), amongst many others. The Tremeloes' version is as good as any of them, with subtle piano, and their usual impeccable harmonies.

First released by Lesley Gore in November 1963, and covered by Dusty Springfield in 1964, **'You Don't Own Me'** has long been regarded as a feminist anthem - even more so since Grace featuring G-Eazy's 2015 revival. Which makes Brian Poole and The Tremeloes' cover all the more remarkable. An involved Brian lead vocal, solid backing and tight harmonies make this quite possibly the definitive version - indeed, it was at one time considered for single release.

April 1965: SINGLE [Decca F 12124]

Danish picture sleeve

AFTER AWHILE (Montgomery)
YOU KNOW (Blakley / Poole)

Brian Poole and The Tremeloes had already proved themselves more than capable of tackling Country material with 'Devil Woman' and 'Out Of My Mind', and **'After Awhile'**, a Jim Reeves song from 1960 that was taped at the 'Someone, Someone' session with Norman Petty on piano, is if anything even better. Unfortunately, gentle Country-Pop was the last thing the record-buying public wanted in 1965, and with very little promotion, it failed to chart. A performance for BBC radio can be found on 'Live At The BBC 1964-67'.

A fast Pop-Rocker with unusual chord changes, and harmonies similar to those heard on the Dave Clark Five's less frantic songs, **'You Know'** contrasts very nicely with the A-side.

April 1965: ALBUM [Decca LK.4685]

IT'S ABOUT TIME

TIME IS ON MY SIDE (Meade / Norman)
SOMEONE, SOMEONE (Petty / Greines)
YOU CAN'T SIT DOWN (Clark / Upchurch / Muldrow)
I COULD MAKE YOU LOVE ME (Jones)
RAG DOLL (Gaudio / Crewe)
AFTER AWHILE (Montgomery)
CHILLS (Keller / Goffin)
TIMES HAVE CHANGED (McCoy)
HANDS OFF (Bowman / McShann)
THE UNCLE WILLIE (Colbert, Jnr.)
MICHAEL ROW THE BOAT ASHORE (Trad. / arr. Carlton)
WHAT DO YOU WANT WITH MY BABY (Shuman)
SONG OF A BROKEN HEART (Leander)
HEARD IT ALL BEFORE (Greenaway / Burrows)
WELL, WHO'S THAT (Manston)

Despite a string of singles and a couple of EPs, it had been over 18 months since their last album, as explained at the time.

Brian: "Time hasn't really been on our side during the past year! We just haven't been able to get into the recording studios, what with heavy commitments we've had touring in South Africa, Australia, New Zealand, Sweden, Denmark, France, Ireland and elsewhere."

'**Time Is On My Side**', '**Someone, Someone**' and '**After Awhile**' had been previously released. '**You Can't Sit Down**' was a 1961 instrumental hit for the Philip Upchurch Combo, but The Tremeloes' version is based on The Dovells' April 1963 vocal single, and is a good dance number that must've gone down well live.

'**I Could Make You Love Me**' is a soulful mid-tempo song written by Paul Jones. It is easy to imagine him doing this with Manfred Mann, but their loss is very much Brian Poole and The Tremeloes' gain.

The 4 Seasons' '**Rag Doll**' features Dave Munden on lead vocals - and was only recorded because Brian turned up late. He does a great job too, surpassing Frankie Valli's vocal on the original. The Fenmen (minus their former leader Bern Elliott) also covered the song in 1964.

First released by Tony Orlando in June 1962, '**Chills**' is a catchy mid-paced Pop song, and was covered by both Gerry and The Pacemakers and Bern Elliott and The Fenmen in 1963. The Tremeloes' version is just as good.

Irma Thomas' Soulful ballad '**Times Have Changed**', a September 1964 single for her, is covered in fine style, and at one was considered for single release by The Tremeloes. At the very least, it would've sounded far more contemporary than 'After Awhile', though whether or not it would've been any more successful, we will never know.

A Rhythm 'n' Blues song first recorded by Jay McShann's Orchestra featuring vocalist Priscilla Bowman in October 1955, '**Hands Off**' was covered by Denny Seyton and The Sabres in 1964, and by both Billie Davis and The Liverbirds in 1965. The Tremeloes' version is typically good British R&B, complete with harmonica and maracas. A performance from BBC radio's 'Saturday Club' is on 'Live At The BBC 1964-67'.

First released by The Daylighters as 'Oh Mom (Teach Me How To Uncle Willie)' in April 1964, The Tremeloes' version of **'The Uncle Willie'** owes more to Zoot Money's August 1964 cover, which also shares the same title. This is even wilder though, with prominent Alan Blakley organ, and both Rick Westwood and Dave Munden playing with an almost Pretty Things-style abandon. The song was performed live on 'Blue Peter, while a 'Saturday Club' version can be found on 'Live At The BBC 1964-67'.

Performing 'The Uncle Willie' on 'Blue Peter', 1965.

Just when one was starting to think they were listening to a Manfred Mann album, The Tremeloes' prove their eclecticism with **'Michael Row The Boat Ashore'**, a song that dates back to at least the mid 19th century, but was perhaps best known at the time via a 1960 revival by The Highwaymen, as well as covers by Lonnie Donegan (1961) and The Kestrels (1963). When performed on stage, it was done in a semi-comedy fashion, but here the song is played completely straight, complete with whistling.

Once in a while, a song pops up that has "HIT!" written all over it, but is, inexplicably, over-looked. Such is the case with **'What Do You Want**

With My Baby', a Mersey-styled Beat number that sounds like a lost classic on very first hearing - yet was kept in the can for almost a year prior to its release on this album. At least German group The Rattles could hear the song's potential, as they covered the song for a single shortly afterwards.

Written by Mike Leander, and recorded by obscure UK group The Chariots in 1962, '**Song Of A Broken Heart**' sounds like a bizarre amalgamation of 'Wimoweh' and 'Johnny Remember Me'. With Dave Munden again featured as the vocalist, this weird but wonderful recording deserves to be more widely known.

A 1964 single for Stevie Lewis, whom despite the name was a female vocalist who sounded not unlike Sandie Shaw, '**Heard It All Before**' is a Soulful Pop song with an unusual time-signature. It was written by two of The Kestrels, who not coincidentally shared Peter Walsh as a manager.

'**Well, Who's That**' was issued as a single by The Wilde Three the same month as Brian Poole and The Tremeloes' recording, a trio that featured Marty Wilde, his wife and former 'Vernons Girl' Joyce, and future 'Moody Blue' Justin Hayward. The Tremeloes' version rocks just as hard, albeit in a more light-hearted fashion - and apparently required 30 takes, as Brian kept inventing his own, rather dubious, lyrics! Highly professional though they were, it wasn't unusual for the band to lighten things up in the studio.

Dave: "In the early days, we never used any dope of any kind in the studio. However, we were recording some of our early hits, aided purely by a few pints of beer and our natural enthusiasm and exuberance, and we used to make a track called an 'idiot' track - featuring lots of shouting and funny voices. The record company thought that we were all stoned, but we weren't."

Two BBC recordings of 'Well, Who's That' (mis-titled as 'Who's That Knocking') are on the 'Live At The BBC 1964-67' collection.

Despite, or perhaps because, of its wide eclecticism, 'It's About Time' was the best album of Brian Poole and The Tremeloes' career, though it would also be their last. A different track listing was released for the American market, under the title 'Brian Poole Is Here!':

I Want Candy / Michael Row The Boat Ashore / You Can't Sit Down / Hands Off / Times Have Changed / Rag Doll / Well, Who's That / I Could Make You Love Me / Love Me Baby / Heard It All Before / Chills / Uncle Willie

When The Tremeloes found some belated USA success in 1967 after they'd split from Brian, the album was reissued with the same track listing and cover photo as 'The Tremeloes Are Here!'.

Brian Poole and The Tremeloes with their mums, 1965.

MY BABY LEFT ME (Crudup)
[BBC Radio - Not released until 2013]
WELL ALRIGHT (Allison / Holly / Petty / Mauldin)
[BBC Radio - Not released until 2013]

Originally released by Arthur Crudup in 1951, '**My Baby Left Me**' is probably best known via Elvis Presley's 1956 cover. However, Brian Poole and The Tremeloes' BBC recording is clearly based on Dave Berry's version, a minor hit for him the previous year, and can be found on 'Live At The BBC 1964-67'. The Tremeloes without Brian tackled it again for the BBC in 1968.

First released by Buddy Holly as 'Well.... All Right' in November 1958, and covered by Bobby Vee with The Crickets in 1962, The Tremeloes' predictably good (albeit a little rushed) version of '**Well Alright**' for BBC radio is on 'Live At The BBC 1964-67'.

July 1965: SINGLE [Decca F 12197]

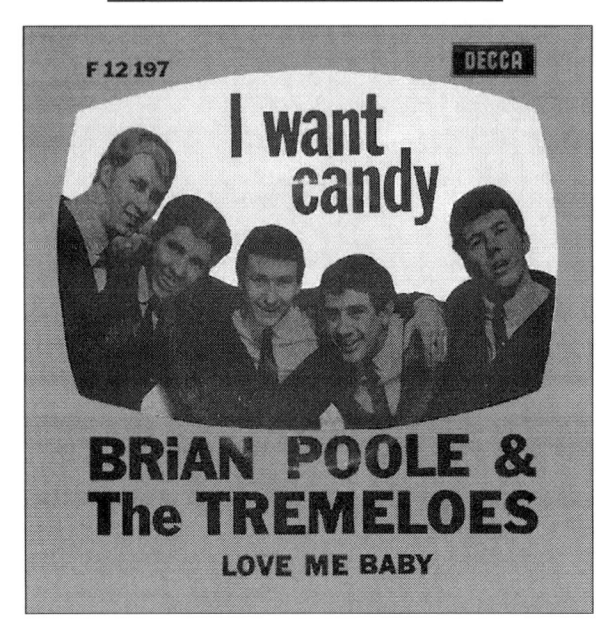

Danish picture sleeve

I WANT CANDY (Gottehrer / Goldstein / Feldman / Berns)
LOVE ME BABY (Poole / Blakley)

Brian Poole and The Tremeloes had already cut some authentic-sounding British Rhythm 'n' Blues for EPs and albums, but they'd never issued any as a single - until now. At first, they needed a little persuading.

Brian: "Dick Rowe at Decca played us The Strangeloves' record, 'I Want Candy', and suggested we cover it. We weren't sure, but he was convinced it was a certain hit."

A US hit for The Strangeloves a couple of months earlier, for **'I Want Candy'** Brian Poole and The Tremeloes upped the Bo Diddley-influence, and came up with one of the toughest-sounding singles of that summer. With promotion on 'Lucky Stars - Summer Spin', 'Top Of The Pops', 'Ready Steady Go!', 'Gadzoooks!' and 'Blue Peter', the No. 25 UK and No. 81 Australia top chart position was a little disappointing, but it remains a fondly remembered classic. A BBC radio 'Saturday Club' performance is on 'Live At The BBC 1964-67', while post-Punk band Bow Wow Wow had a big hit with the song in 1982.

Another driving Rhythm 'n' Blues number, the self-composed '**Love Me Baby**' was performed on 'Gadzoooks!', while a BBC radio 'Saturday Club' version can be found on 'Live At The BBC 1964-67'. Danish group The Hitmakers covered the song in 1967.

I GO CRAZY (Brown)

Instead of 'I Want Candy', which had already been a giant native hit for The Strangeloves, for the US market **'I Go Crazy'** was used instead. Originally released by James Brown and The Famous Flames as *'I'll Go Crazy'* in January 1960, and subsequently covered by P.J. Proby (1964), Tommy Quickly with The Remo 4 (1964) and The Moody Blues (July 1965), The Tremeloes' version is a powerful rendition, but its chances of hitting the American charts were remote in the extreme. A BBC radio 'Saturday Club' performance is on 'Live At The BBC 1964-67'.

Brian Poole and The Tremeloes continued to tour heavily during this period - not that they didn't have time for other things.

Brian: "In 1965, my very first date with Pam, my future wife, was a trip to the cinema - to see 'King Rat' - and then on to the Scotch of St. James where we ran into Keith Moon and the rest of the boys in The Who. He invited us to a party afterwards in his basement flat. It was brilliant - and it was also the first time I'd come across one of those hubble-bubble pipes you see in films set in Morocco, the Far East and exotic places like that. I got Pam back to her family home at 7.30 the next morning, and her Dad was furious. He forbade her ever to go out with me again. Fortunately, I was able to smooth things out."

SHE SAID YEAH (Bono / Jackson)
[BBC Radio - Not released until 2013]
IT'S ALL OVER NOW BABY BLUE (Dylan)

[BBC Radio - Not released until 2013]
BABY IT'S YOU (Bacharach / Dixon / David)
[BBC Radio - Not released until 2013]

First released by Larry Williams in January 1959, **'She Said Yeah'** was covered by The Animals (1964), Cliff Bennett and The Rebel Rousers (1964) and The Rolling Stones (September 1965), amongst others. Surprisingly, The Tremeloes' versions (there are two of them) sounds closer to The Animals' cover than the others, albeit without any organ. Both BBC radio performances are on 'Live At The BBC 1964-67'.

First released by Bob Dylan in March 1965, and covered by Them in January 1966, The Tremeloes' version of **'It's All Over Now Baby Blue'** is faster, with a nice guitar riff, organ, and a strong Brian lead vocal. This BBC radio recording can be found on 'Live At The BBC 1964-67'.

'**Baby It's You**' was first released in November 1961 by The Shirelles and covered by The Beatles (1963), Dave Berry (1964), Helen Shapiro (1964) and Cilla Black (1965). The Tremeloes' lovely version for the BBC owes a debt to The Beatles, albeit with a little more subtlety. It's on 'Live At The BBC 1964-67'.

November 1965: SINGLE [Decca F 12274]

Swedish picture sleeve

GOOD LOVIN' (Clark / Resnick)
COULD IT BE YOU? (Poole / Blakley)

First released by The Olympics in March 1965 and a B-side for The Swinging Blue Jeans in October 1965, The Tremeloes' version of '**Good Lovin'**' is up to the band's usual high standards, with prominent drums, piano and organ, though the guitar only really surfaces for a solo. It failed to chart in the UK, despite promotion on 'Top Of The Pops', 'Thank Your Lucky Stars', 'Five O'clock Funfair' and 'Now!', though it did just about scrape into the Australian Top 100 at No. 98. However, their faith in the song was justified when The Young Rascals topped the US charts with a version in early 1966. A BBC radio recording is on 'Live At The BBC 1964-67'.

With its adventurous harmonies and prominent acoustic guitar, the Folk-Pop-Rock of '**Could It Be You?**' sounds almost like a Beatles 'Rubber Soul' outtake, and could've been an interesting new direction for the band. Sadly though - apart from a 1966 B-side - this single would be Brian Poole and The Tremeloes' final release.

May 1966: SINGLE [Decca F 12402]

PLEASE BE MINE (Blakley / Poole) [B-side]

1966 was the year when *everything* changed for the band, but rather than the big falling-out of some of their rivals (Wayne Fontana and The Mindbenders literally split in the middle of a concert!), Brian Poole and The Tremeloes just gradually drifted apart, staying on largely still-friendly terms. It was also a period that saw the first line-up changes since 1962, with the May 1966 departure of original bassist Alan Howard.

Brian: "I think Alan never wanted to be in a world touring band and was always on the verge of going into other businesses, which he did with success."

First of all, they replaced him with Mick Clarke [Michael William Clarke, b. 10th August 1946], someone who stayed for around 3 months.

Dave: "Our bass guitarist Alan Howard decided to leave the band and start his own business. We replaced Alan with a friend of Rick's who had played with him in another local band. His name was Mick Clarke."

Brian Poole and The Tremeloes' final release was '**Please Be Mine**', the May 1966 B-side of 'Hey Girl' - Brian Poole's debut solo single without the band *(see the Brian Poole Solo section for more details).* Probably still with Alan Howard on bass, it's a softly-sung but soulful ballad, complete with a 'Time Is On My Side'-type spoken part and Bluesy guitar solo.

Rick Westwood, Dave Munden, Brian Poole, Mick Clarke, Alan Blakley.

LIKE A ROLLING STONE (Dylan)
[BBC Radio - Not released until 2013]
WALKIN' MY CAT NAMED DOG (Tanega)
[BBC Radio - Not released until 2013]
HEY GIRL (Goffin / King)
[BBC Radio - Not released until 2013]

On 28th May 1966, Brian Poole and The Tremeloes performed on BBC radio's 'Saturday Club' with their new member Mick Clarke. The three songs chosen were surprising ones. The first, '**Like A Rolling Stone**', was a single for the song's composer Bob Dylan in June 1965.

Brian: "Obviously we always promoted our latest single, but most of the songs that we played at the BBC weren't actually in our live set. The show's producer would say to us 'There's a big interest in

Folk music at the moment, can you go away and learn the latest Bob Dylan number and then play it next time?' So we'd learn the song, and play it live in the studio next time we were on the show."

The Tremeloes' version is distinguished by a unique guitar riff, but otherwise Alan Blakley's organ and even Brian's phrasing stick closely to the original template. It is on 'Live At The BBC 1964-67'.

'Walkin' My Cat Named Dog' was a single for Norma Tanega in February 1966, and for Barry McGuire in March 1966. Judging by the guitar intro, it was the original that inspired The Tremeloes' fine treatment, which can be found on 'Live At The BBC 1964-67'.

But the biggest surprise was **'Hey Girl'** - a Freddie Scott song that also happened to be Brian Poole's solo debut. On the single, he was backed by session musicians and singers, but here it is given a lighter band treatment, with dominant organ and some lovely harmonies.

Brian: "That just proves what a load of nonsense it was to suggest that we'd fallen out. They would hardly have backed me on it if that had been the case, and it was rubbish to say they didn't like the song. Having heard the BBC session again after all these years, I have to say our version is a whole lot better than the single!"

With work steady, but seemingly little hope of the band ever making it big again, Mick returned to his old band The Symbols. Eventually, he would find major stardom as a founder member of '70s band The Rubettes, and The Tremeloes would remain on friendly terms with him, utilising his talents again decades later. He was replaced by someone who would greatly contribute to the band's future survival, becoming very much 'the face' of the band - Len 'Chip' Hawkes [Leonard Donald Stanley Hawkes, b. 2nd November 1945].

Len: "I was called by John Salter, who was our manager's booker, and he said 'The boys are thinking of getting a bass player who can sing'. He picked me up, and we picked Dave Munden up, and went to Rick's bedroom. And then Dave just went, and said 'See ya!'. (Brian) was doing an interview or something, and Al Blakley banged his teeth or something... well it turned out that Rick was the only one who auditioned me, in his bedroom. It was the most bizarre thing."

LOVING YOU IS SWEETER THAN EVER (Hunter / Wonder)
[BBC Radio - Not released until 2013]

A 3rd September 1966 'Saturday Club' performance captured the band metamorphosing: As well as performing both sides of The Tremeloes' 2nd single 'Good Day Sunshine' / 'What A State I'm In', they also included **'Loving You Is Sweeter Than Ever'**, with vocals by Brian. A May 1966 single for The Four Tops, the song has the distinction of being the *only* song to be recorded by Brian Poole and The Tremeloes, *and* Brian Poole solo (on an April 1967 'Saturday Club' performance), *and* The Tremeloes (on their May 1967 debut album). The Brian Poole and The Tremeloes version is as good as any of the others.

Len 'Chip' Hawkes, Rick Westwood, Brian Poole, Alan Blakley, Dave Munden.

Then, almost inevitably, came the final split, though this wasn't until the early weeks of 1967. By then, it wasn't just the music where they differed in opinion.

Brian: "I hated that flower power they started wearing on stage. Instead, I used to wear a big leather jacket. We were all getting on each others' nerves, and by the time The Tremeloes had their first big hit with 'Here Comes My Baby' in 1967, I was looking for a way out. A university gig in the Midlands, our last scheduled show, seemed as good a time to go as any."

Alan: "It wasn't really Brian's fault, you know. He sincerely thought that the way he saw it was the best for all of us. But towards the end it was ridiculous. You should have seen us on stage. Brian was wearing collars and ties and all that, and we were wearing gear that was in. When he saw us in our clothes he'd say, 'Hello, here's the fancy dress party'. What could we do?"

Rick: "Us four have the same ideas on clothes, music, everything. Brian's were entirely different. It just wasn't working. As time went on we changed our outlook."

Dave: "We were still playing together when 'Good Day Sunshine' came out. We were quite happy with reactions to it, so we decided to try again. We found 'Here Comes My Baby' quite by chance, and we were so impressed we had to record it. And it sold. So we thought the time had come for us to tell Brian we were splitting. We were playing at Aston University in Birmingham, and the record had just crept into the bottom of the charts."

Alan: "Why did we make the break? Basically it was a question that we had our ideas - about the kind of numbers to perform, the way to do them, the way we should dress on stage, and so on. Brian had his ideas. They were different from ours. I suppose the break was more or less inevitable."

Brian: "There's been a lot of nonsense written about this period, with people saying that we'd fallen out and were always having arguments. To be honest, we went along with it a little bit because it kept our name in the papers, but it wasn't true at all. The fact is we'd had loads of hits, a few world tours, and we'd kind of got to the end of the road. We thought the time was right to try other things."

PART 3:

BRIAN POOLE - SOLO

SOLO: BRIAN POOLE

THE SINGLES

Brian Poole's post-Tremeloes career can be neatly divided into two parts - with just one solitary 1975 single between them - Half-a-dozen interesting, but ultimately unsuccessful singles during 1966-1969; and the recording and touring return of the past 40 years, kicking off with a pair of 1983 singles. Below are all nine of Brian's singles from 1966 to 1983.

May 1966: SINGLE [Decca F 12402]

Danish picture sleeve

HEY GIRL (Goffin / King)

Originally released by Freddie Scott in June 1963, 'Hey Girl' was covered by Duffy Power (1963), Kenny Lynch (1963) and Barry St. John (as 'Hey Boy', 1965). Brian Poole's ambitions as a Big Band balladeer seemed an unlikely prospect to some, but he proved himself to be surprisingly good at the genre, and remains proud of the record to this day.

Brian: "Mike Smith and me collaborated on a song that I did with an orchestra full of star musicians of the time. One to remember is Don Lusher on Trombone. The song was 'Hey Girl', I think my best vocal at Decca. There's many more but this one stood out I think."

Despite promotion on 'Thank Your Lucky Stars' and 'The Five O'Clock Club', it failed to chart, a fate that was to befall all of his solo singles. This wasn't totally without precedent - Manfred Mann did much better with their new singer Mike D'Abo than Paul Jones ever did solo, and The Mindbenders' 'Groovy Kind Of Love' will always be better-remembered than any of Wayne Fontana's solo hits - but it was still unexpected. Two versions of 'Hey Girl' from 'Saturday Club' - one with The Tremeloes, one without - can be found on 'Live At The BBC 1964-67' (The B-side 'Please Be Mine' is by Brian Poole and The Tremeloes, and is reviewed in that section).

September 1966: SINGLE [CBS 202349]

Danish picture sleeve (note misspelling of 'Touch'!)

EVERYTHING I TOUCH TURNS TO TEARS (Geld / Udell)
I NEED HER TONIGHT (Freemantle / Smith)

EVERYTHING'S WRONG (Alfred / Farrall)
[BBC Radio - Not released until 2013]

March 1967: SINGLE [CBS 202661]

THAT REMINDS ME BABY (Greenaway / Cook)
TOMORROW NEVER COMES (Tubb / Bond)

October 1967: SINGLE [CBS 3005]

JUST HOW LOUD (Schroeck / Lowing)
THE OTHER SIDE OF THE SKY (Greenaway / Cook)

LOVING YOU IS SWEETER THAN EVER (Hunter / Wonder)
[BBC Radio - Not released until 2013]

In August 1966, along with The Tremeloes, Brian Poole was signed to CBS, where he released another three singles. **'Everything I Touch Turns To Tears'** is a piano-led orchestrated ballad that was originally released by Jimmy Clanton in November 1965, and covered by Barry St. John (March 1966) and Cilla Black (April 1966). A BBC radio 'Saturday Club' performance is on 'Live At The BBC 1964-67', an episode that also featured an exclusive cover of Chubby Checker's August 1965 mid-paced song **'Everything's Wrong'**. Far superior to any of these is the single's B-side, the passionately sung Bluesy ballad **'I Need Her Tonight'**, where thankfully the orchestra took a rest.

'That Reminds Me Baby' is more orchestrated middle-of-the-road Pop (and yet again, there's a BBC radio 'Saturday Club' performance on 'Live At The BBC 1964-67', along with an orchestrated version of **'Loving You Is Sweeter Than Ever'**), as is Ernest Tubb's (via B.J. Thomas) **'Tomorrow Never Comes'**, as well as the final CBS A-side **'Just How Loud'**. Infinitively superior is the B-side, **'The Other Side Of The Sky'**, a Northern Soul stomper that should be better known. Now split from The Tremeloes, during this period Brian continued to tour heavily with his backing band The Unity, a band who sounded far better than they looked.

Brian Poole and The Unity, 1967.

March 1969: SINGLE [President PT 239]
(with The Seychelles)

Dutch picture sleeve

SEND HER TO ME (Dickinson / Hayward / Bosher / Dillon)
PRETTY IN THE CITY (Dickinson)

July 1969: SINGLE [President PT 264]
(with The Seychelles)

WHAT DO WOMEN MOST DESIRE (Hill / Hawkins / Coghill)
TREAT HER LIKE A WOMAN (Dickinson / Dillon)

Performing 'Send Her To Me' on 'Beat Club', 1969.

Following a year without a recording contract, Brian signed to President, bringing with him his new band The Seychelles. Things got off to a great start with '**Send Her To Me**', a lost freak-beat classic, complete with fuzz guitar, pounding drums, driving piano and soaring harmonies. It's probably the most exciting thing Brian Poole did post-Tremeloes in the '60s, but despite promotion on shows like The Netherlands' 'Doebidoe' and Germany's 'Beat-Club', it failed to chart anywhere. For '**What Do Women Most Desire**', his final '60s release, Brian went for a lighter treatment, with a sound not a million miles away from the 'Sunshine Pop' of groups like The 5th Dimension.

Brian with Andrew Loog-Oldham and Peter Noone.

After this, legend has it that Brian Poole retired from the music business to work in the family butchers shop - but in fact, as well as continuing to perform, he became a highly successful businessman.

Brian: "I still played non-stop with my own band, called lots of different names. I put some money into a recording company, Outlook. We were doing OK, and then one day my brother Arthur rang to ask me to help him over Christmas in a factory attached to one of our shops, which was about a mile away from Outlook's offices in Manor Park. I gave him a hand, mainly in an administrative capacity, for about six months, though, if I was around, I'd pitch in for a laugh whenever there was a queue in the shop. Neither The Tremeloes nor me started from a deprived background. Our parents were business people, and they worked very hard to give us good security, that still exists to this day. Actually, going into the family business meant a rise in my standard of living! It's still an ongoing company, now owned by the younger members of the family. Very busy time, trying to run two businesses."

The 'butchers shop' story started largely thanks to a TV show.

Brian: "Anglia TV came to shoot a programme about me for a series called 'Where Are They Now?', presented by David Jacobs. Outlook's offices were closed for the weekend, so we did some filming at my house in Barking. Next, I arranged for one of Arthur's shops to open up, just for the camera crew, and they made that the main theme of the programme. They showed a bit of the back fence at the house, and forgot all about Outlook Records and the evening residency I had with the local band at a club called The Three Rabbits. They took me for a ride, and I never got paid."

Meanwhile, there was a one-off single.

August 1975: SINGLE [Pinnacle P 8407]
(with Carousel)

SATISFIED (Renouf)
RED LEATHER (Myers)

'Satisfied' is a contemporary-sounding Pop-Rocker that's not without its charms, though more interesting is 'Red Leather', a song clearly inspired by The Hollies' 'Long Cool Woman (In A Black Dress)', despite the rather strange mix with prominent organ and occasional reverb. Brian is less than satisfied today.

Brian: "Can't think what made me sing those songs, not really to my liking. I kind of find them embarrassing now but OK then I suppose!"

He returned to music full-time after seeing a well-known comedy duo.

Brian: "I went to see Cannon and Ball at Great Yarmouth and they saw me in the audience, stopped the show and said I should be back in the business where I belonged. I talked about it to the wife all the way home and decided I was going back."

Brian Poole with Tramline (above) and Black Cat (below).

April 1983: SINGLE [Outlook OUT 100K]
(with Tramline)

DO YOU LOVE ME - TWIST AND SHOUT (Gordy Jr + Russell / Medley)

(B-side 'Time and Tide' is by Tramline only)

November 1983: SINGLE [Sumatra SUM 4]
(with Black Cat)

SOMEONE, SOMEONE (Petty / Greines)
BYE BYE BABY (Venesse)

The first come-back single was '**Do You Love Me - Twist and Shout**', a Rock-Disco update of two hits from 20 years earlier that was recorded with the band Tramline, and which sounds rather dated now with its squelchy keyboards and brittle drums. Better is the follow-up with Black Cat, '**Someone, Someone**', a song The Tremeloes also remade a couple of times. It's updated enough to make it sound contemporary, but without losing what made it special in the first place. The B-side, '**Bye Bye Baby**', is a good modern Rock 'n' Roll song with honking saxophones, and not the perhaps expected 4 Seasons/Bay City Rollers hit.

Brian: "Tramline was only for a few weeks, but Black Cat was another story. Some of my best few years in the business. Big R'n'R for everyone and a much loved band, some of whom I still have as friends. We played at the very first 'Rockers Reunion' at Cumberland Hotel in London, all the Bikers clubs in massive evidence and a great time with Black Cat and Chris Black."

A highlight of this period was a rather special concert in 1985.

Brian: "Royal Gala for British forces was another great day. As I walked on the stage televised worldwide, my microphone transmitter pack fell off and hung at my side! I was vocally backed by Sue and Sonny who I had worked with in Decca and EMI studios on many tracks, and the band was led by Alan Ainsworth. Met Princess Anne!"

THE TREMELOES - EVEN THE BAD TIMES ARE GOOD!

THE ALBUMS

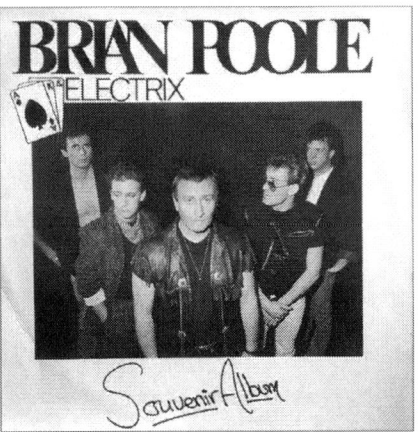

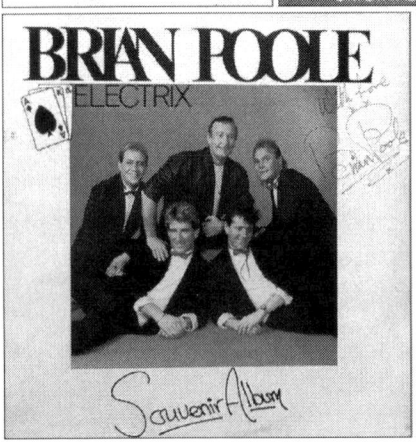

Since the mid-80's, there have been numerous albums on cassette, vinyl and CD, largely consisting of re-makes of 'The Hits' with the occasional covers of '50s/'60s classics. The albums pictured above and listed below are the main ones, but is not definitive.

Brian: "I re-recorded all my hits, both with Alan Blakley producing, and on my own. I also now own the masters to everything I ever did."

<u>1985: ALBUM {cassette} [Autograph Series ASK 773]</u>

GREATEST HITS

(with Black Cat)

DO YOU LOVE ME / GOOD LOVIN' / SOMEONE, SOMEONE / CANDY MAN / GHOST RIDERS / PETER GUNN / TWIST AND SHOUT / FEEL SO LONELY / WANT YOUR LOVE / ROCK 'N' ROLL MEDLEY: JOHNNY B GOODE - CAROL - LITTLE QUEENIE *(some songs are Black Cat only)*

<u>1985: ALBUM {vinyl} [BPCV BPC 1]</u>

THE ALBUM

(with Black Cat)

TWIST AND SHOUT / HEY LITTLE GIRL / FEEL SO LONELY / GOOD OLD ROCK 'N' ROLL / WANT YOUR LOVE / ROCK 'N' ROLL MEDLEY: JOHNNY B GOODE - CAROL - LITTLE QUEENIE / CHEVROLET / DO YOU LOVE ME / GIMME GOOD GOOD LOVIN' / CANDYMAN / GHOST RIDERS *(some songs are Black Cat only)*

<u>1987: ALBUM {CD} [SRT7KL1184]</u>

SOUVENIR ALBUM

(with Electrix)

TIME IS ON MY SIDE / HEY LITTLE GIRL / CANDYMAN / GOOD LOVIN' / THREE BELLS / TWIST AND SHOUT / SOMEONE SOMEONE / GIMME GOOD LOVIN' / I WANT CANDY / LOVE ME BABY

<u>1989: ALBUM {CD} [SRT9KL1918]</u>

SOUVENIR ALBUM
(with Electrix)

PLAY THE OLDIES / DO YOU LOVE ME / CANDYMAN / SOMEONE - SOMEONE / YOU CAN'T SIT DOWN / THREE BELLS / ST. TROPEZ / TWIST AND SHOUT / HEY LITTLE GIRL / COULD IT BE YOU / I WANT CANDY / CHEVROLET / ROCK & ROLL MEDLEY: JOHNNY B. GOODE - CAROL - LITTLE QUEENIE

LATE '80S: ALBUM {cassette} [SRT 91C 2949]

BRIAN POOLE
(with Electrix)

DO YOU LOVE ME / CANDY MAN / SOMEONE, SOMEONE / TWIST AND SHOUT / GIMME GOOD LOVIN' / ROCK AND ROLL MEDLEY / THREE BELLS / I WANT CANDY / ST. TROPEZ / HEY LITTLE GIRL / CHEVROLET / GHOST RIDERS / GOOD OLD ROCK 'N' ROLL / PLAY THE OLDIES / STAR IN A ROCK 'N' ROLL BAND

EARLY '90S: ALBUM {cassette} [private pressing]

30TH ANNIVERSARY SOUVENIR
(with Electrix)

DO YOU LOVE ME / CANDY MAN / SOMEONE, SOMEONE / TWIST AND SHOUT / THREE BELLS / SILENCE IS GOLDEN / FEEL SO LONELY / HOUSE PARTY / SHAKE A TAIL FEATHER / SOMETIMES WHEN WE TOUCH / THE UNCLE WILLIE / TO LOVE SOMEBODY / BRING IT ON HOME TO ME / HEY LITTLE GIRL

2008: ALBUM {CD} [private pressing]

ANTIQUE GOLD
(with Electrix)

DO YOU LOVE ME / TWIST AND SHOUT / CANDY MAN / SOMEONE, SOMEONE / SILENCE IS GOLDEN / I WANT CANDY / GOOD LOVIN' / CAN WE HOLD ON / AIN'T NOTHING BUT A HOUSE PARTY / **BEND ME SHAPE ME** (Electrix only) / **MOVING ON / BAREFOOTIN'**

Brian: "Right up to this year my band Electrix has been Steve Thompson (guitar), Tony Allen - 'Gil' (drums) Andy Wilde (keys) and Rob Swain (bass), all vocals also, and backed myself and Chip Hawkes on many gigs recently. Also Chip and me had the pleasure of working with Vanity Fare on many tours until 2021."

Brian Poole and Electrix, then and now.

May 1989: SINGLE [KORP 1]

AIN'T NOTHIN' BUT A HOUSE PARTY (Sharh / Thomas)

A more high-profile release was in May 1989, when Brian and a handful of other '60s stars got together for a single under the name The Corporation - who were quickly dubbed 'The Travelling Wrinklies'! Sadly, despite a Promo Video and an acoustic performance on 'This Morning', **'Ain't Nothing But A House Party'** - with an instrumental of the same song on the B-side - failed to chart.

Brian: "We asked a lot more singers to take part than actually did it, but in the end it boiled down to me, Clem Curtis from The Foundations, Reg Presley of The Troggs, Mike Pender of The Searchers and Tony Crane from The Merseybeats, no slouches, any of them. We did it at the old Pye studios in London on a Monday, when none of us was likely to be working anywhere else. Two weeks later, we shot the video at the Town & Country Club and in central London. The record got a lot of exposure, but Radio One wouldn't play it because they didn't think we were serious about it. I'd like to remix the Corporation single and issue it again, as it still sounds like a hit to me."

2002: 'REELINANDAROCKIN'' [Private Pressing]

2004: 'REELINANDAROCKIN'' Volume II [Private Pressing]

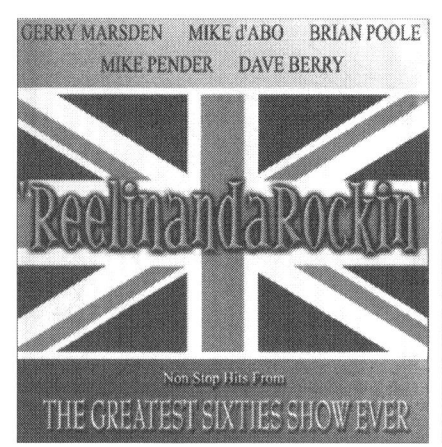

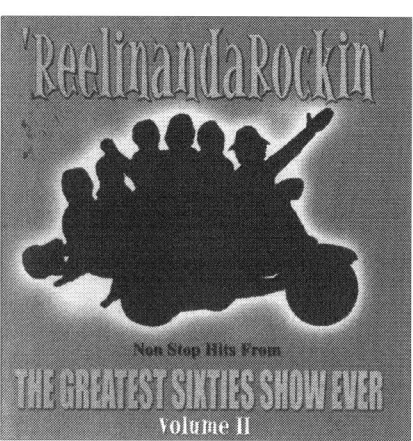

In 2002, Brian got together with Gerry Marsden, Dave Berry, Mike D'Abo and Mike Pender, to both tour and record a CD called 'ReelinandaRockin''. In addition to further re-cuts of **'Do You Love Me'**, **'Someone, Someone'** and **'Twist and Shout'**, Brian contributed to a **Rock 'n' Roll Medley** and a **Buddy Holly Medley**, as well as a cover of the Spencer Davis Group's **'Gimme Some Lovin''**.

In 2004, he did it again for 'ReelinandaRockin' Volume II', this time with Mike Pender, Wayne Fontana, Dave Dee, Tony Crane and Dave Berry. Alongside re-cuts of **'Candy Man'** and **'Do You Love Me'**, Brian contributed to another **Rock 'n' Roll Medley** and an **Everly Brothers Medley**, in addition to a cover of The Rolling Stones'/Chris Farlowe's **'Out Of Time'**.

As mentioned in the Brian Poole and The Tremeloes section, the band were the very first to use Marshall amps. Brian remained close friends with Jim Marshall, right up until his passing at the age of 88 in 2012. The following year, he headed-up a rather special occasion.

Brian: "When I was asked to unveil a plaque commemorating the life and achievements of my good friend Jim Marshall, I was proud and pleased to do it on the 6th April 2013 in Hanwell, Middlesex.

This is where Jim's first shop was and on the day I went and stood outside what used to be No. 76 Uxbridge Road for the first time since the Tremeloes and me were among his very first customers in the early 60's. Just along the road is where Amp No.1 was conceived and built. Beside Jim's family, colleagues and friends, was a large crowd eager to see the plaque which I was to unveil about 10ft up on the building. Just as I was telling a story about Jim in his later years the plaque suddenly unveiled itself causing much surprise and a little chuckle! A great day and as usual Jim Marshall OBE was in control."

With Jim Marshall on his Birthday in 2009, and unveiling the plaque in 2013.

Brian Poole retired from doing tours in 2019, but still does the very occasional one-off gig at the time of writing in 2023, and remains a consummate and hard-working performer.

(© Brian Poole)

PART 4:
THE TREMELOES
(1966 - 1976)

June 1966: SINGLE [Decca F 12423]

BLESSED (Simon)
THE RIGHT TIME (Blakley / Poole)

Although they would continue touring together until early in 1967, on 13th May 1966, Brian Poole released his debut solo single 'Hey Girl', a record which featured the final new Brian Poole and The Tremeloes recording 'Please Be Mine' on the B-side. A month later on 10th June 1966, The Tremeloes released *their* debut single without Brian, with a cover of Simon and Garfunkel's January 1966 album track '**Blessed**', accompanied by their new bassist and singer Mick Clarke. It's a superb piece of harmonised Folk-Rock, but, with rival UK covers by The Kytes and Guy Darrell, it quickly sank without a trace. Curiously, the band revived the song in 1969, complete with an electric sitar makeover, and this arrangement can be heard on both the 'Live in Cabaret' album and on a BBC radio recording that's on 2004's 'BBC Sessions' collection.

A Blakley-Poole co-write, '**The Right Time**' is another harmonised Folk-Rock number, albeit a little faster than the A-side, and includes a rare Alan lead vocal. Despite the lack of sales, The Tremeloes had successfully established their own unique sound from their very first single.

August 1966: SINGLE [CBS 202242]

Spanish picture sleeve

GOOD DAY SUNSHINE (Lennon / McCartney)
WHAT A STATE I'M IN (Blakley / Smith)

Now signed to CBS along with Brian Poole, The Tremeloes' next release was a cover from The Beatles' 'Revolver' album, and again featured Mick Clarke. Their version of '**Good Day Sunshine**' includes a strong Dave Munden lead vocal and a distinctive honky-tonk piano intro - unusually for The Tremeloes, played by a guest musician.

Rick: "'The distinctive honky-tonk piano intro' on 'Good Day Sunshine' was played by Don Gould from The Applejacks."

Just as with 'Blessed' though, the release coincided with two UK rival versions - this time by The Eyes and ex-The Fortunes' Glen Dale.

Even better is '**What A State I'm In**', a freak-beat psych-out with fuzz guitar, a 'Taxman'-styled riff, and Dave's best lead vocal to date. Whereas it is not too difficult to imagine Brian Poole singing 'Good Day Sunshine', it is nigh on impossible to imagine him doing the same on 'What A State I'm In'. Again, a BBC version can be found on both 'BBC Sessions' and 'Live At The BBC 1964-67'.

By the time they promoted the A-side on 'Saturday Club' the following month, Mick Clarke had departed, to be replaced by Len 'Chip' Hawkes, formerly in The Horizons and Davey Sands and The Essex. This version is on both 2004's 'BBC Sessions' and 2013's 'Live At The BBC 1964-67'.

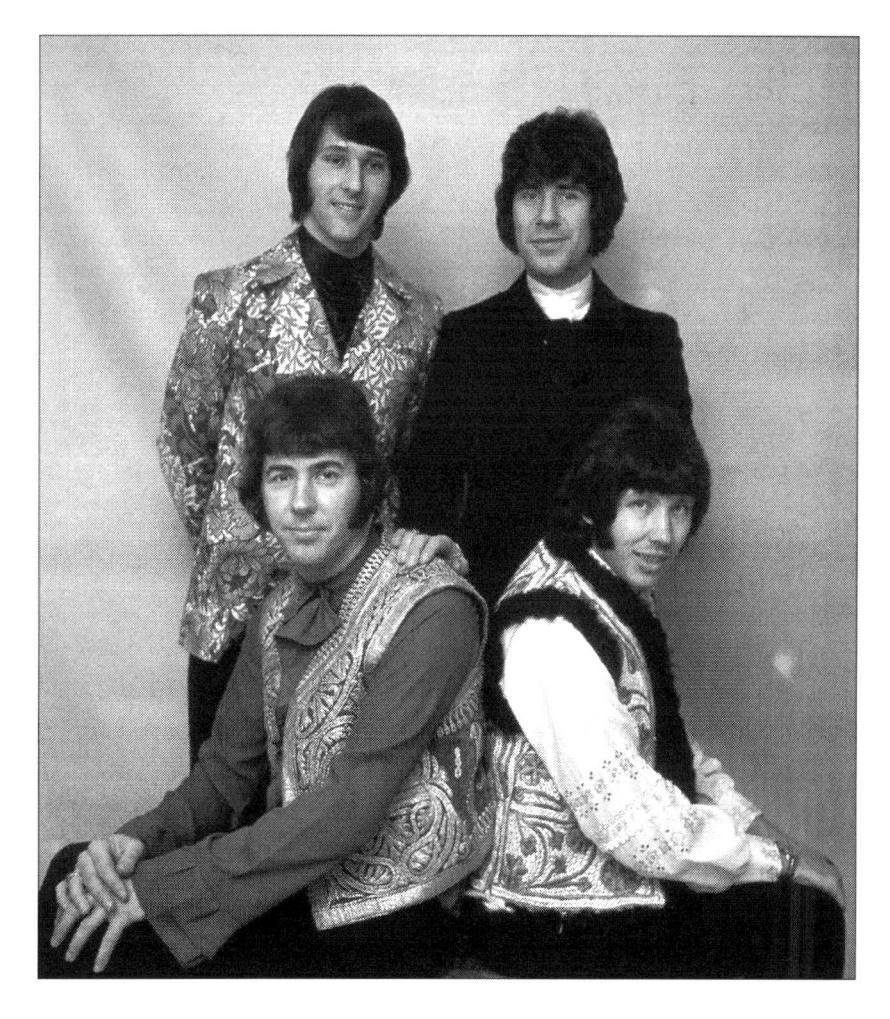

January 1967: SINGLE [CBS 202519]

Dutch picture sleeve

HERE COMES MY BABY (Stevens)
GENTLEMAN OF PLEASURE (Blaikley / Hawkes / Westwood)

Despite two excellent singles, no-one predicted a great future for the by now Brian Poole-less The Tremeloes. After all, with a few notable exceptions (The Beatles of course, as well as The Hollies, Herman's Hermits and The Dave Clark Five), nearly all the Beat groups who'd emerged in 1963/1964 were pretty much washed-up chart-wise, even former multi-chart-toppers like The Searchers and Gerry and The Pacemakers. '**Here Comes My Baby**' was written by then-emerging singer-songwriter Cat Stevens, albeit in a far more relaxed fashion than The Tremeloes' Trini Lopez-inspired version.

Alan: "Cat Stevens had been writing a load of numbers, and he gave us a pile of them, and we selected this one. We put our own terrible arrangement to it, and it came out, we think, good!"

Len: "Alan and I had been to every music publisher in London until we stumbled on our first hit 'Here Comes My Baby'. The record entered the charts after our first TV appearance. I remember being so excited I couldn't believe it! We were immediately added to a Hollies tour along with The Kinks and The Spencer Davis Group."

Instantly catchy and memorable, the record was promoted on such TV shows as 'Top Of The Pops', 'Crackerjack', 'The Record Star Show', 'The London Palladium Show', 'Blue Peter', 'Two Of A Kind' (called 'Piccadilly Palace' when broadcast in the USA), Germany's 'Die Drehscheibe' and 'Beat! Beat! Beat!', and The Netherlands' 'Moef Ga Ga'. All this exposure got the record to No. 4 in the UK, No. 8 in Ireland, No. 13 in the USA, No. 14 in Germany 14 and New Zealand, No. 19 in The Netherlands and No. 47 in Australia. A BBC radio 'Saturday Club' performance can be found on both 'BBC Sessions' and 'Live At The BBC 1964-67', while Chip Hawkes would remake it in a radically different style in 1976.

Performing 'Here Comes My Baby' on 'Beat! Beat! Beat!', 1967.

Establishing what would quickly become a regular feature of The Tremeloes' hit singles, the B-side of 'Here Comes My Baby' is more musically adventurous than the A-side. The self-composed **'Gentleman Of Pleasure'** has the instrumental attack and falsetto harmonies of 'A Quick One'-era The Who, and sounds light years away from what they were doing with Brian Poole.

THE TREMELOES - EVEN THE BAD TIMES ARE GOOD!

April 1967: SINGLE [CBS 2723]

German picture sleeve

SILENCE IS GOLDEN (Gaudio / Crewe)
LET YOUR HAIR HANG DOWN (Blakley / Hawkes / Westwood)

To follow up their smash hit, because of audience reaction whenever they performed it, they decided on an old 4 Seasons B-side that they'd been doing on stage for several months.

Rick: "Mick came into the band in 1966 to replace Alan Howard. We asked Mick if there was a song that he knew that we could play in the band. Mick suggested the B-Side of The Four Seasons 'Rag Doll' - 'Silence is Golden'. We learnt it and played it on stage with Mick singing. Then Mick left the band and we carried on playing 'Silence' with me singing it. Thanks, Mick, you did us a big favour there."

Alan: "We made a follow-up, it's called 'Up, Down, All Around', but in the mean time we'd been on a tour and had been doing one of our old numbers, which is a 4 Seasons number. It's been going down so good on stage we thought we'd release this as our follow-up instead of the one we'd already recorded."

'Silence Is Golden' would quickly become the biggest hit of their career, thanks in no small part to a group member whose voice had previously been rarely heard on record.

Dave: "We did it a bit different, because the original was obviously the B-side of 'Rag Doll' from the 4 Seasons. Unbeknown to us, our lead guitarist Ricky Westwood had a freak falsetto voice. We thought we'd record that and Rick can do it, go in the studio, put the lead vocals on it, and we did all the harmonies and it worked out wonderfully well for us. And it's probably our biggest ever track, which we're very grateful to the 4 Seasons for."

With promotion on 'Top Of The Pops', 'Dee Time', 'As You Like It', 'Joe and Co.', 'The London Palladium Show', 'Two Of A Kind' (aka 'Piccadilly Palace'), Germany's 'Beat! Beat! Beat!' and The Netherlands' 'Moef Ga Ga', it got to No. 1 in the UK, Ireland, Norway, New Zealand and Zimbabwe, No. 5 in Australia and New Zealand, No. 8 in Germany and No. 34. Belgium. Significantly, it also got to No. 11 in the USA, a country where they'd had very little success in previous years.

Len: "We were playing 'Silence Is Golden' on stage and the audience reaction was so good that we decided to record it on our only day off in the middle of the tour. By the end of the tour it had entered the Top 20 and made Number 1! This was our biggest number one international hit, selling more than three million copies world-wide. I recollect Tony Hicks from The Hollies telling me that they had planned to record the song straight after the tour but we beat them to it! We all got up in the middle of the night when the charts came out in London, we walked down The Strand and saw that we were number one. It was great!"

A version from BBC radio's 'Saturday Club' is on 'BBC Sessions', and it became so much their signature tune that they reprised the song on 'Top Of The Pops' specials in 1969, 1973 and 1988.

'**Let Your Hair Hang Down**' is another song that owes a debt to the 'Mod' sounds of The Who and The Small Faces, with a falsetto lead vocal, distorted fuzz-guitar and all-over-the-place drums. The low voice singing the title line is producer Mike Smith.

Rick: "The fuzz sound on 'Let Your Hair Hang Down' was either my Gibson Fuzz or a British Pedal Company Tone Bender... or maybe the Solar Sound Tone Bender, which looked the same. I cut out a space below the tone and volume controls of a Fender Jaguar and fitted the Gibson Fuzz into the guitar and also included an on/off switch for the fuzz. My Dad cut out a steel-plate and shaped it to fit around the fuzz pedal controls and the volume and tone controls of the guitar. He then had it chrome plated."

Performing 'Silence Is Golden' on 'Moef Ga Ga', 1967.

With this new-found success in their own right, the "new boy" suddenly found himself to be the pin-up of the band.

Dave: "All the girls fancied him, he was a good-looking boy. He was really the focal point of The Tremeloes for quite a few years."

Inevitably, there were the occasional disagreements, but by and large the band got on well.

Len: "We were all such different characters, but somehow it worked. We didn't have many disputes but of course we did. Then in the next minute we were in the pub having a drink. We were just mates and it worked."

In April 1967, The Tremeloes taped a pilot episode for a TV series called 'Presenting The Tremeloes'. The only episode made was called 'Seven League Boots', and was taped on location in Brighton and Scotland, but despite plans for a possible 26-part series and the band's enthusiasm, no more were made, and the whole thing was quickly forgotten.

Alan: "Well there's this series we're hoping to get, in America to start with, and with a bit of luck it should be on our screens as well. We're only going to be ourselves for a fraction of the time, and the rest of the time we're playing all the other people in the films, with beards and false moustaches and everything, and just ourselves as I say for a fraction of the time. We've done the first one, so as soon as it is done and passed, we'll be starting full time. 9 to 5 men!"

Dave: "Next on our list is to get this TV series together, it is definitely due to be shown in America, but the televising date has yet to be fixed. We've already shot one piece. The style has been compared to the Monkees' show. We did act before, if you can call it that, in 'A Touch Of Blarney', which we made in Ireland. On the strength of that comedy film we were picked for this series. The man who's doing these films is an English fellow who was responsible for that great series, 'The Telegoons'! Just look at our faces and you'll see why he picked us! Seriously though, the film is about a firm who will undertake to do anything. We have to test boots for the Army by marching from Land's End to John O'Groats! Only in the film that is. Ricky here, plays a young girl and an old woman, apart from himself! It was very difficult filming all day and playing in the evenings. That's why it took two weeks to get that one in the can. But it will be planned much better in future."

I'LL TAKE YOU WHERE THE MUSIC'S PLAYING (Barry / Greenwich)
[BBC Radio - Not released until 2004]
IT TAKES TWO (Stevenson / Moy)
[BBC Radio - Not released until 2004]

Just as they had during the Brian Poole era, The Tremeloes continued to occasionally feature exclusive song performances on their BBC radio radio guest spots. '**I'll Take You Where The Music's Playing**' was a July 1965 single for The Drifters, and covered by fellow Essex band The Fingers in October 1966, as well as performed by The Fortunes for BBC radio the same year (a performance that wasn't released until 2018). The Tremeloes had a knack of, more often than not, surpassing the originals when covering Soul and Motown material, and such is the case here. It is on 2004's 'BBC Sessions'.

Even better is '**It Takes Two**', a song that was first released by Marvin Gaye and Kim Weston in August 1966 and covered by Otis Redding and Carla Thomas in March 1967. On The Tremeloes' BBC 'Saturday Club' recording, the very heterosexual Dave and Len perform a male-male duet without any irony, with prominent accompaniment from Alan's organ (Ooh, Mrs!). Again, this is on the essential 'BBC Sessions' set.

THE TREMELOES - EVEN THE BAD TIMES ARE GOOD!

May 1967: ALBUM [CBS 63017]

HERE COME THE TREMELOES

HERE COMES MY BABY (Stevens)
RUN BABY RUN (BACK INTO MY ARMS) (Gant / Melson)
MY TOWN (Atkins)
ROUND AND ROUND (Weston / Freemantle / Duncan)
WHAT A STATE I'M IN (Blakley / Smith)
LOVING YOU (IS SWEETER THAN EVER) (Hunter / Wonder)
GOOD DAY SUNSHINE (Lennon / McCartney)
YOU (O'Sullivan)
LET YOUR HAIR HANG DOWN (Blakley / Hawkes / Westwood)
SHAKE HANDS (AND COME OUT CRYING) (Kershaw)
WHEN I'M WITH HER (Hawkes)
EVEN THE BAD TIMES ARE GOOD (Murray / Callander)

With a title that references their first big hit, the debut album 'Here Come The Tremeloes' is a satisfying mix of old, new, covers and originals. It peaked at No. 15 in the UK album charts, while a shorter 10-song version in the USA under the title 'Here Comes My Baby' peaked at No. 119. Of the songs on the UK album, **'Here Comes My Baby'** - heard in extended form here, **'What A State I'm In'**, **'Good Day Sunshine'** and **'Let Your Hair Hang Down'** had been previously released.

'Run Baby Run (Back Into My Arms)' was previously released by The Newbeats in September 1965. The Tremeloes' cover is faster and more robust, and a good showcase for Rick's falsetto. They liked it enough to also use it as the opening song on their 1969 live album, 'Live In Cabaret', while a BBC version can be found on both 'BBC Sessions' and 'Live At The BBC 1964-67'.

A Chet Atkins instrumental from 1965, The Tremeloes' version of **'My Town'** is again a showcase for Rick, but this time for his country pickin', backed up by some wordless harmonies, while the catchy Pop-Rocker **'Round and Round'** is most notable for a bass riff that would later be recycled for the hit single 'Suddenly You Love Me'.

The Four Tops' **'Loving You (Is Sweeter Than Ever)'** is a song that had previously been sung by Brian Poole, both with a without The Tremeloes, at the BBC, but Dave is the vocalist here. They performed the song on German TV's 'Beat! Beat! Beat!', also, as part of a medley with 'Reach Out I'll Be There', for BBC radio. The latter can be heard on 'BBC Sessions'.

The excellent Beatle-esque **'You'** was written by a pre-fame Gilbert O'Sullivan, when he was still using his real name Ray. A good song, made even better by the brief instrumental freak-out, The Tremeloes dug it out again for BBC radio's 'Radio One Club' in September 1969, and again this can be found on 'BBC Sessions'.

Len: "Mike Smith brought Ray to light. He used to record his demos on an old upright piano in a shed in his back garden, and had been known to bring it in the studios and sit in on some sessions. Alan Blakley and I were stupid, really. At the time we were dabbling in management, and we let Ray go! He was a phenomenal talent and had some amazing songs, most of which were never recorded."

'**Shake Hands (and Come Out Crying)**' is another song originally released by The Newbeats, in January 1966, and again is beefed up by The Tremeloes and utilises Rick's unique falsetto. It was performed as a medley with 'Run Baby Run (Back Into My Arms)' for the 'Live In Cabaret' album.

The jangly, Byrds-like '**When I'm With Her**' was written solely by Len, but would quickly lead to a highly prolific and creative songwriting partnership with Alan Blakley.

Len: "I used to write songs on my own anyway, but I didn't play them to anyone. We'd just finished our first album - well we hadn't finished our first album, we had one song that was missing. Al said 'We should at least put on one that we've written', and I said 'I've got a song', and Al said, 'Wha... well, let's hear it!'. And I played it to him, and he said 'Well that's great for an album, let's do it!'... It wasn't a single, it was an album track, but we ended up recording it, and then I started writing with Al."

The closing '**Even The Bad Times Are Good**' was initially a contender for Sandie Shaw to sing at the 1967 Eurovision Song Contest, but somehow ended up with The Tremeloes instead. This early version, with its "Go on Len, have a sing!" intro, spoken by Rick, differs from the single release a couple of months later, but essentially all of the hit ingredients are already there.

Fan Pics by Doreen Higgs, circa 1967 (© Valerie Slater)

July 1967: SINGLE [CBS 2930]

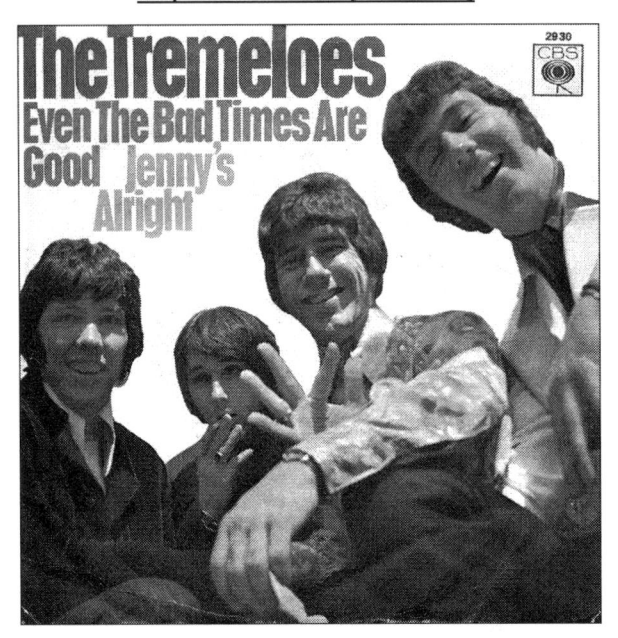

German picture sleeve

EVEN THE BAD TIMES ARE GOOD (Callender / Murray)
JENNY'S ALRIGHT (Blakley / Hawkes)

For the re-recorded single version of '**Even The Bad Times Are Good**' - distinguished by its "Parrot Face!" intro, spoken by Alan - they increase the silliness even further, coming up with something instantly memorable.

Alan: "Originally it was a track on the LP, but everywhere we went everyone said 'That's a fantastic song' and all that, and really we didn't even notice it when we recorded the LP. We just took it as another song, but then we started listening to it, and thought it is a good song. So went back to the studio, worked out a new arrangement and everything, and put it out as a single."

With promotion on 'Top Of The Pops', 'Dee Time', 'Billy Cotton's Music Hall', 'As You Like It' and Austria's 'Gogo-Scope', it got to No. 1 in the UK and Zimbabwe, No. 2 in New Zealand, No. 3 in The Netherlands, No. 7 in Ireland, No. 8 in Belgium, No. 18 in Germany, No. 36 in the USA and No.

46 in Australia. A BBC radio 'Saturday Club' performance is on 'BBC Sessions', while overseas covers include South Africa's Dickie Loader and The Blue Jeans, Germany's The Pick-Ups, Spain's Los Tamara, Elio Roca, José Luis, and Grupo 15 (all as 'Contigo Es Mejor'), The Netherlands' Ellis De Waal (as 'Als De Zon Mij Een Dag Vergeet'), Finland's Jukka Kuoppamäki (as 'Kaiken Uudeksi Teet') and Italy's Quelli (as 'Questa Città Senza Te').

Far more restrained than all their other B-sides to date, the organ and piano-dominated '**Jenny's Alright**' contrasts very nicely with the more in-yer-face A-side.

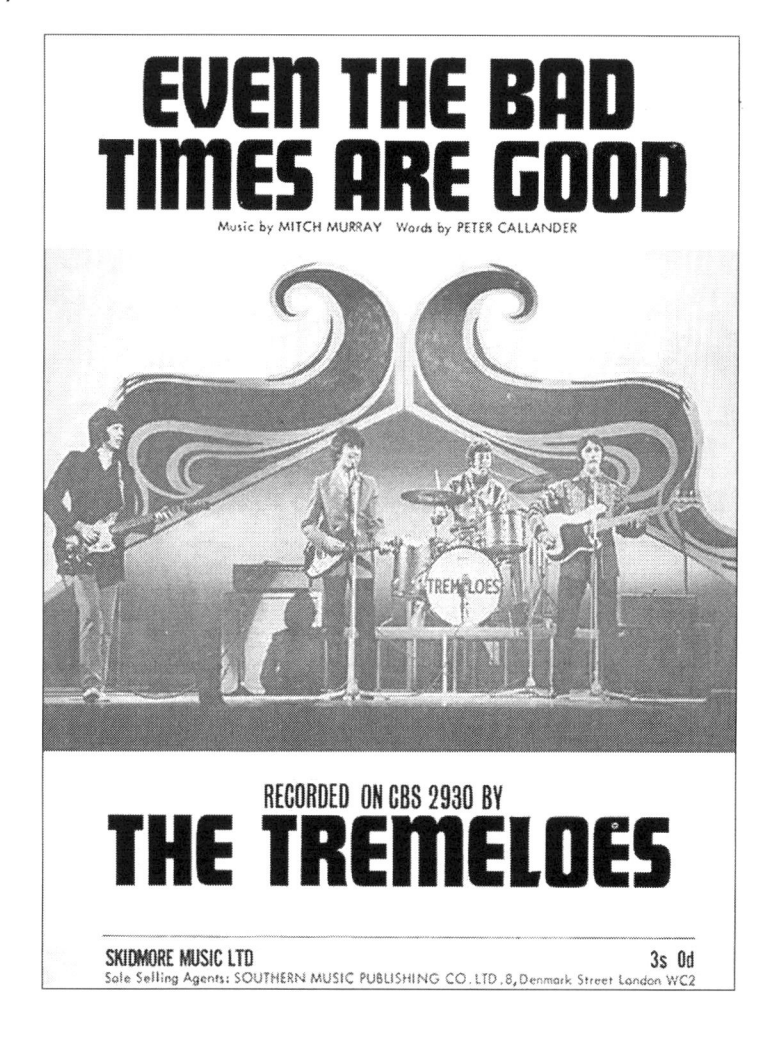

THE TREMELOES - EVEN THE BAD TIMES ARE GOOD!

Performing 'Even The Bad Times Are Good' on 'Gogo-Scope', 1968.

October 1967: SINGLE [CBS 3043]

Norwegian picture sleeve

BE MINE (MI SEGUIRAI) (Ferrari / Moschini / Pallavicini / Sorrenti / Smith)
SUDDENLY WINTER (Blakley / Hawkes)

After three smash hits in a row, '**Be Mine**' was The Tremeloes' first misstep. It's hard to pinpoint why, as it's a lovely Beach Boys-styled ballad, with Rick's falsetto as delicately beautiful as Brian Wilson's. Maybe the lack of dynamics didn't help, unlike the original version by Italian group Gli Scooters (as 'Mi Seguirai), which had more of a quiet/loud arrangement.

Len: "We thought it would really go. That's the only one really, that I had all the confidence in, and it's the only one that didn't go!"

Despite appearances on 'Top Of The Pops', 'Crackerjack' and 'Dee Time', it stalled at No. 39 in the UK, got to No. 17 in Zimbabwe, and failed completely pretty much everywhere else. A performance from BBC radio's 'Happening Sunday' is on 'BBC Sessions'.

With its way-out backwards guitar and hi-hat intro, one could be forgiven for thinking they were listening to The Jimi Hendrix Experience rather than The Tremeloes - *that's* how far-out **'Suddenly Winter'** starts off. Instead, it quickly evolves into a melodic Pop-Rocker with soaring harmonies with just the occasional Hendrix-inspired touches, and wouldn't have sounded out of place on The Pretty Things' 'S.F. Sorrow' album. An extraordinary record that could perhaps have been a bigger success than the A-side.

November 1967: ALBUM [CBS 63138]

ALAN, DAVE, RICK AND CHIP

HAPPY SONG (Pattison / Hawkshaw)
RUNNING OUT (Simpson / Ashford)
NEGOTIATIONS IN SOHO SQUARE (Colton / Smith)
SUDDENLY WINTER (Blakley / Hawkes)
SUNSHINE GAMES (Woolfson)
SILENCE IS GOLDEN (Gaudio / Crewe)
NORMAN STANLEY JAMES ST. CLARE (Pattison / Hawkshaw)
COOL JERK (Storball)
I'M WITH YOU ALL THE WAY (Colton / Smith)
SING SORTA SWINGLE (Blakley / Hawkes)
TOO MANY FISH IN THE SEA (Whitfield / Holland)
COME ON HOME (O'Sullivan)

Just seven months after their debut, and in time for Christmas, came The Tremeloes' 2nd UK album, 'Alan, Dave, Rick and Chip'. Two of the songs, '**Suddenly Winter**' and the by now eight-months-old '**Silence Is Golden**' were previously released, leaving ten new songs.

Despite its title, '**Happy Song**' is an unusual up-tempo minor key song about someone feeling sad, with harpsichord and pounding double-time drums as the main instrumentation.

'**Running Out**' is a tough modern Soul song, originally released by Vernon Garrett in October 1967, and quickly covered by duo Bongi and Judy the same month. Ably sung by Dave, a version for BBC radio's 'Saturday Club' is on 'BBC Sessions'.

Perhaps one of the more disposable tracks on the album, '**Negotiations In Soho Square**' has a Beatlesesque feel, but the "Baa-be-doo-be-dum-dum" lyrics, that take up far too much of the song, are more than a tad irritating.

First released by American band The Music Explosion in August 1967, The Tremeloes' version of '**Sunshine Games**' lacks the proto-punk garage feel of the original, but more than compensates by some nice The Searchers-styled jangling guitars and harmonies. It was written by Eric Woolfson, later of The Alan Parsons Project fame - someone who contributed several good songs to The Tremeloes around this time.

Complete with harpsichord and amusing-but-sad lyrics, '**Norman Stanley James St. Clare**' sounds like something the late Neil Innes of The Bonzo Dog Doo-Dah Band fame would've come up with.

Alan: "It's about a statue, in a park, and this fellow's looking at him and really just taking the mick out of him, the statue. He's standing there in the nude - the statue that is!"

First released by The Capitols in March 1966, and covered by Ian and The Zodiacs (1966), The Mindbenders (1967) and The Creation (1967), '**Cool Jerk**' is Soul song about a supposed dance craze. Although not the greatest song ever written, The Tremeloes' version is as good as any. Despite this, songs like these were a cause of frustration.

Len: "The whole thing was live gigs, and we used to have to work between the shows. Personally, I think the second album was a bit of desperation all round. Some tracks were those we were doing onstage such as 'Cool Jerk', an American Soul song. We all knew it and didn't have to work out the chords, we could just go in and record it, it was all wrong really. With hindsight, I think if we'd had a proper manager at the time, we could've afforded to take six months out, get in the studio and get some original stuff down."

'**I'm With You All The Way**' is a rather mediocre mid-paced piano-led song with falsetto harmonies, though Dave sings it well.

The Swingle Singers were a vocal group who specialised in acapella arrangements of classical works, and used their voices to imitate instrumentation. '**Sing Sorta Swingle**' is a light-hearted but un-amusing 'comedy' tribute to them, with Rick's biting guitar licks being its one saving grace. A version from BBC radio's 'Saturday Club' is on 'BBC Sessions'.

The Tremeloes might've been frustrated at being forced to record cover versions due to time constraints, but '**Too Many Fish In The Sea**', originally released by The Marvelettes in October 1964, is one of their very best Motown covers. A BBC 'Saturday Club' performance can be found on 'BBC Sessions'.

Another song written by Ray (Gilbert) O'Sullivan, '**Come On Home**' is a superb bluesy Soul ballad with organ and electric piano, though it's a bit of a strange way to end an otherwise mostly upbeat album. A version from BBC radio is on 'BBC Sessions', while Czechoslovakian act Jiří Helekal and Shut Up covered it as 'Zeptej Se, Kam Plují Lodi' in 1970.

Although not as successful as 'Here Come The Tremeloes', 'Alan, Dave, Rick and Chip' sold well. Yet despite their continuing success with single releases, it would be three years before The Tremeloes released another UK studio album.

ON LOVE (Bell / Turnbull)
[Not released until 2000]
EVERY LITTLE BIT HURTS (Cobb)
[Not released until 1990]
NO, NO, NO (Woolfson)
[Not released until 2000]

Despite the frequent record releases, The Tremeloes left quite a few recordings 'in the can' over the years, with many of them only surfacing decades later. First released by UK psychedelic band Skip Bifferty in August 1967, The Tremeloes' version of '**On Love**' is if anything even better, even if the vocals could do with being higher in the mix. Taped in late 1967 or early 1968, it was first released on 'Here Come The Tremeloes - The Complete 1967 Sessions' in 2000.

Brenda Holloway's classic Soul ballad from March 1964, **'Every Little Bit Hurts'** was covered in 1965 by Cilla Black, The Spencer Davis Group and Petula Clark, and by The Small Faces in 1968. The Tremeloes' version blows 'em all away, with one of Dave's greatest vocal performances, an excellent guitar solo, and lush but appropriate strings. Clearly a lot of effort went into making it, but perhaps they thought it was just too well-known to put out? Whatever, it stayed unreleased until 1990's 'The Ultimate Collection'.

'**No, No, No**' has fast, minor key verses and a la-la-la chorus, and although a little forced structurally it's well worth a listen. The Tremeloes themselves must've thought it needed more work, as they would re-record it in 1971, but the original 1968 version finally surfaced on 'Suddenly You Love Me - The Complete 1968 Sessions' in 2000.

January 1968: SINGLE [CBS 3234]

Dutch picture sleeve

SUDDENLY YOU LOVE ME (Pace / Panzeri / Palat / Callander)
AS YOU ARE (Murray / Callander)

After the relative failure of 'Be Mine', the group returned to the party sounds of 'Here Comes My Baby' and 'Even The Bad Times Are Good'. **'Suddenly You Love Me'** was another English re-write of an Italian song, this time Riccardo Del Turco's 'Uno Tranquillo' (translated as 'Quiet One'), a No. 21 hit in his native country in 1967. The Tremeloes omit the brass of the original by going for a more Rock-arrangement, adding a bass and drums intro previously heard on 'Round and Round'. With promotion on 'Top Of The Pops', 'Crackerjack', 'Dee Time', 'New Release', 'Doddy's Music Box' and 'The Golden Shot', as well as Sweden's 'Popside', it peaked at No. 6 in the UK and New Zealand, No. 7 in Zimbabwe, No. 9 in Ireland, No. 20 in Australia, No. 43 in Belgium and No. 44 in the USA. A BBC radio 'Saturday Club' performance is on 'BBC Sessions', while in France it was recorded by Joe Dassin as 'Siffler Sur La Colline', and Cilla Black covered the song for an album a few months later.

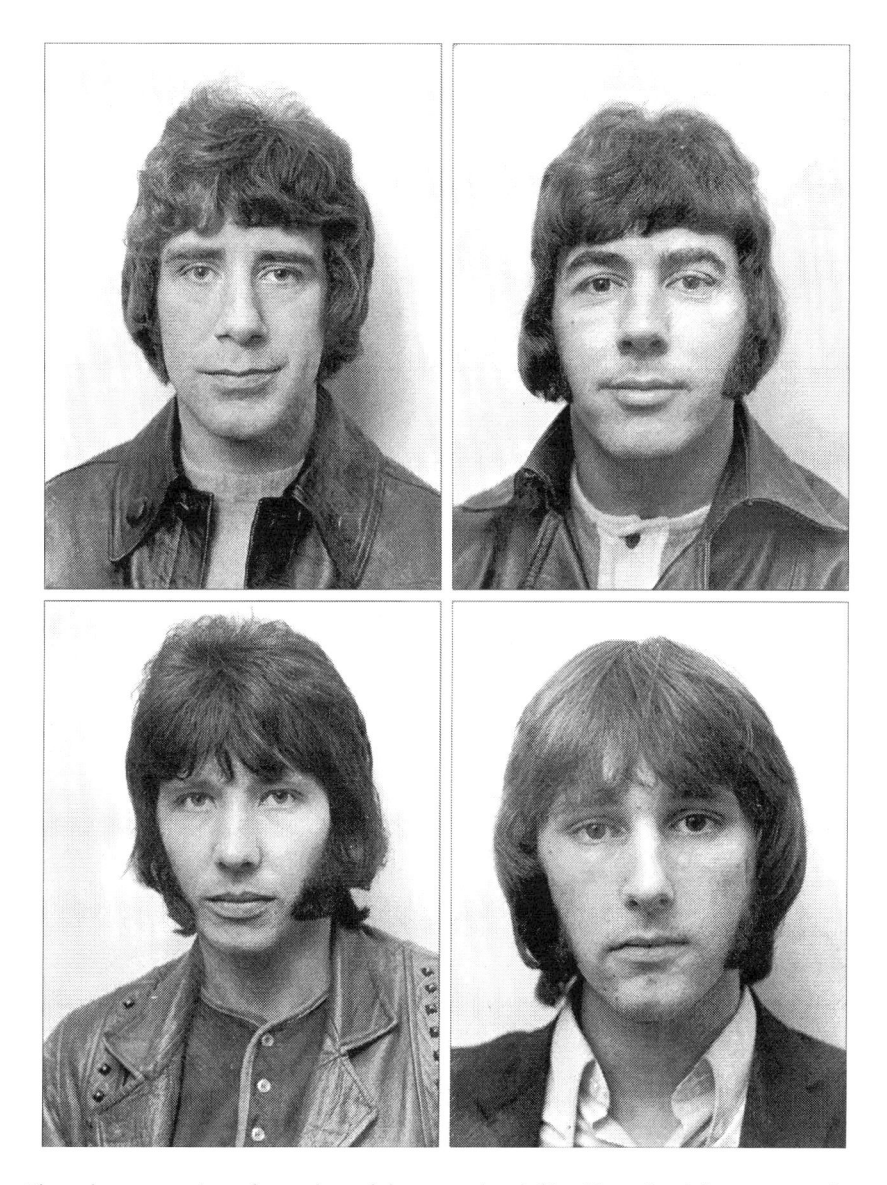

The slower, minor-keyed and harmonised '**As You Are**' keeps up the tradition of B-sides that are at least as memorable as the A-sides. So much so, it was promoted as the A-side in The Netherlands and Germany, reaching No. 35 in the latter (in the USA and Canada, 'Suddenly Winter' was the B-side to 'Suddenly You Love Me', while in New Zealand it was 'Negotiations in Soho Square'). Spanish group Los Junior's covered 'As You Are', translating it as 'Como Tú' in the process.

THE TREMELOES - EVEN THE BAD TIMES ARE GOOD!

Performing 'Suddenly You Love Me' on 'Popside', 1968.

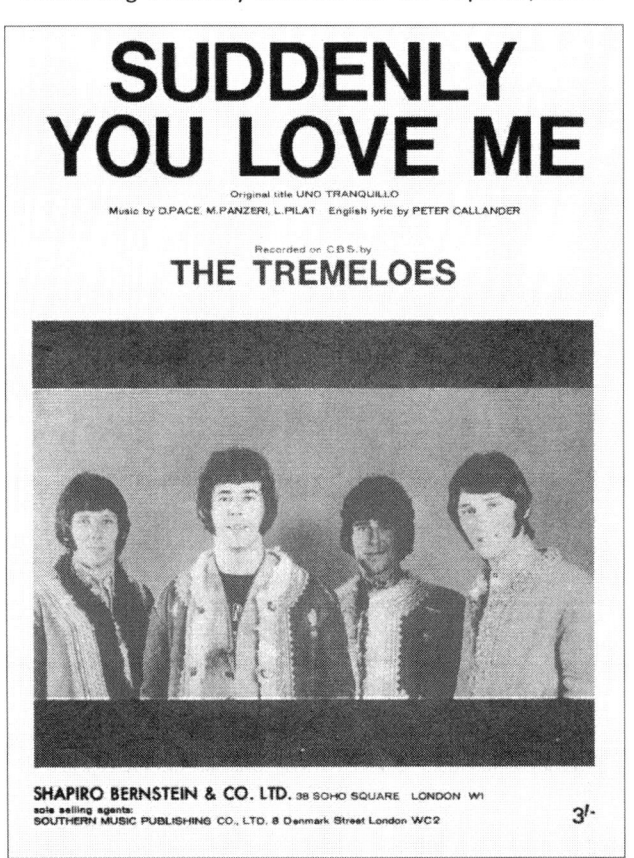

E IN SILENZIO (Parazzini / Crewe / Gaudio)

After recording, with new English lyrics, a couple of Italian songs, The Tremeloes did the exact opposite by recording '**E In Silenzio**' - a new version of 'Silence Is Golden' - in Italian, for exclusive single release in that country. As well as being in a different language, it has a slightly alternative vocal arrangement, lacking the usual "Ooohs" during the intro.

GIMME LITTLE SIGN (Smith)
[BBC Radio - Not released until 2004]
WALK AWAY RENEE (Brown / Calill / Sansone)
[BBC Radio - Not released until 2004]

Along with a performance of 'Suddenly You Love Me', a January 1968 'Saturday Club' broadcast included a couple of exclusive covers. '**Gimme Little Sign**' was a July 1967 single for Brenton Wood, and is performed in a rather relaxed manner by The Tremeloes.

More successful musically is '**Walk Away Renee**', a single for The Left Banke in February 1966 and covered by UK duo The Truth in March 1967. The Tremeloes' version however, was almost certainly inspired by The Four Tops' memorable July 1967 hit, and features a superb Dave lead vocal and an organ break from Alan. Both songs are on 'BBC Sessions'.

YOU DON'T KNOW LIKE I KNOW (Hayes / Porter)
SHOW ME (Tex)
I TAKE WHAT I WANT (Porter / Hayes / Hodges)
REACH OUT I'LL BE THERE (Holland / Dozier / Holland)

Instead of the 'Alan, Dave, Rick and Chip' album, for the USA and a few other markets - including Canada, South Africa and Mexico - The Tremeloes' 2nd album was 'Suddenly You Love Me'. It largely consists of songs from singles and the UK albums, but amongst the eleven tracks are four exclusive songs, all of them Soul covers that they could probably have played in their sleep.

First released by Sam and Dave in November 1965, **'You Don't Know Like I Know'** quickly became a much-covered Soul classic in the UK, with versions by Keith Powell and Billie Davis (1966), Geno Washington and The Ram Jam Band (1966), Jimmy James and The Vagabonds (1966), Zoot Money's Big Roll Band (1966), Cliff Bennett and The Rebel Rousers (1967) and Paul and Barry Ryan (1967). The Tremeloes' version is a glorious duet between Dave and Len, proving once again just how great Dave in particular was at singing Soul.

The Tremeloes' version of Joe Tex's March 1967 release **'Show Me'** is, if anything, even better. Also covered by The Foundations in 1967, Dave Munden never sounded more like a black Soul man, singing with more passion than Joe Tex did on the original. Surprisingly, the song got an outing on TV, when the band performed it on the TV special 'Liberace in London', a show that also featured a unique collaboration with Liberace on Simon and Garfunkel's 'The 59th Street Bridge Song (Feelin' Groovy)'. Perhaps even more surprising - when so much '60s and '70s TV has been lost forever - the TV special still survives.

Another Sam and Dave song, **'I Take What I Want'** was first released by the duo in August 1965, and covered the following year by both The Artwoods and The Hollies. The Tremeloes' performance is exciting, and features some great organ and drumming, but it is a little too rushed, having an almost "Let's get this one out of the way!" feel to it.

Already performed for BBC radio the previous October as a medley with 'Loving You Is Sweeter Than Ever' - which can be found on 'BBC Sessions' - a full version of The Four Tops' August 1966 Motown classic **'Reach Out I'll Be There'** was released on the US 'Suddenly You Love Me' album. Also covered by Chris Farlowe (1966) and P.J. Proby (1967), as well as by Petula Clark (1967) and Jackie Trent (1967), The Tremeloes' version sticks close to the original template. On the Spring 1967 tour with The Hollies, there were some heated "debates" over which band were going to perform the song on stage... allegedly!

May 1968: SINGLE [CBS 2889]

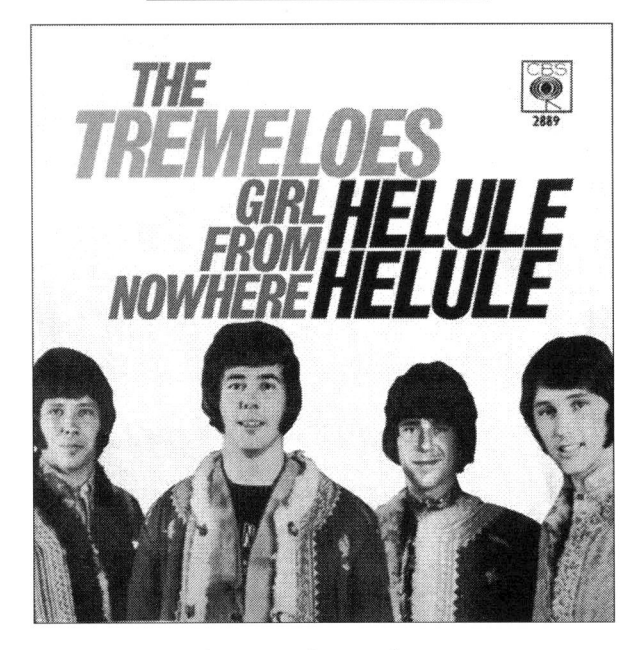

German picture sleeve

HELULE HELULE (Kabaka / Hawkes / Blakley)
GIRL FROM NOWHERE (Blakley / Hawkes)

Prior to mid-1969, by far the most musically adventurous Tremeloes A-side was '**Helule Helule**', with its African chant 'nonsense' lyrics and percussion. Based on a rough demo sung in Swahili by Kenyan duo Daudi Kabaka and George Agade from 1966, there really was nothing else quite like it around at the time, with perhaps Dave Dee & Co's 'Zabadak' from the previous year a distant cousin.

Alan: "We like the sound of African numbers, African war chants, and we went up to Manchester believe it or not. Darkest Manchester! And found this African song, and between us we wrote some more lyrics and tune to go with the song. It's the real African-Dagenham sound!"

Promoted on 'Top Of The Pops', 'Time For Blackburn!', 'Whistle Stop', 'Billy Cotton's Music Hall' and 'Dee Time', it got to No. 14 in the UK, No. 13 in New Zealand and Zimbabwe, No. 16 in Ireland, No. 20 in Germany,

No. 29 in Australia and No. 46 in Belgium - not bad going for something so *out there!* A BBC radio 'Saturday Club' performance is on 'BBC Sessions'.

'**Girl From Nowhere**' is *almost* just a Beatles/Bonzos-styled piano-led Pop-Rock song - but what kicks it into another stratosphere are Rick's ground-breaking 'bagpipes' interludes played on his guitar, which when combined with Dave's drum rolls, sounds just like a Scottish marching band.

MY BABY LEFT ME (Crudup)
[BBC Radio - Not released until 2004]

Arthur Crudup's (via Elvis Presley) '**My Baby Left Me**' had previously been taped at the BBC by Brian Poole and The Tremeloes back in 1965. The Tremeloes' 1968 recording is faster, with an echo-drenched Len doing his best to sound like Elvis, but the actual arrangement still owes more to Dave Berry's 1964 hit. It can be found on 'BBC Sessions'.

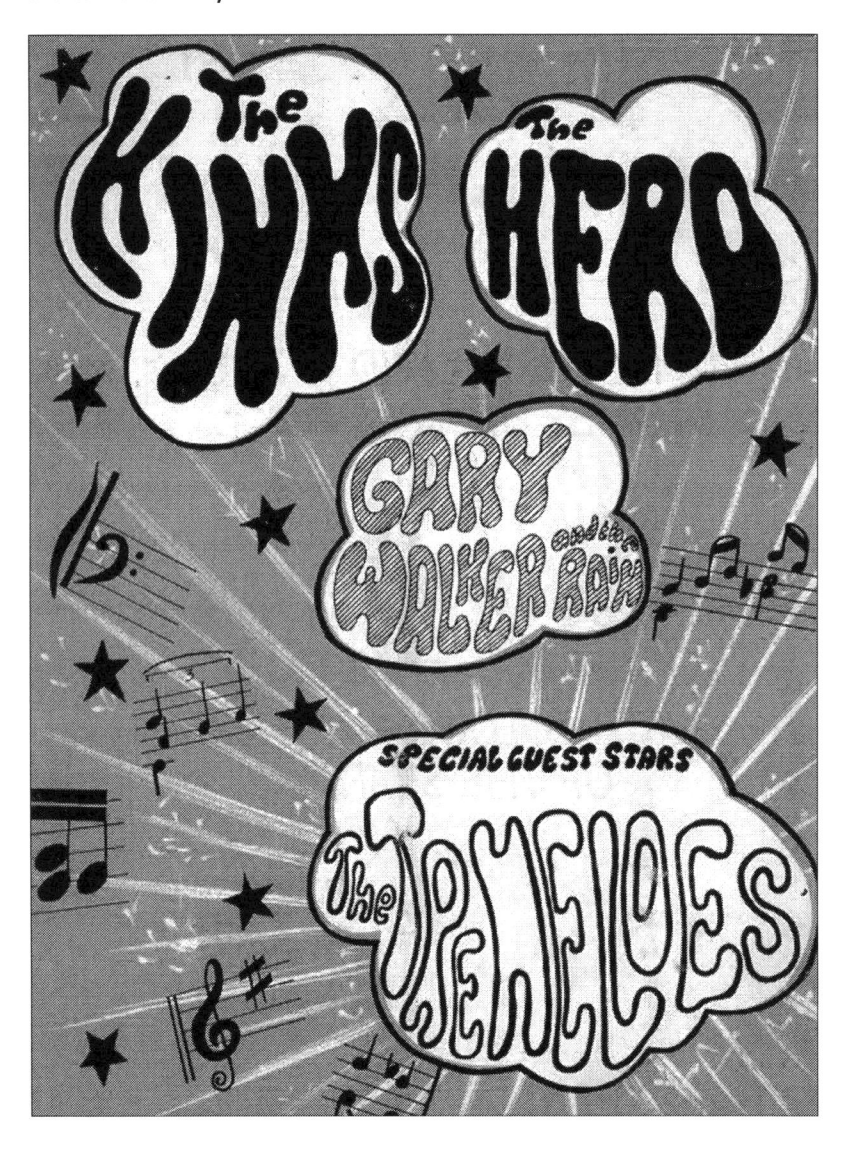

July 1968: ALBUM [Epic BN 26388]
WORLD EXPLOSION! {USA only}

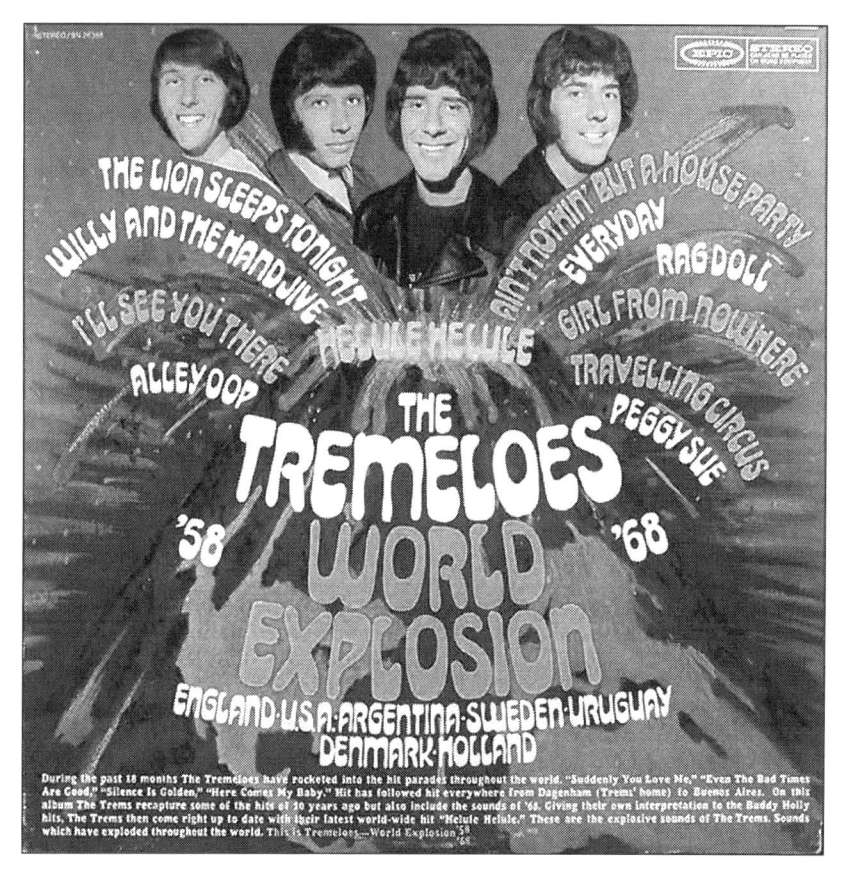

PEGGY SUE (Holly / Petty / Allison)
EVERYDAY (Petty / Hardin)
THE LION SLEEPS TONIGHT (Campbell)
RAG DOLL (Gaudio / Crewe)
I'LL SEE YOU THERE (Blakley / Hawkes)
WILLY AND THE HAND JIVE (Otis)
HELULE HELULE (Kabaka / Blakley / Hawkes)
GIRL FROM NOWHERE (Blakley / Hawkes)
ALLEY OOP (Frazier)
TRAVELLING CIRCUS (Blakley / Hawkes)
AIN'T NOTHIN' BUT A HOUSE PARTY (Sharh / Thomas)

In some overseas territories, including the USA, Canada, Australia, New Zealand, Spain and Japan, there was an exclusive Tremeloes album that wasn't released in the UK and most other European countries. Unfortunately, consisting largely of covers of songs from the '50s and early '60s, it was very much a retrogressive move - if Len was dissatisfied with 'Alan, Dave, Rick and Chip', what he thought of this album is probably unprintable! **'Helule Helule'** and **'Girl From Nowhere'** had already been released, but nine of the other eleven songs were "new".

The 1957 Buddy Holly classic, it is easy to imagine Brian Poole and The Tremeloes doing a good and faithful cover of **'Peggy Sue'**. Here however, it sounds like no more than a warm-up jam, with a slower pace, laid-back vocal, and uninspired guitar and drums.

The B-side of Buddy Holly and The Crickets' 'Peggy Sue' was **'Everyday'** - also featured here. It's pleasantly sung by Len, with largely sympathetic backing, but it still somehow lacks "oomph".

'The Lion Sleeps Tonight' was a 1961 hit for The Tokens, though it was based on 'Wimoweh', first released by The Weavers in 1952 - which itself was based on the old Zulu chant 'Mbube'. Rick does a fine job of the falsetto vocal, but it is then all-but-ruined by what sounds like a kazoo solo, and it is clear that no-one is taking these recordings particularly seriously.

'Rag Doll' had previously been included featuring Dave Munden on lead vocals on Brian Poole and The Tremeloes' 'It's About Time' album in 1965 - and here it is again, sounding almost identical.

One of only two newly-composed songs on the album, **'I'll See You There'** with its "la, la, la, las" is a bit Tremeloes-by-numbers, but on *this* album it's like a breath of fresh air! The song would resurface in more ragged form a few months later - under the title **'I Will See You There'** - as the Israel-only B-side of the 'I'm Gonna Try' single. Despite its lack of UK release, the song was performed on BBC radio's 'David Symonds Show', released on 'BBC Sessions', while it also received at least three covers - all as 'I Will See You There' - by Ireland's The Dreams (1968), the UK's Linda Kendrick (1969) and New Zealand's The Chicks (1969).

'**Willie and The Hand Jive**' (under the title '*Willy* and the Hand Jive') was first released by The Johnny Otis Show in April 1958, but is probably better known in the UK via Cliff Richard and The Shadows' 1960 cover. The Tremeloes' version could be improved by a better mix, but otherwise it's pretty good, with some nice piano work.

Hollywood Argyles' '**Alley Oop**' was previously recorded by Brian Poole and The Tremeloes for 1963's 'Twist and Shout' album, where it featured a suitably daft vocal from Brian. This time Dave Munden does the vocals, where it is (mainly) spoken in an over-the-top "posh" voice - similar to The Bonzo Dog Doo-Dah Band's Vivian Stanshall. It's genuinely funny, but it is difficult to imagine what the Americans and the Japanese would've made of it!

With some very "Jewish"-sounding instrumental interludes and a good

Len vocal, **'Travelling Circus'** is an interesting slice of self-composed Pop-Psych that deserved to be heard more widely.

Originally released by The Show Stoppers the previous year, the Soulful **'Ain't Nothin' But A House Party'** quickly received UK covers by The Boston Show Band (who would later evolve into The Glitter Band) and The Paper Dolls. The Tremeloes' exciting cover has more in common with the Soul performances on the 'Suddenly You Love Me' album than the sometimes tired covers on here, and was deemed good enough to perform on TV with Lulu on her TV series 'Happening For Lulu', as well as on BBC radio's 'Saturday Club', as heard on 'BBC Sessions'. Two decades later, Brian Poole would re-record the song as part of The Corporation, aka 'The Travelling Wrinklies'.

(IF YOU THINK YOU'RE) GROOVY (Marriott / Lane)
[BBC Radio - Not released until 2004]

For a BBC radio performance on 'David Symonds Show' in August 1968, The Tremeloes included an exclusive cover of **'(If You Think You're) Groovy'**, a song written by The Small Faces' Steve Marriott and Ronnie Lane, and a January 1968 single for P.P. Arnold. It is absolutely superb! A great song anyway, Dave sings with passion, and the band play with commitment and vigour, giving a foretaste of the more serious direction The Tremeloes would go in the not-so-distant future. This essential performance is on 'BBC Sessions', while they also performed it on the sadly long-lost 'Colour Me Pop' TV show.

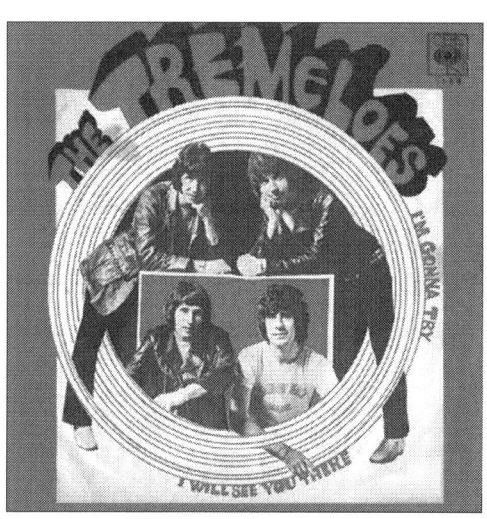

I'M GONNA TRY (Del Turco / Bigazzi)

Israeli picture sleeve

In July 1968, an exclusive song was released as a single A-side in parts of Europe, Chile and Israel only, namely '**I'm Gonna Try**'. Based on 'Luglio' by Italian singer Riccardo Del Turco, it featured one of two sets of completely new English lyrics by Jack Fishman. A catchy Pop-Rocker, it didn't do much chart-wise, but with the *other* set of lyrics as 'Something Is Happening', it became a world-wide smash hit for Herman's Hermits.

EN TU MONDO (Casal)

Despite only moderate success in the USA, The Tremeloes found superstardom in other new and unexpected territories.

Dave: "During 1967 and 1968 we flew to the US again, after our hits with 'Here Comes My Baby' and 'Silence Is Golden'. But we had somehow run our course. Instead though, we became the first British band to conquer South America. During March and

November 1968, we became a sensation in Argentina and Brazil. In Rio de Janeiro and Sao Paulo, we appeared in huge stadiums. CBS Records had a branch in Mexico at the time. Their agent really liked us and worked hard for our success. On our first tour, the plane had to stop over in Rio, and then we arrived in Buenos Aires - and in both cases it was like the Beatles, fans waving madly everywhere. Of course, later on bands like The Police and Sting played there, but for many years we were the first, until that wave eventually subsided. We also visited Scandinavia, Australia, South Africa, Iceland, Germany, Israel, The far East, The Eastern Bloc, to name but a few."

Alan: "We recorded in Spanish down there, for instance ´En Tu Mundo´, and stuff like that sold surprisingly well - not only in Argentina and Brazil, but also in Spain and at home in England!"

Featuring convincing Latino vocals by Dave, and fabulous flamenco guitar playing by Rick, The Tremeloes even performed it on BBC radio's 'Symonds On Sunday', as heard on 'BBC Sessions', as well as on the 'Live In Cabaret' album.

September 1968: SINGLE [CBS 3680]

Spanish picture sleeve

MY LITTLE LADY (Pace / Panzeri / Pilat / Blakley / Hawkes)
ALL THE WORLD TO ME (Blakley / Hawkes)

'**My Little Lady**' is another foreign-language song with new English lyrics, this time Orietta Berti's 'Non Illuderti Mai' (which translates as "Never Deceive Yourself"), from April 1968. The new lyrics, written primarily by Len, were inspired by an attractive actress, model and TV host named Carol Dilworth, whom he met when the band appeared on popular TV show 'The Golden Shot' earlier in the year. Instantly catchy, the song is enhanced by Mexican-style mariachi horns, and with appearances on 'Top Of The Pops', 'Time For Blackburn!', 'Crackerjack', 'Dee Time' and Germany's 'Beat Club', it got to No. 6 in the UK, No. 1 in Ireland and New Zealand, No. 2 in Belgium and Zimbabwe, No. 3 in Germany and The Netherlands, No. 5 in Norway and No. 51 in Australia. A BBC radio performance from the 'Dave Cash' show is on 'BBC Sessions', while Joe Dassin covered it in French as 'Ma Bonne Étoile'.

Although lacking the Pop-Psych touches of most other recent B-sides, '**All The World To Me**' is a good Pop-Rocker, with prominent harpsichord.

THE TREMELOES - EVEN THE BAD TIMES ARE GOOD!

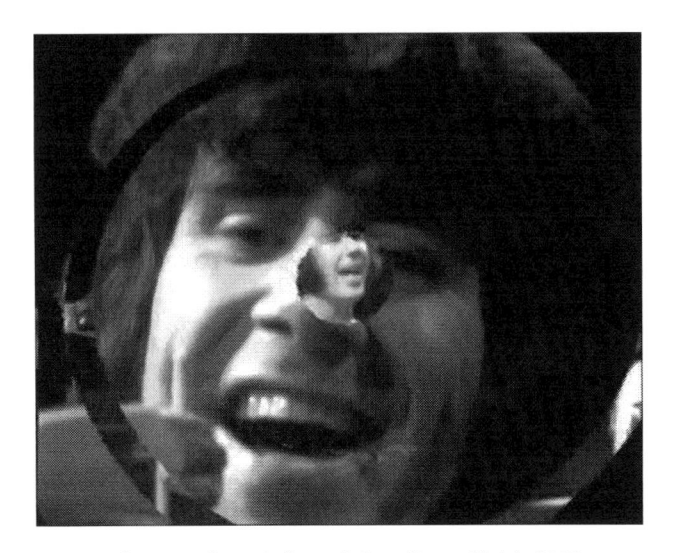

Performing 'My Little Lady' on 'Beat Club', 1969.

134

Carol Hawkes (née Dilworth): "He came up to me and was the most popular one in the band - he was the pretty one and the one the girls liked and the face of '67 or whatever. Number one in the charts and he obviously thought he was God's gift to women. We used to wear very short skirts on the show and he came up to me and said 'Ooh, I can see your knickers!' I thought 'You flash git. Who do you think you are?' (Laughs) And I just tried to avoid him and he kept on following me around. I think I became a bit of a challenge!"

November 1968: SINGLE [CBS 3873]

Dutch picture sleeve

I SHALL BE RELEASED (Dylan)
I MISS MY BABY (Blakley / Hawkes)

As was obvious by their B-sides, albums and BBC performances, there was so much more to The Tremeloes than their catchy Pop hits, something which was becoming increasing frustrating for the band. With '**I Shall Be Released**', they attempted to show off their more serious side on a single A-side. Written and recorded by composer Bob Dylan in late 1967 (though not released until 1991), it had previously been covered by Boz (aka Boz Burrell) in May 1968 and The Band in July 1968, but The Tremeloes' fabulous Len and Dave duet blows 'em all away, with the tight musicianship and harmonies enhanced by strings courtesy of Mike Mansfield. It was promoted on 'Top Of The Pops', 'Crackerjack', The Netherlands' 'Jam', and Germany's 'Beat Club' and 'Die Drehscheibe', but stalled at No. 29 in the UK, No. 47 in Australia, and flopped completely in most other countries. A BBC radio performance from 'Pete's Sunday People' is on 'BBC Sessions'. Marmalade released a cover of the song the following month as an album track, as did The Hollies early in the new year.

Even better is '**I Miss My Baby**'. Starting gently and acoustically with Len's solo vocal, the song gradually builds with stunning harmonies, subtle organ, and wild drumming. Len and Alan were by now writing songs the equal of the best of their contemporaries; all they needed was the confidence to release one as an A-side. Again, a performance from BBC radio's 'Pete's Sunday People' is on 'BBC Sessions'.

Performing 'I Shall Be Released' on 'Beat Club', 1969.

March 1969: SINGLE [CBS 4065]

German picture sleeve

HELLO WORLD (Hazzard)
UP, DOWN, ALL AROUND (Blakley / Hawkes)

After the relative flop of 'I Shall Be Released', and still apparently lacking the confidence to put out one of their own songs as a UK A-side, they once again recorded a song by an outside writer.

Tony Hazzard already had a track record for writing hits by some of the UK's top groups, including The Hollies ('Listen To Me'), Manfred Mann ('Ha! Ha! Said the Clown' and 'Fox on the Run') and Herman's Hermits ('You Won't Be Leaving'). He'd also written 'The Sound of The Candyman's Trumpet', a song that was recorded by Cliff Richard, and was in the running to represent the UK in the Eurovision Song Contest, though eventually that honour went to 'Congratulations'.

Tony Hazzard: "The next year I decided to try to write a proper Eurovision winner and came up with the title, 'Hello World', which seemed an obvious title to me. It was a straightforward pop song with a generally uplifting lyrical theme. I was pleased with my demo, which was included on my first album. During the MPA selection process, Mickie Most was sitting on the panel, and complained that the panel was rejecting songs which he thought were hits, including mine and one by (Roger) Greenaway and (Roger) Cook. I can't remember the title of the Rogers' song, but it was subsequently a hit, as was mine. I remembering moaning to a songwriting acquaintance, Peter Callender, and he retorted 'Well, at least it got you to write a hit!' The set-up in those days was that I would book a studio and musicians, and record a demo which they would then offer to an A&R man of their choice. In this case I think the song was pitched to the Tremeloes' producer, Mike Smith, or it could have been one of the band. The Tremeloes decided to keep the double speed for the first half of the chorus, which I thought lessened the impact."

Apart from the afore-mentioned double-speed in part of the chorus (the chorus on Tony Hazzard's version is slow throughout), The Tremeloes follow the demo template surprisingly closely, though whether purposely or accidentally, they sound a bit like The Bee Gees - a group who were having considerable success with similar Pop-Rock material at the time. Not everyone in the band was happy though.

Alan: "I didn't really want this record released. I didn't expect 'Hello World' to even be a Top Twenty hit, I really didn't like it. 'I Shall Be Released' on the other hand, wasn't a commercial proposition, but it was a worthwhile record and better than the usual things we do."

It was promoted on 'Top Of The Pops', 'The Golden Shot', 'The Basil Brush Show', 'Pop Scotch' and The Netherlands' 'Jam', but was only a moderate hit at No. 14 in the UK and No. 20 in New Zealand. A performance on BBC radio's 'Symonds On Sunday' is on 'BBC Sessions', and the original demo was released on 1969's 'Tony Hazzard Sings Tony Hazzard' album.

Fading in at the beginning (and fading out at the end), and sounding like little more than a studio jam, '**Up, Down, All Around**' is a loose and wild 3-chord rocker, with some bluesy guitar playing from Rick, and Dave sounding *totally* unhinged vocally. It is unlike anything the band had done previously... which makes it all the more surprising that a song of this title was originally planned as the follow-up to 'Here Comes My

Baby' two years earlier. If it had sounded anything like this, it could've ended The Tremeloes' chart career as quickly as it had began!

Dave: "I'm not saying that I never indulged in a few illegal substances. We did. I think everybody did. But we knew when enough was enough. You know, we had the presence of mind to think, no, that's it, you know, done that, been there, done that, seen that, got the T-shirt - now should get on with life, you know."

JACQUELINE (Pace / Hazzard)

For the Italian market, The Tremeloes re-recorded 'Hello World' with new lyrics in Italian - but instead of a straight translation, it was about a girl called '**Jacqueline**'!

CAN'T TURN YOU LOOSE (Redding)
[BBC Radio - Not released until 2004]

Originally released by Otis Redding in November 1965, the up-tempo Soul number '**Can't Turn You Loose**' was covered by Johnny Kidd and The Pirates (1965, not released until 1983), The Alan Price Set (1966), Jimmy James and The Vagabonds (1966), Zoot Money's Big Roll Band (1966) and Geno Washington and The Ram Jam Band (1967). Kicking off with a drum roll and a screaming Dave Munden vocal, The Tremeloes' BBC recording may not have broken new ground musically, but it's one of their very best Soul covers, and can be heard on 'BBC Sessions'.

June 1969: SINGLE [CBS 4313]

German picture sleeve

ONCE ON A SUNDAY MORNING (Aguile / Kusik / Snyder / Blakley / Hawkes)
FA LA LA, LA LA, LA LE (Blakley / Hawkes)

With their last two singles selling less well than expected, The Tremeloes harked back to the party sounds of 'Here Comes My Baby', 'Even The Bad Times Are Good' and 'Suddenly You Love Me', in the hope of putting them back at the top. Their plan back-fired spectacularly. Based on Luis Aguilé's 1967 Spanish-language single 'Cuando Salí De Cuba' with newly-written English lyrics, '**Once On A Sunday Morning**' is not a *bad* record. But, despite promotion on 'Top Of The Pops' and 'The Basil Brush Show', it failed to chart completely, though it did get to No. 17 in Zimbabwe and No. 25 in The Netherlands. Both the public and the band were getting bored with this type of Pop-Rock song, and it was time for change. A BBC radio recording from the 'Jimmy Young' show is on 'BBC Sessions'.

Even the B-side of this single is rather run-of-the-mill. '**Fa La La, La La, La Le**' starts off OK, with odd, syncopated timing and piano, but then evolves into a mediocre sub-Eurovision type song, complete with a predictable La-La-La-ing chorus.

SADNESS OF TOMORROW (Blakley / Hawkes)
[Not released until 2000]

Recorded around this time, '**Sadness Of Tomorrow**', is a song that wasn't released until 2000 on 'Boxed'. Again, it has that "La, La, La" chorus, and is nothing special, but it does perhaps have the edge on 'Fa La La, La La, La Le'.

October 1969: SINGLE [CBS 4582]

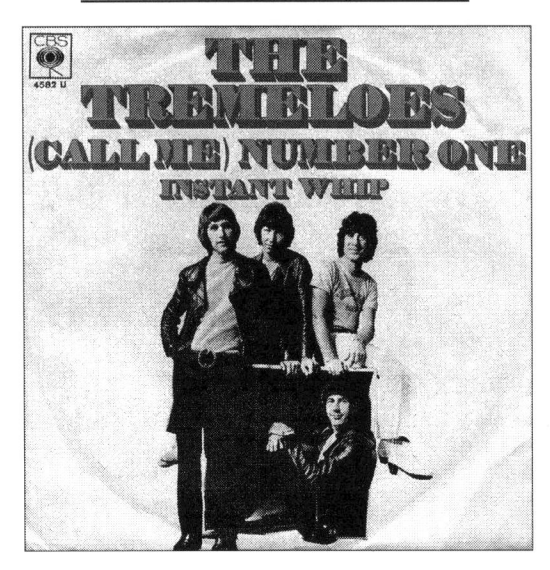

German picture sleeve

(CALL ME) NUMBER ONE (Blakley / Hawkes)
INSTANT WHIP (Munden / West)

Up until now, The Tremeloes had relied at least partially on other writers for their single A-sides, and their one attempt at a more serious-sounding record with 'I Shall Be Released' pleased the critics more than the record buyers.

Len: "We had gotten into the carefree, sing-along thing and we found the more it worked for us, the harder it became to get out of the rut."

Something they'd had for some time, **'(Call Me) Number One'**, with its superb Lennon-like vocal from Dave, was a complete change of style for the band.

Alan: "The only way you can describe it, is it's sorta like what The Traffic were doing when they first started. It's something like that."

Promoted on 'Top Of The Pops', 'Crackerjack', and Germany's '4-3-2-1, Musik Fur Junge Leute' [aka '4-3-2-1, Hot and Sweet'], the record was a major success almost everywhere, including No. 2 in the UK and Ireland,

No. 3 in Germany and Zimbabwe, No. 4 in Norway and New Zealand, No. 17 in The Netherlands, No. 22 in Belgium and No. 27 in Australia. A performance from 'Radio One Club' is on 'BBC Sessions', while a new stereo mix appeared on 2000's 'Master - The Early 70's Sessions' CD.

Alan: "(We've) come to hate all those happy records, even the ones that sold hundreds and hundreds of thousands. People have bought it thinking it was a good record, and not because it was the Tremeloes."

'**Instant Whip**' is even more of a shift in styles. An instrumental jam with wild drumming, screams, riffing guitars and maracas, it's closest cousin was probably Chicago's version of the Spencer Davis Group's 'I'm A Man', but this is far more crazed. Can this really be the same band that were Fa-La-La-ing on the B-side of the previous single?

THE TREMELOES - EVEN THE BAD TIMES ARE GOOD!

Performing '(Call Me) Number One' on '4-3-2-1, Musik Fur Junge Leute', 1969.

The Tremeloes with their better halves, 1969: Alan and Lin, Len and Carol, Dave and Andree, Rick and Lynn. All four members of The Tremeloes, as well as Brian Poole and his wife Pam, remained with the women that they married in the '60s, something that is probably unique in the music industry!

October 1969: ALBUM [CBS 63547]

LIVE IN CABARET

MEDLEY: RUN BABY RUN (BACK INTO MY ARMS) (Gant / Melson)
- **SHAKE HANDS (AND COME OUT CRYING)** (Kershaw)
- **HELLO WORLD** (Hazzard)
- **MY LITTLE LADY** (Pace / Panzeri)
ANGEL OF THE MORNING (Taylor)
MEDLEY: GAMES PEOPLE PLAY (South)
- **PROUD MARY** (Fogarty)
BLESSED (Simon)
HERE COMES MY BABY (Stevens)
EN TU MONDO (Casal)
MEDLEY: MOUNTAIN DEW (Trad.)
- **F.B.I.** (Gormley)
I SHALL BE RELEASED (Dylan)
MEDLEY: SILENCE IS GOLDEN (Gaudio / Crewe)
- **EVEN THE BAD TIMES ARE GOOD** (Murray / Callander)
- **SUDDENLY YOU LOVE ME** (Callander / Pace / Panzeri / Pillat)
GOOD TIMES (Vanda / Young)

Even back in the pre-record contract days of The Tremilos, the band had a reputation for being great live, and this stayed with them throughout their career. Taped at 'The Showboat' in Manchester and the 'Top Hat' in Spennymoor in June 1969, this captures the band just before they went "serious" with '(Call Me) Number One'. It remains one of the finest live albums of the '60s, even with the somewhat unappealing cover and title ('Live In Cabaret' was never going to sound as cool as 'Got Live If You Want It!' or 'Live at The Star Club!'). There is some distortion on the vocals, but for what it loses in fidelity, it gains in atmosphere.

Len: "It's a great album. We were one of the best live bands of the sixties!"

'Live In Cabaret' is a mixture of hits, misses, album tracks and stage favourites, and although most of the songs would already have been known to keen fans, there are a number of "new" songs on the album. The one down-side is that many of the big hits are thrown away in medleys or performed in edited form, something that would become unthinkable in later years.

First recorded by Evie Sands in 1967, and covered in fine style by both Billie Davis and P.P. Arnold, **'Angel Of The Morning'** is beautifully sung by Dave. He obviously loved the song, as it pretty much remained in The Tremeloes' set lists for the next half a century, and was re-cut for both an '80s single and a '90s album. They performed it on 'Colour Me Pop' the previous year, while a 1968 BBC radio performance is on 'BBC Sessions'.

Joe South's much-covered **'Games People Play'** features Rick's electric sitar, as well as a strong Len vocal - but it very quickly segues into a great version of Creedence Clearwater Revival's **'Proud Mary'**, with a powerhouse vocal from Dave and the sitar still much in evidence. The latter song was performed on BBC radio's 'Jimmy Young' show, as heard on 'BBC Sessions'.

An instrumental, **'Mountain Dew'** is an old Appalachian folk song which dates back to at least the 1920's, and is a great showcase for Rick's accomplished hillbilly pickin', heard here along with an all-too-brief snippet of The Shadows' '**F.B.I.**'.

The raucous rocker '**Good Times**' is a song originally recorded by The Easybeats, and covered by both Amen Corner and Cliff Bennett. It's the closing song on this album, but when the band taped it for the 'Doing Our Thing' live TV show the following year, it was used as the opener. A performance from BBC radio's 'Pete's Sunday People' is on 'BBC Sessions'.

February 1970: SINGLE [CBS 4815]

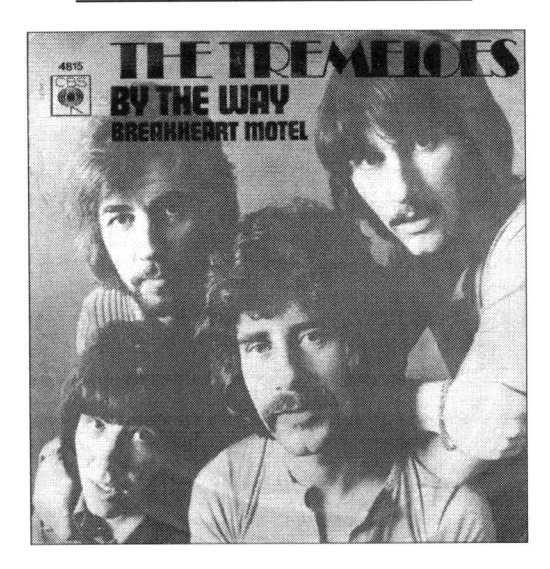

Dutch picture sleeve

BY THE WAY (Blakley / Hawkes)
BREAKHEART MOTEL (Munden / West)

A slow ballad that starts with gentle acoustic guitars, strings and a delicate, beautifully-sung Len lead vocal, '**By The Way**' gradually builds with impeccable harmonies, a soulful Dave counter-vocal - and pioneering, layered guitars, similar to what Queen were doing years later.

Rick: "I was the first British guitarist in a Pop group to use multi-track guitar on records. Brian May from Queen used it a lot on their records many years later. I must say that Brian May is a much better guitarist than I am!"

It is arguably the most sublime piece of music the band ever made, but even with appearances on 'Top Of The Pops' and 'The Basil Brush Show', it stalled at a disastrous No. 35 in the UK, with New Zealand being the only country that bettered it at No. 18. Perhaps it was a little *too* sophisticated and subtle for the public at large. Certainly there were some far more catchy and instant-memorable songs around in early 1970. Songs like 'Yellow River'.

'Breakheart Motel' is an affectionate and accurate Elvis Presley tribute/parody, with boogie woogie piano, Rockabilly Scotty Moore-like guitar licks, Jordanaires-styled backing vocals - and a great lead vocal from the Elvis-fanatic in the band.

Len: "I wish I'd met Elvis Presley, because he was the best! The best singer, the best artist the world has ever had, I think. That's my opinion."

Performing 'By The Way' on 'The Basil Brush Show', 1970.

WHAT CAN I DO (O'Sullivan)
[Not released until 2000]

Not released until 2000, the Pop-Psych, piano-led '**What Can I Do**' features nasal, compressed vocals, and more 'Queen'-like guitar. When the song first surfaced on 'Boxed', it was credited to Alan and Len, but on some subsequent releases, Gilbert O'Sullivan is correctly listed as the writer. It's certainly a highly worthwhile track that didn't deserve to remain in the can for 30 years, and the band themselves must've liked it, as they still performed it on BBC radio's 'Saturday People' in late 1969, as heard on 'BBC Sessions' *(Note: The Tremeloes continued to tape sessions for the BBC regularly during 1970-1972, but sadly the cut-off point for the official CDs is 1969. Many of these fascinating later sessions survive, and circulate amongst collectors).*

YELLOW RIVER (Christie)
[Not released until 1990]

As 'By The Way' was sliding down the charts from its not-so-lofty top chart position of No. 35, a song called **'Yellow River'** - featuring The Tremeloes but composed by a promising new writer by the name of Jeff Christie - was racing up the charts. It would peak at No. 1 in the UK, as well as be a major hit pretty much everywhere else. Here's the 'Yellow River' story in the words of Dave, Len and Jeff Christie.

Dave: "A Young guy came in one afternoon when we were rehearsing, and he said he had some songs for us to listen to. Would we be interested in hearing them and maybe recording some? So he played, I think it was the first song, was 'Yellow River'. And then started singing. And instantly it was much better than anything that he'd played us on the cassette. It was obviously a hit record. It's just waiting to be put down and sung and done whatever way, but it was instantly a hit record."

Jeff: "It was not the first song at all. I had played them a substantial number of songs including a song I'd specifically written with them in mind called 'Tomorrow Night' which they immediately said was the type of song they were trying to get away from, even though it was in the vein of several of their hits. I was about to call it a day and just asked them to listen to the 'Yellow River' demo which I think was the last song and that really did hit the spot and they asked for a copy tape to take to London. Dave mentions I played my songs on a cassette but it was on a Grundig Reel to Reel tape recorder. I was very interested in songs about America and in particular Americana. Confederate soldier on leave, going back to his sort of hometown area which was called 'Yellow River'."

Dave: "We recorded it, put it down, maybe two or three different versions of it, with me singing the lead vocal on it and the Tremeloes playing the whole backing and doing the vocal backing as well."

Len: "And funny enough, it was like a typical Tremeloes record.

Happy, up-tempo, typical."

Jeff: "First of all, they were going to release it as an album track, and then second of all, they were going to release it as a B-side, and then they were going to release it as an A-side. This is the way I remember it. And when they were going to release it as an A-side, as a single, I really thought, that's it, that's fantastic! Then after all that, they decided, change of plan, they weren't going to do it, they were going to release one of their own songs."

Dave: "When we recorded it, 'Yellow River', we thought that it was definitely a hit record, but Alan (Blakley) wanted it to be released with his brother. His brother was in a little group called The Epics and he said, 'Look, we've got a single. Why don't we release this, give it to my brother and put this new band together and let them have the record?'"

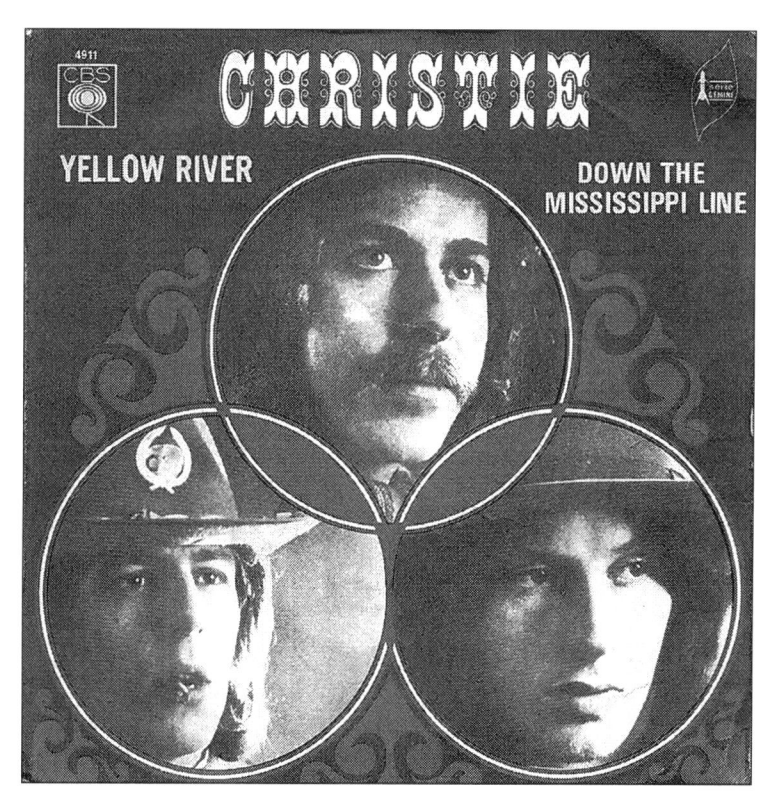

French picture sleeve for Christie's 'Yellow River', 1970.

Len: "Because he wanted to get his brother in the charts. You can't blame him you know. So we thought, well, let's get Jeff down from Leeds, take the lead voice off 'Yellow River' and just let Jeff sing on our track and have Jeff as the front-man for this little band. It's exactly what happened. And the name was like, well, what can we call it? And it was so natural. 'Christie', he wrote the song and 'Christie' sounded a good name for a band. That was it."

Jeff: "It was number one in 26 countries and the UK, and it reached 16 in the US Cashbox top 100 chart and 22 in the US Billboard top 100 chart."

Len: "I have to admit that probably, as far as I'm concerned, it was one of the biggest mistakes that we ever made. Really, not releasing 'Yellow River' because it would have made The Tremeloes profile up that little bit more at the end of the '60s, going into the '70s, because it would have been a '70s record and took us into that decade as well. But it would have been a huge hit, it would have been number one, no question about it. So, yes, a few regrets!"

Perhaps surprisingly, The Tremeloes performed the song on 'The Basil Brush Show' - along with 'By The Way' - about a month prior to the release of Christie's version, and even then it must've been apparent that they'd made a mistake. However, their 1970 studio recording wasn't released until 1990's 'Ultimate Collection', while an alternate version about 35 seconds longer and with less backing vocals appeared on 'Boxed' in 2000. 'Yellow River' remained an integral part of The Tremeloes' live act for most of their remaining career (indeed, their first release of the song was a then-recent live version on a 1985 compilation), perhaps as a reminder to everyone what they'd let slip away. A performance for BBC radio circulates unofficially.

NO COMPRENDES (YELLOW RIVER) (Christie / Gale)

The Spanish version of 'Yellow River' was recorded as 'No Comprendes', but as with 'Hello World' and the Italian 'Jacqueline' a year earlier, the foreign version has lyrics entirely unrelated to the original.

Dave: "The Tremeloes went to South America and it was decided to make a version for South America, which was called, as you know, 'No Comprendes'. And the lyrics were written by, I think, probably the promoter in South America. And I learnt the lyrics off just phonetically. Paraphrased, learnt to sing the song, and we recorded it. And when we went to South America, I think we were number one in the charts with it. And Christie's version of 'Yellow River' was something like number three or number four, the same record, just with Jeff singing in English and the Tremeloes backing it. And we were at number one with me singing in Spanish with the same track. It was quite a unique, unusual situation, really strange."

Released in various Spanish-speaking countries, remarkably, the song was also performed on British TV, as part of their 30 minute appearance on Granada TV's 'Doing Their Thing'.

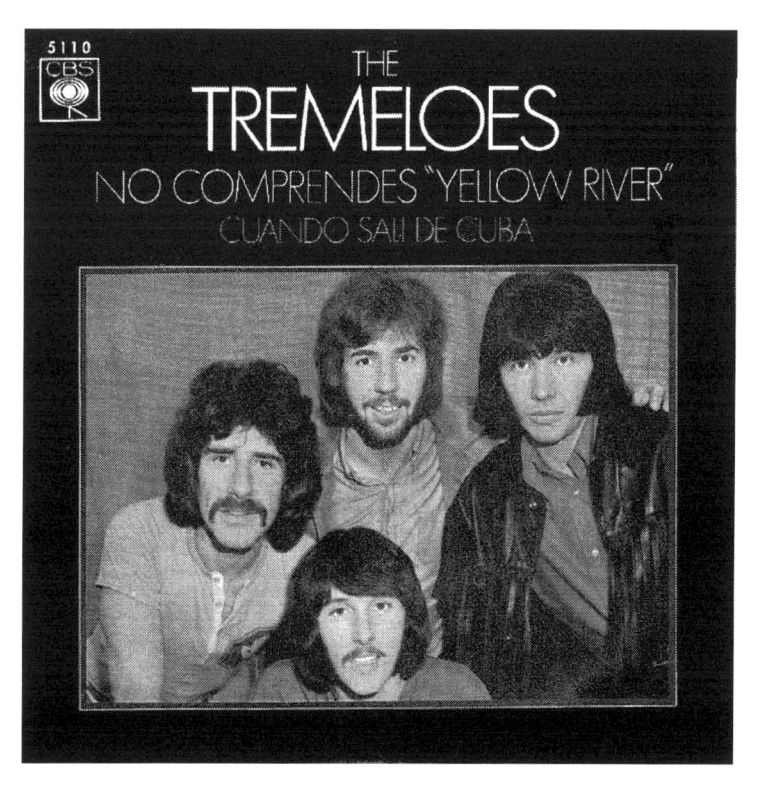

Spanish picture sleeve

Early 1970: ALBUM [Castle Music CMRCD 025]

MAY MORNING *[Not released until 2000]*

MAY MORNING (Blakley / Hawkes)
ALL PULL TOGETHER (Blakley / Hawkes)
TILL THE SUN GOES DOWN (Blakley / Hawkes)
TURN ON WITH THEE (Blakley / Hawkes)
I CAN'T EVEN BREATHE DOWN HERE (Blakley / Hawkes)
MAY MORNING (REPRISE 1) (Blakley / Hawkes)
ANYTHING (Blakley / Hawkes)
THINK OF WHAT YOU SAID (Blakley / Hawkes)
BEER DUEL (Blakley / Hawkes)
HARD TIME (Blakley / Hawkes)
I'LL TAKE YOU HOME (Blakley / Hawkes)
BUNCH OF RAPES (Blakley / Hawkes)
MAY MORNING (REPRISE 2) (Blakley / Hawkes)
I YOU KNOW (Blakley / Hawkes)

In the early months of 1970, The Tremeloes were commissioned to write and perform the music for 'May Morning', a movie directed by Ugo Liberatore, and starring Jane Birkin, Alessio Orano and John Steiner. Alan and Len were due to fly over to Italy in advance to compose the sound-track, but then disaster occurred when Alan became ill. Undeterred, Len went ahead, and largely composed the soundtrack himself, doing a stellar job of coming up with imaginative material while watching movie rushes, timing material to the second. With Alan recovered, the others joined him to record the music, but it was all in vain: the movie was a major flop, so the soundtrack wasn't released. Fortunately, the master tapes survived, and the album was given a very belated release some 30 years later, when it quickly gained a reputation as a lost gem, becoming essential listening for connoisseurs of British Pop-Psych.

The movie itself, shot on location in Oxford in the summer of 1969, reflects the 'Swinging Sixties gone sour' mode that was very much in vogue at the time - think 'Performance' and 'If' rather than 'Blow Up' and 'The Knack'. The Tremeloes' sound-track has a curiously retro feel, with acoustic guitars to the fore, as well as a sometimes blatant Beatles influence.

The song '**May Morning**', appears in three forms. The first is a laid-back mid-paced Boogie, with acoustic and electric guitars, and a vocal shared by Len and Dave; '**May Morning (Reprise 1)**' is faster, with vocals by Dave, and a flute similar to the one heard on Canned Heat's 'Going Up The Country' - which was probably done on Len's newly-acquired mellotron; '**May Morning (Reprise 2)**' is again fast, but this time purely an instrumental, with more 'flute', as well as harmonica and electric sitar. Two years after this, in April 1972, The Tremeloes recorded a version for BBC radio - though without any mention of the words 'May Morning' - and featuring an inspired John Fogerty-styled vocal from Dave. Like all of their post-1969 BBC recordings though, this extraordinary recording still awaits an official release.

'**All Pull Together**', not surprisingly, is an acoustic sing-a-long, quite similar to The Beatles' 'All Together Now' - though with the added attraction of The Goons-inspired ad-libs.

MAY MORNING

With its descending chords, and Lennon-like phrasing, the nearest reference point for **'Till The Sun Goes Down'** is 'Dear Prudence', though the double-tracked solo voice without harmonies and with sparse instrumentation sounds more like some of the gentler moments on the 1970 'John Lennon/Plastic Ono Band' album - which wasn't even recorded when this song was cut.

After a brief piano introduction, the near-instrumental **'Turn On With Thee'** starts as an 'I've Got A Feeling' type jam, but then it quickly becomes slower and more melodic, with soft wordless harmonies and synthetic strings.

'**I Can't Even Breathe Down Here**' is a short laid-back boogie instrumental, featuring just a solitary acoustic guitar and a harmonica.

This time probably taking their inspiration from The Faces and The Rolling Stones, '**Anything**' starts off sounding gloriously ragged and rustic, but then develops into a powerful Country-tinged Rock song, complete with wah wah guitar and some pretty powerful drumming. An alternate take is on 'The Complete CBS Recordings 1966-72', while a more electric version for BBC radio circulates unofficially. Three years later, the chorus for 'Anything' would be recycled for the song 'Make Or Break'.

With acoustic backing and strings, **'Think Of What You Said'** is a gentle and melodic song sung by Len. The only thing wrong with it is the short running time of under two and half minutes in length.

Another instrumental, the first half of **'Beer Duel'** features acoustic guitar pickin', but then evolves into a weird space-age mellotron noise, but it's all over in under a minute.

MAY MORNING

'Hard Time' is another all-too-brief instrumental, all slow and heavy, with timpani, effects-laden guitar and mellotron.

Kicking off with saxophone, the Dave-sung **'I'll Take You Home'** features distant backing vocals and a beefy guitar riff. With a bit more work, this interesting song had the potential to turn into a minor classic.

The instrumental '**Bunch Of Rapes**' features just a fast-strummed acoustic guitar and Bluesy harmonica, and was written to accompany the film's notorious rape scene.

If it weren't for the slide guitar and somewhat weird mellotron touches, the excellent closer '**I You Know**' could almost be mistaken for a 'Rubber Soul' / 'Revolver'-era Beatles song. An alternate version is on 'The Complete CBS Recordings 1966-72'.

August 1970: SINGLE [CBS 5139]

French picture sleeve

ME AND MY LIFE (Blakley / Hawkes)
TRY ME (Blakley / Hawkes)

After the poor chart-showing of 'By The Way', and despite the mistake in not releasing 'Yellow River' as a single, The Tremeloes persevered with using their own composition as a single A-side. With superb lead vocals by Len, and Dave singing the bridge, central to the success of '**Me and My Life**' is a memorable guitar riff.

Len: "I'd written the riff and rang Al at two in the morning, I was so excited by it. At the time, I was really into Roy Wood, and I remember asking myself what would Roy do with it. Al and I spent the rest of the night finishing the song."

With promotion on 'Top Of The Pops', 'Stewpot', 'Lift Off', 'The Basil Brush Show', 'The Golden Shot' and 'Ev', the single peaked at No. 4 in the UK, No. 2 in Ireland, No. 6 in Germany and Zimbabwe, No. 27 in The Netherlands and No. 46 in Belgium. A BBC radio performance circulates unofficially, while covers include those by Italian Le Particelle (as 'Oh, Mia Bambina', 1970), the Spanish Albert Band (as 'Quiero Vivir', 1970), and, decades later, hardcore Punk group Anti-Nowhere League (2017).

As with '(Call Me) Number One', the band had succeeded with a song that was progressive musically, and pleased the critics just as much as the record buyers. It proved to be their last hit of any significance.

The Dave-sung **'Try Me'** is a mid-paced boogie with tough, arpeggio guitars, and a layered lead that would've made Brian May listen in awe - showing just how far the band had progressed in recent months.

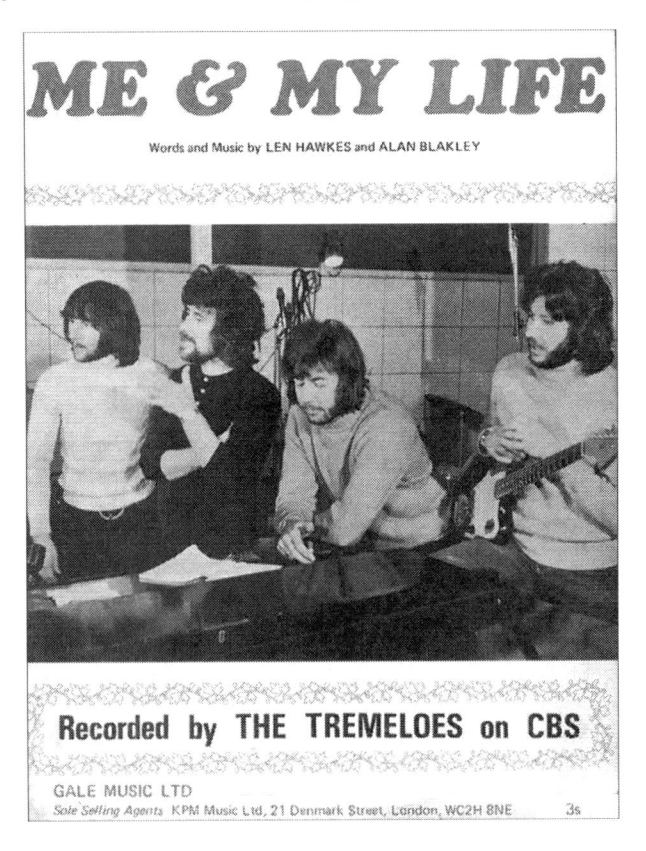

REMEMBER LOOKING BACK (Blakley / Hawkes)

A foreign-language song with new lyrics by Len and Alan, **'Remember Looking Back'** has a nice happy/sad melody similar to some of The Move's lighter moments, but is spoilt by a weak "Sha-la-la-la-la" chorus. Not released in the UK at the time, it first surfaced on a Mexican EP in early 1971 - an EP that also featured 'Me and My Life', 'Breakheart Motel', and, oddly, 'The Lion Sleeps Tonight'.

November 1970: ALBUM [CBS 64242]

MASTER

WAIT FOR ME (Blakley / Hawkes)
LONG ROAD (Blakley / Hawkes)
NOW'S THE TIME (Blakley / Hawkes)
TRY ME (Blakley / Hawkes)
BUT THEN I... (Blakley / Hawkes)
BEFORE I SLEEP (Blakley / Hawkes)
BOOLA BOOLA (Blakley / Hawkes)
I SWEAR (Blakley / Hawkes)
BABY (Blakley / Hawkes)
BY THE WAY (Blakley / Hawkes)
WILLOW TREE (Blakley / Hawkes)
ME AND MY LIFE (Blakley / Hawkes)

Following the success of their self-penned singles and the (unreleased) 'May Morning' soundtrack, The Tremeloes' self-confidence was at an all-time high, so they recorded the album THEY wanted to make.

Alan: "Don't really know how to describe it, but it is completely home grown, and music we really like. I'll admit that we have been influenced, and don't mind saying The Beatles had a tremendous influence on us. So have the Stones. You can't help being influenced by them, they are incredible. But what pleases us about the new stuff is that it's completely spontaneous. No longer are we sitting down and penning out the standard hit formula."

The first flaw in their (Master) plan though was CBS releasing the album prior to them finishing it.

Len: "We had finished the backing tracks and basic guide vocals and were supposed to fly to South America for a tour. None of the tracks had been properly finished, with the exception of the projected single 'Me and My Life'. But still, CBS Records had (literally unfinished) 'Master' mastered and pressed and threw it onto the market. We were all absolutely disappointed!"

A far bigger problem occurred when Alan - with some encouragement from Len - spoke out during a notorious 'Melody Maker' interview. With the heading "We'd Get Backstage and Just Kill Ourselves Laughing at an Audience", their fans were dismissed as "Silly Suckers" (something which has somehow been changed to "Morons" over the years - not a word that was used). The backlash was incredible, with the band getting a lot of publicity for the wrong reason.

Len: "It was devastating. Alan didn't mean to do it like that. He had so much exuberance and energy, he was great for pushing people along. We got booed when we were on stage. You can't retract that kind of thing. To say we were getting cool receptions was an understatement!"

Dave: "Alan was the spokesman for the band. I loved him, but he had a big mouth!"

Rick: "We should have released the LP without any comments at the time."

'**Try Me**', '**By The Way**' and '**Me and My Life**' - all highly worthy songs - had previously been released, but what about the rest?

With Dave sounding like a more powerful John Fogerty, '**Wait For Me**' has a very fuzzy Hard Rock guitar riff, an incredible guitar solo, and a catchy chorus that is backed by just bass and drums. In fact, throughout, there are some oddly under-produced touches - but if this is the "unfinished" album that Len complained about, it largely works in its favour. A very different alternate take can be found on 2000's 'Master - The Early 70's Sessions' collection.

The mid-paced '**Long Road**' features Cliff Bennett and The Rebel Rousers-styled brass and piano, as well as both guitar and trumpet solos. A more stripped-back version recorded for the BBC circulates unofficially.

'**Now's The Time**', after some very brief backwards guitar, is a largely acoustic Len-sung song, with harmonies similar to what Crosby, Stills and Nash were doing at the same time, but if anything The Tremeloes sound tighter.

Again acoustic and harmonised, though with a more upbeat and up-tempo chorus, '**But Then I...**' sounds uncannily like The Hollies. Subtle strings (or mellotron) and a couple of acoustic guitar solos enhance things further. A performance for BBC radio circulates unofficially.

'**Before I Sleep**' is a very touching Len-sung and piano-led ballad about becoming a father, complete with yet more superb guitar from Rick. Again, a BBC radio performance is available in collecting circles.

Largely an instrumental apart from some chanted, wordless harmonies, '**Boola Boola**' is really little more than an (inspired) guitar and drums workout.

'**I Swear**' is a piano-driven mid-tempo song with Dave doing his best John Lennon impersonation, with some brilliant 'Brian May' layered guitar. A more basic-sounding version from the BBC circulates unofficially.

Another impersonation, with Len doing Elvis Presley, '**Baby**' is a light-weight quasi-Rockabilly song, similar to Elvis' 'Teddy Bear'.

'**Willow Tree**', with its three-part harmonies and an exciting guitar riff, is one of the more obviously Beatles-influenced songs, even if one could do without the silly Goons-styled ad-libs. Instead of fading out, the song eventually breaks down into laughter.

In some respect, 'Master' accomplished what they were trying to achieve, proving that The Tremeloes were a highly capable band who could hold their own against pretty much anyone with original material. Ultimately though, sales of the album were disappointing, and they wouldn't make another one until 1974. Regardless, it remained something that the band were justly proud of.

Dave: "The album 'Master' possesses a real cult status with true Tremeloes fans now. If you know 'Master', you know the band pretty well. Here, and on the follow-up 'Shiner', we surely played in a more adventurous way compared to earlier times."

January 1971: SINGLE [CBS 5429]

German picture sleeve

RIGHT WHEEL, LEFT HAMMER, SHAM (Blakley / Hawkes)
TAKE IT EASY (Blakley / Hawkes / Munden / Westwood)

'**Right Wheel, Left Hammer, Sham**' is a tough Blues Boogie, similar to what Status Quo were doing around this time on their 'Ma Kelly's Greasy Spoon' album. Impressive stuff, particularly Dave's vocal and Rick's guitar, but the terrible title didn't help things at all (how many people would've asked for that in a record shop?). Consequently, despite promotion on 'Top Of The Pops', 'Stewpot', The Netherlands' 'TopPop' and Germany's 'Hits A Go Go', it only got to No. 46 in the UK, No. 27 in The Netherlands and No. 31 in Germany. A BBC radio performance circulates unofficially, and a quite different alternate take in stereo surfaced on 'Master - The Early 70's Sessions' in 2000.

An instrumental, '**Take It Easy**' is a loose, funky Blues jam. Good fun though.

THE TREMELOES - EVEN THE BAD TIMES ARE GOOD!

Performing 'Right Wheel, Left Hammer, Sham' on 'Stewpot', 1971.

June 1971: SINGLE [CBS 7294]

German picture sleeve

HELLO BUDDY (Blakley / Hawkes)
MY WOMAN (Munden / Westwood)

A song that somehow harks back to the past while looking forward, '**Hello Buddy**' has the sing-a-long quality and trade-mark harmonies of the big hits (and the "Hello Buddy, Hello Buddy" refrain giving 'Yellow River' a sly nod), but with Country music instrumentation of banjo, fiddle and steel guitar - largely courtesy of Rick Westwood.

Rick: "Many years ago I learnt to play 5-string banjo, Dobro and pedal steel guitar as well as the guitar and bass. I did many recording sessions for other artistes using my 5-string banjo and pedal steel guitar as there were not many musicians who could play those instruments. The men I listened to were Jerry Reed, Chet Atkins, Lloyd Green, Les Paul, Doug Jerrnigan, Albert Lee. We played with Albert Lee in 1965 when he was with a band called 'Chris Farlowe and The Thunderbirds'. They were not very well known and they were supporting us as we were in the charts at the time. They were a brilliant band, much better than us."

With promotion on 'Top Of The Pops', 'Lift Off', 'Whittaker's World Of Music', 'The Basil Brush Show', 'The Golden Shot' and Germany's 'Disco', the UK No. 32 chart placing was a disappointment, though it did do a little better at No. 15 in New Zealand and No. 16 in Germany. A BBC performance circulates unofficially, while foreign-language covers include Spain's Los Huracanes (1971) and La Brigada (as 'Hola Buddy', 1972), Czechoslavakia's Jiří Hromádka (as 'Černá Mária', 1972) and Finland's Kalmar Union (as 'En Oo Vaari', 1973).

A very fast - *too* fast - Chuck Berry-styled Rock 'n' Roll number, **'My Woman'** isn't the greatest song ever written, but it did potentially earn Dave and Rick some publishing royalties.

Performing 'Hello Buddy' on 'Whittaker's World Of Music', 1971.

NO, NO, NO (Woolfson)
[Not released until 2000]

'No, No, No' was first recorded - but rejected - around early 1968. The early 1971 re-cut is a little slower and with beefier production that includes brass and guitar-sitar, but again it was left in the can. Instead, it was given to The Symbols, featuring their old mate Mick Clarke, who simply used the same backing track and overdubbed their own vocals, 'Yellow River' fashion, but it failed to chart. The Tremeloes' own 1971 recording finally surfaced on BR Music's 'Boxed' in 2000.

NO MORE SAD SONGS (Lynne)
[Not released until 2000]

Originally released as '*Please* No More Sad Songs' by Idle Race in November 1969, The Tremeloes' version as '**No More Sad Songs**' is faster and rockier, but otherwise largely retains the Pop-Psych feel of the original. Not released until 2000's 'Boxed', where it was credited to Blakley and Hawkes, on 2020's 'The Complete CBS Recordings 1966-72' both Jeff Lynne's writing credit and the full title were corrected.

Rick: "We were in America and our record company was CBS, and I bought a Mosrite double neck guitar from the company. I got a really good deal but when I declared it at London customs, they would not believe that I got it that cheap and confiscated it. I even had the genuine receipt but they said it was counterfeit. There was nothing I could do and the customs stole my guitar. I found it in a London music shop a couple of years later - I knew it was mine because I put my initials under the plastic pick-guard. It was being sold for twice the price I paid for it in America. No, I didn't buy it back."

October 1971: SINGLE [CBS 7579]

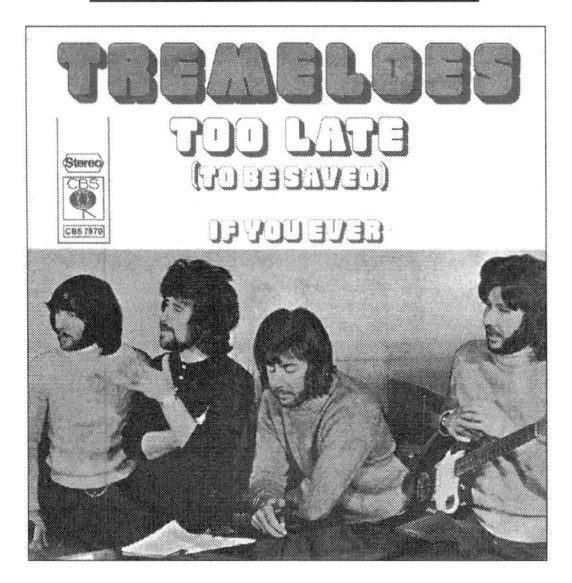

Dutch picture sleeve

TOO LATE (TO BE SAVED) (Blakley / Hawkes)
IF YOU EVER (Blakley / Hawkes)

With both acoustic and country-ish guitars and an unexpected brass-accompanied solo, the harmonised sing-a-long chorus on '**Too Late (To Be Saved)**' contrasts nicely with Dave's Soulful, almost Gospel, sung verses. It was promoted on 'Top Of The Pops', 'Lift Off', and Germany's 'Disco' and 'Hits A Go Go', but only got to No. 33 in Germany and No. 13 in Zimbabwe, and failed to chart completely in the UK. A BBC radio performance circulates unofficially.

'**If You Ever**' is a mid-tempo song with flutes and piano, distinguished by some unusual falsetto scat singing in the solo. Again, a BBC radio performance circulates unofficially.

HOW CAN YOU SAY GOODBYE (Blakley / Hawkes)
[Not released until 2000]

With a dominant electric keyboard riff that sounds a bit like The Archies' 'Sugar, Sugar' as well as organ, '**How Can You Say Goodbye**' is no more than mediocre. The Tremeloes must've thought so too, as it remained unreleased until 2000's 'Boxed'. Despite this, they did do a performance for BBC radio, which is available unofficially.

Performing 'Too Late (To Be Saved)' on 'Hits A Go Go', 1972.

May 1972: SINGLE [CBS 8048]

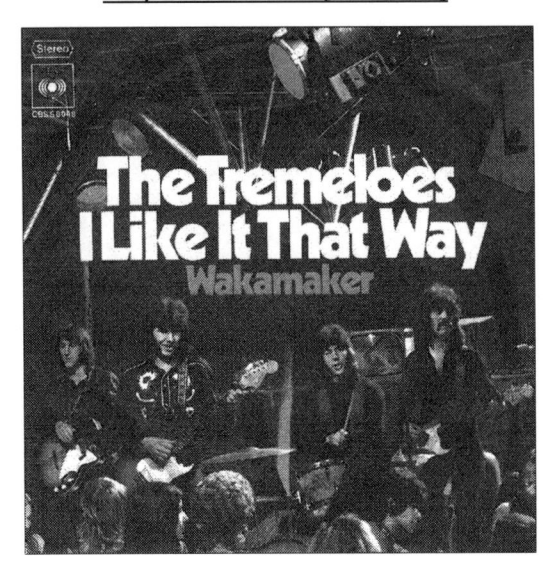

German picture sleeve

I LIKE IT THAT WAY (Blakley / Hawkes)
WAKAMAKER (Blakley / Hawkes)

Another commercial-sounding song, the piano-led '**I Like It That Way**' is enhanced by strings and a 'Penny Lane'-inspired trumpet solo. It's quite catchy, but a tad monotonous, and only really comes to life when Dave does his Soul-Gospel bit. Promoted on 'Lift Off With Ayshea', 'The Basil Brush Show', 'The Golden Shot', The Netherlands' 'Eddy Ready Go' and Germany's 'Disco', it flopped at home, but did get as high as No. 10 in The Netherlands, as well as No. 49 in both Germany and Belgium. A BBC radio performance circulates unofficially.

One of the biggest UK Rock-Pop bands of the early '70s was Slade, who - not unlike The Tremeloes - knew how to write a catchy chorus, yet could Rock out with the best of them. '**Wakamaker**' has a noticeable Slade influence, particularly on Dave's vocal phrasing, while the chorus is both daft and catchy.

HEAVEN KNOWS WHY (Blakley / Hawkes)
[Not released until 2000]

'**Heaven Knows Why**' is slightly retro-sounding melodic Pop-Rocker, complete with "Ooh-wah" backing vocals and a steel guitar solo. It could've made a nice album track if they were releasing such things in 1972, but instead it remained unreleased until surfacing on 'Boxed' in 2000.

Performing 'I Like It That Way' on 'The Basil Brush Show', 1972.

November 1972: SINGLE [EPIC EPC 1019]

German picture sleeve

BLUE SUEDE TIE (Blakley / Hawkes)
YODEL AY (Blakley / Hawkes)

With just four singles - none of them particularly successful - since the 'Master' album nearly two years earlier, The Tremeloes parted company with CBS to sign with Epic records. This coincided with the first line-up change since the Brian Poole and The Tremeloes days back in 1966.

Dave: "Rick Westwood left the Tremeloes for a while, because of his mounting tinnitus problems. His doctor had warned him against loud bands."

Len: "Rick left the band in 1972 and was replaced by Bob Benham. We continued recording our own material and (eventually) produced our album 'Shiner'."

A talented and charismatic singer, guitarist and songwriter, Bob Benham came from Jumbo, a band that had been managed by The Tremeloes, as former colleague (and future Tremelo himself) Aaron Woolley recalls.

Aaron: "Jumbo was a band made up of two guys from London, Bob Benham and myself, and two from Swansea, Stuart Hallyday and Paul Carman. We supported The Tremeloes in 1970 at the Swansea Top Rank Ballroom. They watched us, and after the gig we chatted etc, Alan and Len had recently set up a management and production company called 'Gale Music'. They contacted us a few weeks later for a meeting in London and we became part of Gale Managements' entourage so to speak. They liked our original compositions, and over the next couple of years we recorded three singles and had about twelve other tracks more or less completed for an album."

TREMELOES LEN HAWKES and ALAN BLAKLEY in their plush London offices with JUMBO, a group who they are managing. "They're just what the business needs," enthuses Alan, "there's not another group who look the part and are talented musicians as well."

Aaron: "I think things were pretty tough for them in 1972, the scene was changing, they were trying to keep their own career moving along and together, as well as producing and managing us. Shortly after our 3rd single was released, they sent us off to Asia (Singapore, Thailand, etc) for 3 months, I think basically to get rid of us! Maybe, I dunno. Around July 1972, I decided to take up an offer I'd received from Singapore to be the guitar player MD for an Indonesia 3 girl act called The Nidya Sisters (Motown type stuff), which were about to embark on a tour of Australia and then onto New Zealand etc. So I left Jumbo, I think around 3 or 4 months later, and Bob Benham joined The Tremeloes, as Rick had decided to leave the band."

The first single for Epic, and the first to feature Bob Benham, was '**Blue Suede Tie**', a sort of Elvis Presley tribute via The Beatles' 'Get Back'. The latter's rolling drums and electric piano are present and correct, but with Len doing his best Elvis impersonation (even if he does come across sounding more like Mud's Les Gray), while the "My-My-My-My-My!" and "Blue-Blue, Blue Suede Tie!" refrains fit right into the '50s Revival/'70s Glam sounds popular at the time. Despite promotion on 'Lift Off With Ayshea', 'The Golden Shot', 'Frankie Howerd In Ulster', The Netherlands' 'TopPop' and Germany's 'Disco', this highly worthy record somehow failed to chart in the UK, and only reached No. 38 in Germany and No. 48 in Belgium. A BBC radio recording circulates unofficially, as does a live German radio broadcast.

'**Yodel Ay**' is evidence of Len's growing interest in Country music, even if it is closer to the Country-tinged Rock 'n' Roll of Creedence Clearwater Revival than it is to Hank Williams, with Len's laid-back vocals contrasting sharply against Dave's Fogerty-like roar.

Chip Hawkes, Alan Blakley, Dave Munden, Bob Benham.

LAUREE LEE (Blakley / Hawkes)
[Not released until 2000]

Although slower than 'Yodel Ay', another CCR-influenced track is '**Lauree Lee**', complete with a vocal that could've convinced most that John Fogerty was moonlighting with The Tremeloes. It was not released until 2000's 'Boxed', while a BBC radio performance circulates unofficially.

Performing 'Blue Suede Tie' on 'TopPop', 1973.

April 1973: SINGLE [Epic EPC 1399]

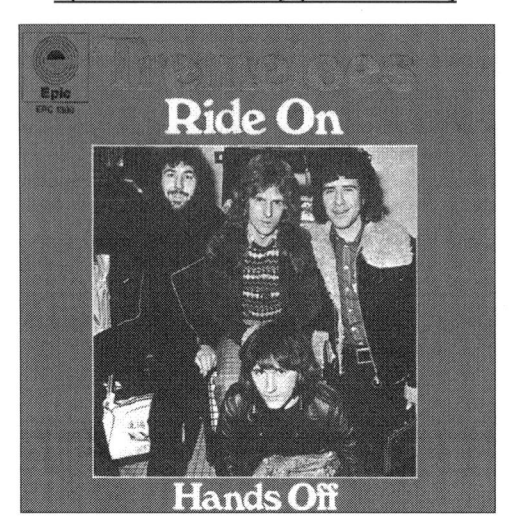

German picture sleeve

RIDE ON (Blakley / Hawkes)
HANDS OFF (Blakley / Hawkes)

Just as they had with Chip Hawkes in 1966 (and would do so again with Davey Fryer in 1988), The Tremeloes very quickly promoted Bob Benham to lead singer status - and it is Bob who does the lead on here. '**Ride On**' is a mid-tempo Blues-influenced commercial Rock song, and with its The Sweet-styled harmonies, weird keyboard touches and effects-laden guitar, it was their most blatant nod to Glam Rock yet.

By this time, they'd almost given up on the UK, with 'Lift Off With Ayshea' being their only known TV promotion for this single, but in Europe they performed the song on The Netherlands' 'TopPop', Austria's 'Spotlight', and Germany's 'Disco' and 'Hits A Go Go'. The latter obviously worked, as it got as high as No. 16 in the German charts.

Not to be confused with the Rhythm 'n' Blues song of the same name that Brian Poole and The Tremeloes recorded in 1965, *this* '**Hands Off**' is a melodic mid-tempo Pop song led by piano, complimented by a guitar effect that makes it sound more like an organ - or is it the other way around? A BBC radio performance circulates unofficially.

THESE DAYS (Hawkes)
[Not released until 2000]

Not released until 'Boxed' in 2000, **'These Days'** is a lovely Len-sung Country song, with acoustic and Steel guitars, as well as a piano solo. With a little work, the song would be re-recorded in 1975 as Chip Hawkes' 1st solo single, where it would be re-titled 'Friend Of A Friend'.

'Ride On' performed on 'Disco', 1973.

July 1973: SINGLE [Epic EPC 1660]

Dutch picture sleeve

MAKE OR BREAK (Blakley / Hawkes)
MOVIN' ON (Blakley / Hawkes)

With ever-declining sales, the band changed their name to 'The Trems' for this and the next single - a name that would also resurface in very different circumstances decades later.

The Bob Benham-sung '**Make Or Break**' kicks off with crashing minor chords and a scream, and is an excellent Glammed-up story of The Tremeloes so far, and how they are not finished yet ("and now Bob is here, putting life in the old dog!"). Despite the fact that the "Make It, Break It" chorus was recycled from the as-yet-unissued 'Anything' from the 'May Morning' soundtrack, it is yet another highly worthy release, but with even their overseas TV appearances drying up, it failed to chart anywhere. The song was issued in Germany under the alternate title '**Make It - Break It**'.

'**Movin' On**' is a fast boogie-guitar Rock 'n' Roll song, not dissimilar to Status Quo - until the 2nd half, when it descends into a stoned-sounding slow jam.

October 1973: SINGLE [Epic EPC 1972] {Europe only}

Dutch picture sleeve

YOU CAN'T TOUCH SUE (Blakley / Hawkes)
STORY FOR THE BOYS (Benham)

More up-tempo Glam Rock, complete with Brian Eno-type bleeps and squeaks, on **'You Can't Touch Sue'** Bob's shouty vocals are complimented by Len's more restrained 'Elvis' voice. It failed chart-wise, though it did get an outing on the Austrian 'Spotlight' TV show.

The harmonised Funk-Rock of The Doobie Brothers made a major impact on the mid-'70s Tremeloes, with their songs often popping up in set-lists at the time. **'Story For The Boys'** is clearly their take on the band, with Dave Munden's soulful voice closer in style to Stevie Wonder than it is to the Glam sounds of late.

THE LADY'S GOT STYLE (Blakley / Hawkes)
[Not released until 2000]
A Pop-Rocker with electric keyboards, **'The Lady's Got Style'** sounds like a cross between 10cc's 'Rubber Bullets' and The Bay City Rollers. It was

rejected, and didn't surface until 2000's 'Boxed', but, under the title 'My Friend Delaney', a new version would be recorded for 1974's 'Shiner' album.

SADIE (Blakley / Hawkes)
[Not released until 2000]

Passionately sung and Soulful, the mid-tempo '**Sadie**' sounds like something The Temptations or The Ch-Lites would do, and even features a saxophone solo. It remained in the can until 'Boxed' in 2000.

January 1974: SINGLE [Epic EPC 2047]

Malaysian picture sleeve

DO I LOVE YOU (Blakley / Hawkes)
WITCHCRAFT (Munden / Benham)

Probably written at least as early as 1971, The Tremeloes actually performed '**Do I Love You**', a mid-tempo Beach Boys type song, for BBC radio in February 1972 - a recording that circulates unofficially, but remains unavailable commercially. The song was then released on a single by obscure singer Jacqueline (Jacqueline Beason from Barking in Essex) the following month, with a production credit by Alan and Len. By the summer of 1973, the song was being performed live, and then it was finally issued on a single at the start of 1974. The superior BBC version features prominent piano throughout and some fine steel guitar towards the end, but this otherwise similar arrangement is more stripped back. They performed the song on 'The Golden Shot', their final appearance on the show, but once again it did nothing chart-wise.

A riff-heavy fast Rocker, '**Witchcraft**' has similarities to what The Sweet were doing at the time, bridging the gap between Glam and Hard Rock.

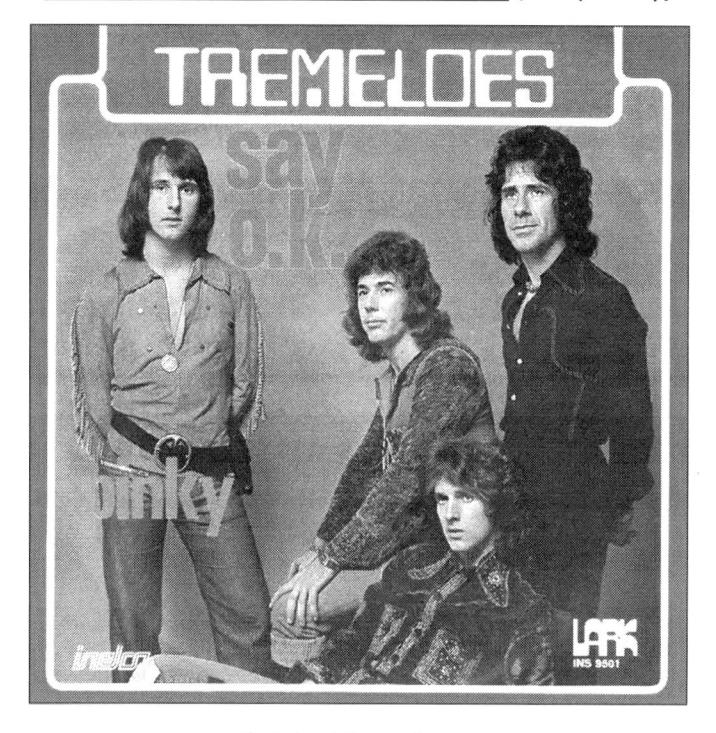

July 1974: SINGLE [Telefunken 6.11 501] {Europe only}

Dutch picture sleeve

SAY O.K. (SAY OLE YOU LOVE ME) (Andrews)
PINKY (Blakley / Hawkes / Munden / Benham)

After several flops in a row, The Tremeloes were dropped by Epic, so they released their next single on a variety of small labels in Europe - Telefunken in Germany, Lark in The Netherlands, Catoca in France, Italy and Sweden, Poplandia in Spain and Portugal - failing to even include the UK. They also released an A-side by an outside writer for the first time in years: Chris Andrews had written many highly memorable hits, both for himself and for artists such as Sandie Shaw and Adam Faith. However, he must've been having an off-day when he wrote '**Say O.K. (Say Ole You Love Me)**', a disposable piece of Euro-Pop that's as mediocre as its title, something in between Middle Of The Road and Boney M, but without any of those bands' panache. Surprisingly, they got to perform it on top-rated German TV show 'Disco', and there was even a cover by Dutch band Lions a couple of years later.

A bit better is **'Pinky'**, though not by much. A largely acoustic melodic Pop-Rocker, this song, written by all four members, is let down by some rather trite lyrics.

Performing 'Say O.K. (Say Ole You Love Me)' on 'Disco', 1974.

SINGLE [Bellaphon BF18529] {Germany only}

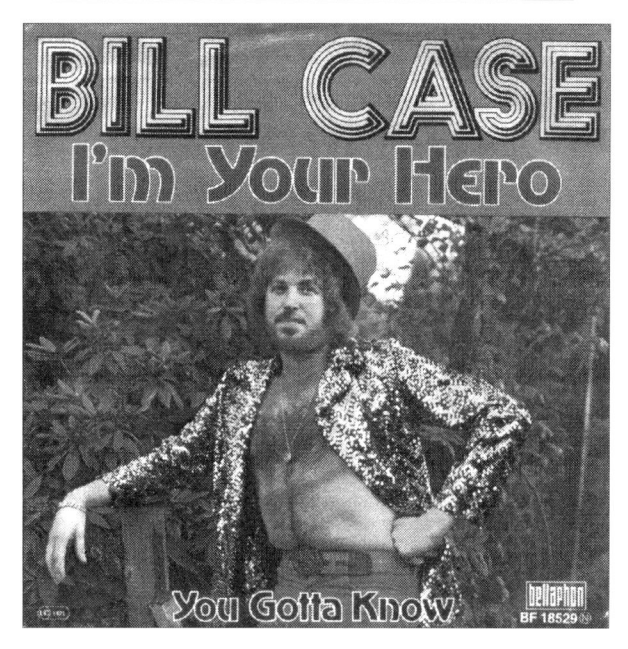

German picture sleeve

I'M YOUR HERO

(Blakley / Hawkes)

YOU GOTTA KNOW

(Blakley / Hawkes)

This fascinating Coda to The Tremeloes' Glam era, and one of their very best, is also one of their least-known. Recorded circa 1974, '**I'm Your Hero**' is a ferocious Gary Glitter inspired track, with lead vocals by Dave, pounding tribal drums, hard riffing distorted guitars, a bizarre wayward guitar solo, and call-and-response backing vocals.

The moodier Len-sung '**You Gotta know**' takes its inspiration from Alvin Stardust, with a Bluesy acoustic guitar riff, hand-claps, another way-out guitar solo, and an unexpected fast Slade-like ending. Issued under the pseudonym Bill Case, it didn't see the light of day until the height of Punk in 1977, and even then only in Germany, but it's received cult status since then - largely by people who are completely unaware of the real identity of the musicians involved.

October 1974: SINGLE [DJM DJS 336]

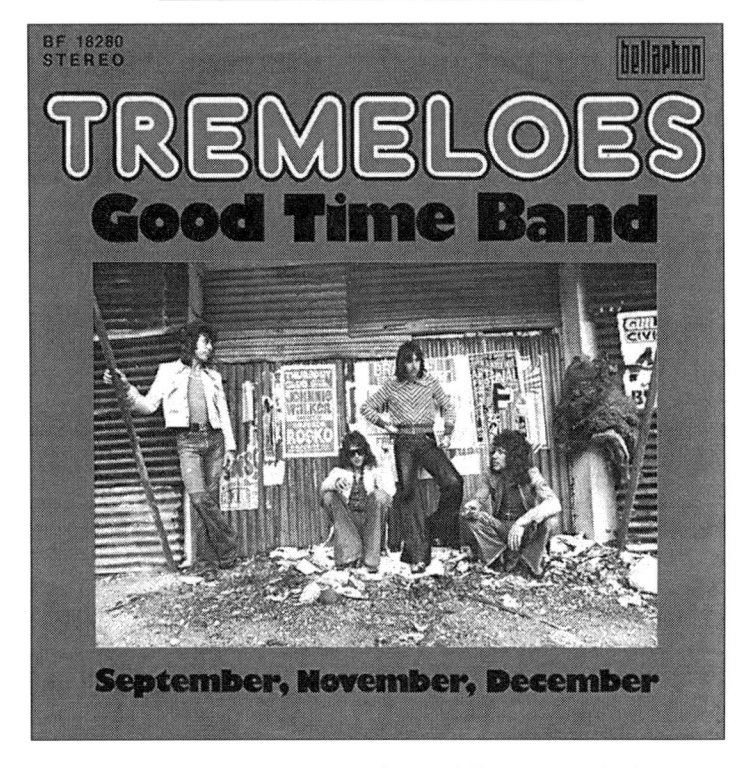

German picture sleeve (note different B-side!)

GOOD TIME BAND (Blakley / Hawkes)
HARD WOMAN (Munden / Benham / West)

Now signed to Dick James' DJM label, '**Good Time Band**' starts with fake crowd noise and the words "Ladies and gentlemen, the good time band!", before proceeding with a mid-paced Funk-Rock guitar riff, and a semi-spoken vocal, similar to Cockney Rebel's Steve Harley. The best thing about it is probably the brief drum break with the "Keep on movin'" chant, but otherwise both song and performance are a tad on the weak side. A flop everywhere else, it did get to No. 43 in Germany.

A bit better is '**Hard Woman**', a song that would also feature on their forthcoming album 'Shiner'. It starts with a sparse guitar riff and cowbell, similar to The Rolling Stones' 'Honky Tonk Women', and even has a soaring chorus like that song.

THE TREMELOES - EVEN THE BAD TIMES ARE GOOD!

November 1974: ALBUM [DJM DJLPS 441]

SHINER

ONE OF THE BOYS (Benham)
MY FRIEND DELANEY (Blakley / Hawkes)
SAD GOODBYE (Blakley / Hawkes)
I WANT IT EASY (Blakley / Hawkes)
SEPTEMBER, NOVEMBER, DECEMBER (Blakley / Hawkes)
HARD WOMAN (Munden / Benham / West)
LONELY DOLLY (Blakley / Hawkes)
BIG BAD BOOGIE (Munden / Benham)
LOVE SONG (Benham)
HELP (Benham)

During their 1974-1975 tenure with DJM, as well as issuing a handful of singles, The Tremeloes released two albums of new material for the first time since 'Master' in 1970. With their ever diminishing circumstances and change of line-up, they had a lot to prove. The first of these albums, 'Shiner', isn't totally successful musically, and at times sounds nothing like The Tremeloes of old, but there are some inspired moments that show just how well the group could adapt to the changing times.

With minor-key piano, similar to that in Paul McCartney's 'Nineteen-Hundred and Eight-Five', **'One Of The Boys'** features Bob - rather low in the mix - on vocals, and there's some meaty guitar work throughout.

Previously recorded and rejected the previous year as 'The Lady's Got Style', the re-titled **'My Friend Delaney'** features prominent harmonica and a real piano, making it far more bluesy than the bubblegum of the older version.

The gentle ballad **'Sad Goodbye'** features electric piano and occasional bongos, and is very 10cc-ish.

Mid-paced and with steel guitar, **'I Want It Easy'** has a very 'affected' vocal, not unlike Steve Harley or David Essex.

'September, November, December' is a nice breezy, Country song sung by Len, a genre that he was clearly very much at home with, while the Stones-influenced **'Hard Woman'** had already been issued on a single the previous month.

A Pop-Rocker, **'Lonely Dolly'** has typically excellent Tremeloes harmonies, though the synthesizer and steel drums make it more than just business as usual.

The band most closely connected to The Tremeloes are probably The Rubettes: former Tremelo Mick Clarke was a key member, Bob Benham joined them for a while in the late '70s, former Rubette Tony Thorpe was recruited by The Tremeloes for at least one TV appearance, Rick Westwood guested on a couple of their albums, and Alan Blakley produced the band. **'Big Bad Boogie'** has a similar Glammed-up Rock 'n' Roll-meets-Bubblegum sound to that band's big hits.

'**Love Song**' is another Country-ish song, and would be no more than mediocre if it wasn't for the trippy instrumental coda which lasts a full minute.

Bob Benham's '**Help**' is modern Country-Rock, closer to The Eagles than Hank Williams, with some interesting Hollies-like harmonies.

'Shiner' was not a commercial success, but few fans could've been prepared for what happened next.

Len: "In 1975 Alan and I were getting more and more disillusioned. As the hits had dropped off by then we both decided to leave the band and embark on our own solo projects. Alan went into producing, and I was signed as a solo artist with RCA records, and moved to Nashville and stayed, with my family, for almost 5 years until 1979."

Dave: "Alan was disillusioned when it came to the Tremeloes, he felt exhausted. Instead he had started producing and wanted to record with Len Hawkes. It wasn´t fun for him anymore. Chip wanted to try for a country career in Nashville, but it was rather a non-career. There was another new member, Aaron Woolley, like

Benham, he came from the band Jumbo. They shared their management with The Tremeloes."

Alan, Chip, Aaron, Bob, Rick and Dave with Bren Goodwin, January 1975.
(© Bren Goodwin)

Aaron: "In December 1974, I was playing in a band touring around Australia, when I got a telegram from Bob, asking me if I'd be interested in joining The Trems. In January 1975 I flew back to the UK and spent around 15 months in the band. They were just finishing off a new Album, and I got to play on the final 3 songs being recorded at DJM. By this time the band was Bob, Rick who had come back onboard, Dave and myself. Alan was involved in the album production etc, but had decided touring was over for him. Len had gone to Nashville, to pursue a solo career in Country Music. Rick by the way was now on bass guitar."

February 1975: SINGLE [DJM DJS 348]

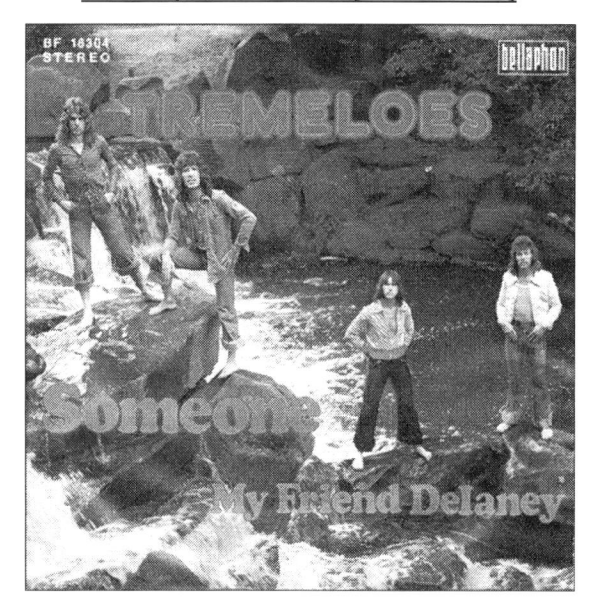

German picture sleeve

SOMEONE SOMEONE (Petty / Greines)
MY FRIEND DELANEY (Blakley / Hawkes)

For The Tremeloes first performance with Aaron Woolley in Uxbridge on the 22nd January 1975, the group appeared as a unique 6-piece line-up of Alan, Dave, Rick, Len, Bob and Aaron - nicely captured on camera backstage with Bren Goodwin, President of The Tremeloes Fan Club at the time. Later that month, they performed as a 5-piece - without Len - at the MIDEM Gala in Cannes, and after that the 4-piece were pretty much on their own.

Considering that they were trying to establish a new line-up, their next move was a surprising one: a re-recording of '**Someone, Someone**', their classic hit with Brian Poole, eleven years earlier in real time, but light years away musically. Softly sung by Dave, and with subtle organ and piano behind the usual band line-up, it is competent without being outstanding. Nevertheless, a strange move indeed. The B-side '**My Friend Delaney**' had previously been released on 'Shiner', and would probably have made a better A-side.

THE TREMELOES - EVEN THE BAD TIMES ARE GOOD!

Cannes, 1975: Aaron, Bob, Dave, Rick, Alan.

Cyprus, 1975: Aaron, Bob, Dave, Rick.

Aaron Woolley, Bob Benham, Rick Westwood, Dave Munden.

April 1975: SINGLE [DJM DJS 373]

ROCKING CIRCUS (Munden / Blakley)
DON'T LET THE MUSIC DIE (Benham)

From the pointless to the sublime. Starting with distant circus-style music and crowd noise, this is a brilliant Beatles pastiche, with Dave sounding more like Lennon than the man himself, and some spot-on SGT. Pepper/Magical Mystery Tour instrumentation and production. The lyrics even mention John Lennon being "top of the bill" at the "Rock 'n' Roll Circus". Sadly, **'Rocking Circus'** was released without the fanfare it deserved, and passed by the world largely unnoticed. Incidentally, when the band performed the song on stage, they used a recording of Alan's piano on a reel-to-reel tape, playing the rest of the song live.

A song that would, eventually, be the title track of their next album, **'Don't Let The Music Die'** has a very West Coast (California, not Cornwall) Soft-Funk-Rock feel to it. It is musically highly accomplished, even if it doesn't sound like the band of old.

THE TREMELOES - EVEN THE BAD TIMES ARE GOOD!

June 1975: ALBUM [DJM DJLPS 447]
DON'T LET THE MUSIC DIE

DON'T LET THE MUSIC DIE (Benham)
CELEBRATION (Benham)
WINDOWS ARE NICE (Blakley)
I'M SORRY (Blakley)
MANDY DOWNS (Benham)
TRIFLE TOWER (Benham)
ROCKING CIRCUS (Blakley / Munden)
SONG FOR ANDRE (Munden)
LOST AND FOUND (Hawkes / Munden)
VICTORIA BOOTS (Benham)

Dave: "In order to make people listen seriously, we used the band name Space for the album 'Don't Let The Music Die' in 1975. There are a lot of horns on it, supplied by the band Gonzales, with Mick Eve on tenor saxophone. Mick used to be the concert booker for the Tremeloes' agency, ´Starlight´ - after his time in Georgie Fame´s Blue Flames, and before he worked for the Ronnie Scott´s Club in Soho. By the way, the Soho club was situated above the Playboy Club. Via the connection to Mick Eve, I met my wife there, an ex-Playboy-bunny, haha!"

Aaron: "The album never had a title! Stupid, really. The Trems had a 'poppy' persona which they/we were trying to kill. So this new album didn't actually mention the Tremeloes at all, but had 'Space' as the band name. Later, after my association was over, the album was re-packaged and called 'Don't Let the Music Die' - The Tremeloes. The album cover is Bob and Rick along with Paul Carman from Jumbo and some other guy who I don't know at all. I've even read some articles online where it's been said that the recordings were with Paul etc, but that's not true."

'**Don't Let The Music Die**' and '**Rocking Circus**' had already been issued as a single. As well as the Funk sound that's also featured on several other songs on the album, '**Celebration**' has an additional light Reggae feel.

Despite Alan Blakley being the band's spokesman, one of the main creative forces, and a key harmony vocalist, he had largely to date avoided being the lead singer on Tremeloes records. Released the previous month as Alan's debut solo single (which indicates little probable involvement from other band members), '**Windows Are Nice**' is the first of two consecutive songs featuring his lead, and with its punky vocals, prominent synthesiser, and a saxophone solo, it has more in common with Berlin-era David Bowie than it does with The Tremeloes' own past. It segues into '**I'm Sorry**' (titled 'Sorry (Lyn's Song)' on the solo single), a John Lennon-styled ballad that again features Alan's vocals, as well as the squeaks and pings of the synthesisers.

A Blues-Soul ballad, '**Mandy Downs**' starts with the sound of a telephone ringing, followed by more than a minute of guitar, before some passionately-sung Bob vocals. '**Trifle Tower**' is a hot Rock-Funk number, complete with brass.

Dave's '**Song For Andre**' is a heartfelt ballad dedicated to his wife Andree, complete with layered electric guitars and some rather weird timing. Very sadly, Andree Munden passed away on 22nd October 2023, during the final stages of writing this book.

'**Lost and Found**' is a Doobie Brothers type work-out, and the only song on the album both co-written and featuring Len, though the Disco strings ill-fit the track - to the degree that at times it sounds like two different songs playing at once.

The closing '**Victoria Boots**' is discordant, piano-led Pop-Rock, and a rather anonymous-sounding ending to The Tremeloes' strangest album. Without Len's distinctive lead vocals, and his knack for composing memorable melodies, The Tremeloes had by now become almost a different band, and despite its at times considerable musical merits, the album sold poorly.

Dave Munden, Bob Benham, Rick Westwood, Aaron Woolley.

August 1975: SINGLE [DJM DJS 406]

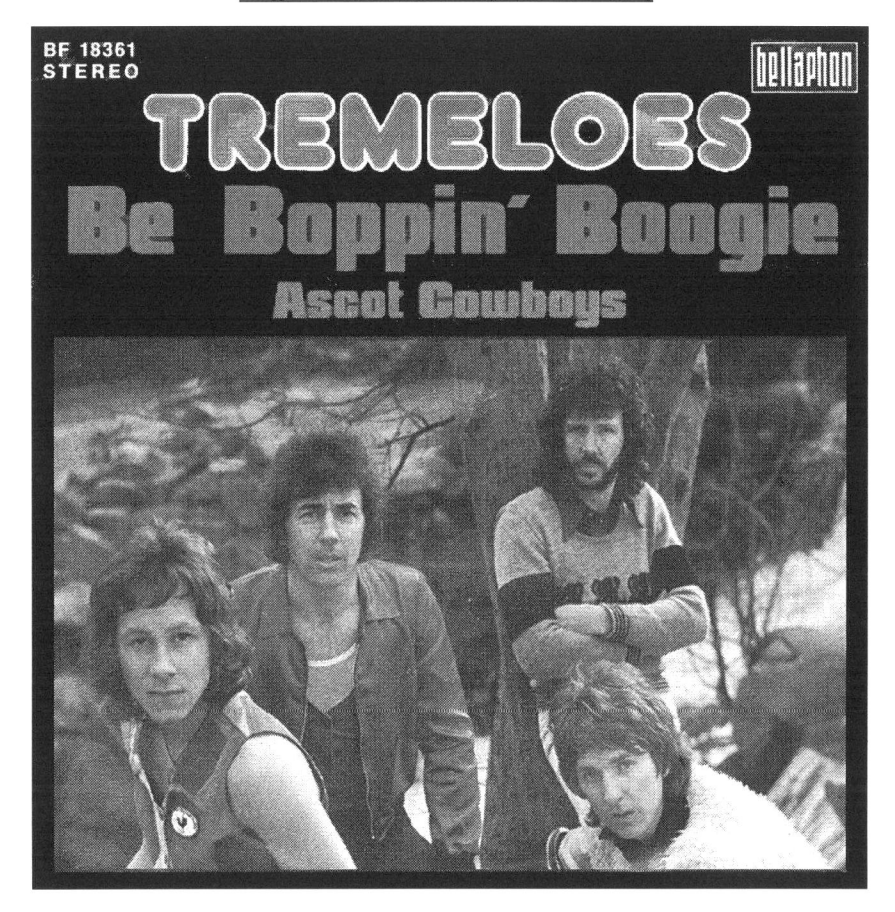

German picture sleeve

BE BOPPIN' BOOGIE (Blakley)
ASCOT COWBOYS (Benham)

With the notable exception of 'Rocking Circus' - already a flop single - there was nothing on the album that really screamed "hit!". '**Big Bad Boogie**' has all the right ingredients - Rubettes-styled Glammed-up '50s Rock 'n' Roll, twin duetting lead guitars - courtesy of Bob and Aaron- and harmonies somewhere inbetween The Andrews Sisters and The Beach Boys. But with TV appearances even in Germany having dried up, few got to hear it, and even fewer went and bought it.

'**Ascot Cowboys**' is one of The Tremeloes' most overtly Funk-Disco recordings, not a million miles to what Earth, Wind & Fire and Kool & The Gang were doing.

Far from being the hit they wished for, this would not only be the group's final single for the label, but their last single for two and half years. Next, both Rick (again) and Aaron jumped ship.

Aaron: "To me it was a great experience, but I soon tired of playing the same songs over and over, and it seemed to be going nowhere. So I decided to leave and return to Australia to start a 4 year course in Music Teaching, and rejoin the band I'd left in Perth."

The next line-up featured Dave, Bob, Paul Isaacs (guitar) and ex-Jumbo, the late Paul Carman (bass) - prompting some commentators to dub the band "The Tremelo", due to Dave being the only remaining member from their hit-making peak.

Paul Carman, Dave Munden, Bob Benham, Paul Isaacs.
(photo by Rick Westwood)

Then Bob Benham and Paul Carman left, and Rick returned, so the line-up was Dave, Rick (back on guitar), Paul Isaacs (guitar) and Joe Breen (bass).

Joe Breen, Dave Munden, Rick Westwood, Paul Isaacs.

Rick: "The picture (above) was taken in Guernsey with the camera on a tripod and using time delay… complete with the arrow in Dave's head, which I didn't notice until I printed it out."

The group were still getting gigs - albeit rarely as prestigious or as they once were - but with the ever-changing line-ups and little hope of getting a major record contract, sometime in late 1976 or early 1977 (the exact date seems to be forgotten), they decided to call it a day.

Len: "Rick pursued a session musician career and ended up as guitarist with The Nashville Teens, whilst Dave continued to play under the name The Tremeloes until 1976/1977 when he went into the insurance business. Eventually he became a croupier at The Cromwell Mint Casino in London."

PART 5:

DAVE, RICK, ALAN, CHIP - SOLO

SOLO: DAVE MUNDEN

February 1971: SINGLE [CBS 7069]

WAKE ME I AM DREAMING (Battisti / Mogol / Scott)
WAIT A MINUTE (Munden)

Dave Munden always put The Tremeloes first, and apart from a brief period in the late '70s when the band didn't exist, he *never* left the band to pursue other projects. Which makes it all the more surprising that he was the first member besides Brian Poole to release a solo record.

Dave: "The song was in a pile of demos we were listening to, and although we liked the song we couldn't see it as a group number. Alan suggested I record it as a solo, and, frankly, no-one was more amazed than myself."

First released in Italy by Lucio Battisti as 'Mi Ritorni In Mente' in October 1969, 'Wake Me I Am Dreaming (Mi Ritorni In Menti)' isn't the perhaps expected quasi-operatic Italian language song, but instead is a pleasant orchestrated Pop ballad. It was also released as a single the same year by Love Affair, but like Dave's version, that also failed to chart. The superior mid-tempo B-side '**Wait A Minute**' is clearly a Tremeloes track in all but name, with harmonies, guitar-sitar and pounding drums, and wouldn't have sounded out of place on the 'Master' album.

SOLO: RICK WESTWOOD

April 1972: SINGLE [CBS 7990]

HELLO SAILOR (Westwood)
TAURUS (Westwood)

There were persistent rumours in the early '70s that Rick was going to record an album of instrumentals, and while that never happened, he did get as far as issuing a single under the name 'Gone West'.

Rick: "I recorded 'Hello Sailor' and 'Taurus' in my front bedroom at home on a Teac 4-track reel-to-reel recorder. We took them to CBS and added the drums and my silly voice to 'Hello Sailor'. No silly voice on 'Taurus', and I used 2 boxes for drums at home. We then tidied the sound up at CBS."

Punctuated throughout by a camp "Hello Sailor!" and manic laughter, **'Hello Sailor'** is a Reggae-ish keyboard near-instrumental, similar to what Dave and Ansil Collins were having chart success with at the time. Though purely instrumental, the B-side **'Taurus'** is in a similar style, and while not exactly the greatest showcase for Rick's considerable talents, they are good fun.

Around this time, Dave and Rick also collaborated with Eric Woolfson on a couple of singles as 'The Shepherds Bush Comets'.

SOLO: ALAN BLAKLEY

May 1975: SINGLE [DJM DJS 367]

SORRY (LYN'S SONG) (Blakley)
WINDOWS ARE NICE (Blakley)

Although Brian and Len were far more prolific, arguably the most musically adventurous Tremeloes solo material was by Alan Blakley - albeit more often than not released under pseudonyms. Both sides of his UK-only debut solo single - '**Sorry (Lyn's Song)**' (re-titled 'I'm Sorry') and '**Windows Are Nice**' - were *also* released by The Tremeloes on the 'Space' (aka 'Don't Let The Music Die') album, and are reviewed in more detail in that section. Suffice to say, they are the most eccentric tracks on the album.

April 1976: SINGLE [Private Stock PVT 55]

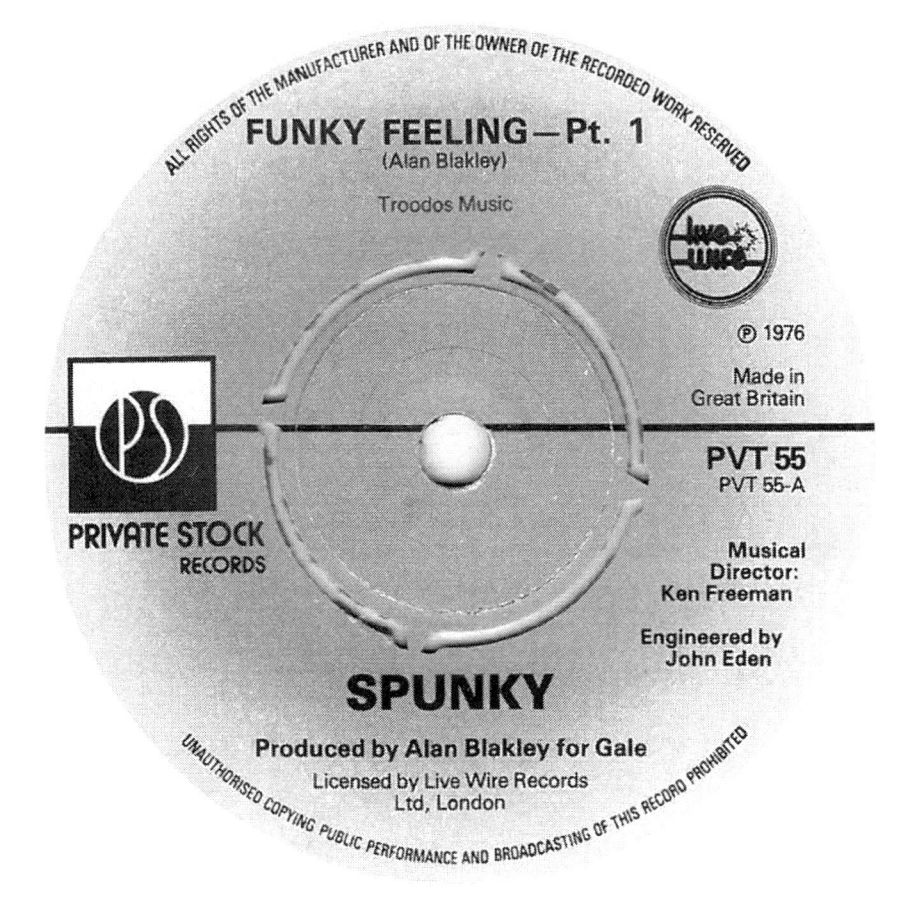

FUNKY FEELING - PT. 1 (Blakley)
FUNKY FEELING - PT. 2 (Blakley)

Then it starts getting complicated. Released under the name 'Spunky', **'Funky Feeling'** (Pts 1 & 2) is a keyboard-orientated spoof Disco song, in much the same vein as some of Bill Wyman's solo recordings - but greatly enhanced by Alan's wife Lin, who provides some genuinely erotic-sounding whispers and groans. The song popped-up again on the 1989 CD 'The Tremeloes - All The Best & Rarities', where it was *wrongly* credited to 'Jack The Lad', a pseudonym Alan would use for a different record in 1983.

1976: SINGLE [Maritim New 17 384 AT] {Europe only}

German picture sleeve

LOST WITHOUT YOU (Blakley)
GIMME ROCK'N'ROLL (Blakley)

Alan's most widely released single was 'Lost Without You', but even that was only issued in Germany and Belgium in 1976, and, where it was re-titled '***I'm* Lost Without You**', The Netherlands in 1977. The song is an odd combination of T-Rex guitar riffs, electronic keyboard sounds and New Wave-ish vocals, and sounds very much like the missing link between Glam Rock and Synth-Pop. '**Gimme Rock'n'Roll**' is faster, again with more than a hint of T-Rex, as well as a Kenny/The Bay City Rollers fag-end-of-Glam feel.

July 1978: SINGLE [Atlantic K 11162]

ROCKIN' BAND (The Intelligents)
WARDANCE (The Intelligents)

June 1979: SINGLE [Atlantic K 11292]

TAKE IT FROM THE TOP (The Intelligents)
SUPERDRAIN (The Intelligents)

November 1979: SINGLE [Atlantic K 11408]

SORRY (Blakley)
WHEN WE DANCE (Blakley)

DOLE Q (Devlin / Blakley)
[Not released until 1989]

(LOVE LEFT ME) BLEEDING (Devlin / Benham)
[Not released until 1989]

Continuing his Glam-meets-New Wave sound, Alan then issued three late '70s singles as The Intelligents. Two additional tracks appeared on 'The Tremeloes - All The Best & Rarities' in 1989, curiously with '**(Love Left Me) Bleeding**' featuring Bob Benham on vocals and as a co-writer - that said, the same album also lists Brian Poole and Electrix's 'Star In Rock'n'Roll Band' as The Intelligents, as well as renaming '**Rockin' Band**' as 'Rockin' Good Band', so it's hard to know what is accurate and what is not.

1983: SINGLE [Polydor 813 798-7]

German picture sleeve

REGGAE MUSIC (Ree)
TANGO TORROMOLINUS (Bennett)

Last, and definitely least, is a 1983 single credited to Jack The Lad, though, as the picture sleeve features what looks like half-a-dozen Frankie Goes To Hollywood rejects rather than Alan Blakley, it is probable that his involvement was minimal. '**Reggae Music**' (which also appears on 'The Tremeloes - All The Best & Rarities', albeit about 20 seconds shorter than the German Polydor single), is a Calypso-tinged Reggae number, not dissimilar to Eddie Grant, and '**Tango Torromolinus**' (credited to 'Jack The Lad's Dad') is an instrumental in the same mode.

SOLO: CHIP HAWKES

1974: SINGLE [Ariola 13150 AT] {Italy}

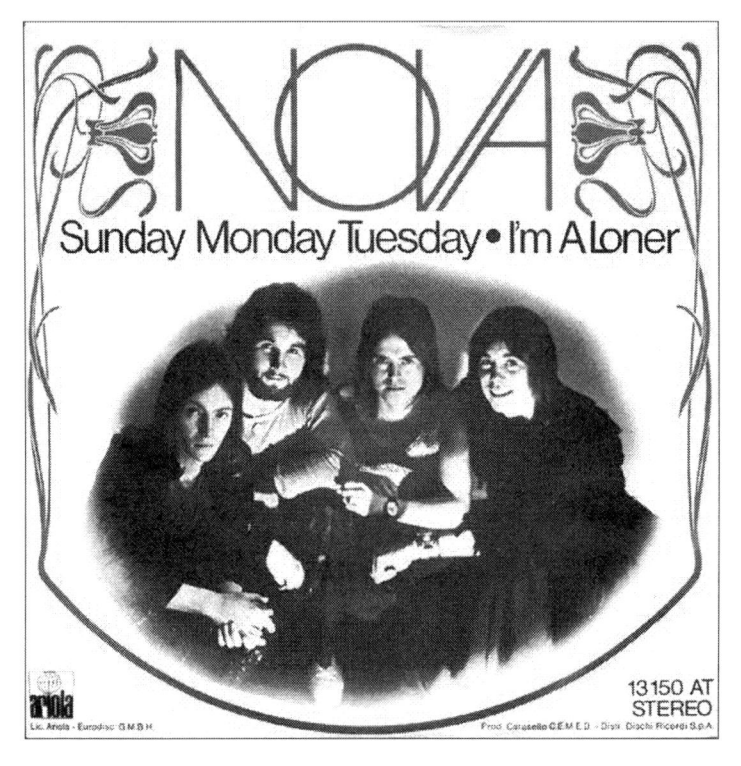

SUNDAY MONDAY TUESDAY (Morris)
I'M A LONER (Butts)

Apart from Brian Poole, Chip Hawkes has been the only Tremelo to make a serious attempt at a solo career outside the band, despite him being the last one to issue a solo single - at least officially. He did in fact do lead vocals on a single by obscure UK band 'Nova', released in Italy and France in 1974, and in Australia (where the songs had different composer credits) in 1976. For some unknown reason, the cover for the European releases are of a group called Kindness - who would later find fame as Smokie - despite the fact that Kindness/Smokie had nothing whatsoever to do with this record. '**Sunday Monday Tuesday**' is up-tempo Cajun-ish Pop-Rock, ideally suited to Len's vocals, while the B-side '**I'm A Loner**' is far more downbeat and largely acoustic.

August 1975: SINGLE [Chelsea 2005 027]

FRIEND OF A FRIEND (Hawkes)
TIMES ARE CHANGING (Hawkes)

With Len now living in Nashville (where he and his family would stay for the best part of five years), he released his debut single proper with the Country-ish **'Friend Of A Friend'**. A couple of years earlier, the song had been attempted with The Tremeloes under the title 'These Days', and in some ways that version was more typically-Country thanks to its steel guitar. The new version eschews that for tinkly piano and mandolin, as well as female harmony vocals. **'Times Are Changing'** is slightly more rockin' and with male harmonies, and sounding far more like his band of old.

THE TREMELOES - EVEN THE BAD TIMES ARE GOOD!

<u>1976: ALBUM [RCA Victor PL 25044]</u>

NASHVILLE ALBUM

ONE MORE DUSTY ROAD (Hawkes)
ELEANOR RIGBY (Lennon / McCartney)
LOVE IS A GUESSING GAME (Bryant / Bryant)
READY FOR THE TIMES TO GET BETTER (Reynolds)
WILMA LOU (McDill)
HERE COMES MY BABY (Stevens)
RIDERS IN THE SKY (Jones)
IT'S SO EASY TELLING LIES (Cook)
ALL I WANNA DO IN LIFE (Theoret / Reynolds)
THE FACE (Hawkes)
WALK RIGHT BACK (Curtis)

After the one-off single on Chelsea, Len signed to the more major RCA Victor label - the same one as his idol Elvis Presley. He was instantly impressed with the high standard of musicianship in Music City, USA.

Len: "It had been an ambition of mine for a good three years to record in Nashville, and I finally got to realize this dream when Alan Sizer signed me to RCA UK. The first day in the studio was a real experience. I was knocked out with the musicians and the way they moulded my songs into shape. The first song we recorded was 'One More Dusty Road' and I was very pleased with the way it turned out. Garth, the engineer, fixed up a vocal mic in the studio and we played it almost live. Apart from one guitar overdub by Reggie Young and one harmony vocal by Garth, that was it - finished."

Album highlights include a radically re-arranged Country-Rock version of The Beatles' 1966 classic '**Eleanor Rigby**', complete with banjo and violin; the timeless 1949 Vaughn Monroe classic '**Riders In The Sky**'; the superb mid-tempo original '**The Face**'; the more Rock-than-Country '**All I Wanna Do In Life**' (later a single for Marianne Faithfull); and a Doo-Wop meets Boogie-Woogie arrangement of The Everly Brothers' 1961 hit '**Walk Right Back**'.

<u>January 1977: SINGLE [RCA Victor PB 5002]</u>

ONE MORE DUSTY ROAD (Hawkes)
SHE COULDN'T FIGURE MY REASON (Hawkes)

<u>June 1977: SINGLE [RCA Victor PB 5033]</u>

ELEANOR RIGBY (Lennon / McCartney)
SAVE YOUR PITY (Hawkes)

There were two singles taken from the album the following year, but like the album, their sales were unspectacular, and Len was dropped by the label - despite rumours of enough songs recorded for a 2nd album. The self-composed B-sides 'She Couldn't Figure My Reason' and 'Save Your Pity' were both exclusive to these releases.

DREAM BABY DREAM (Campbell / Hawkes)
[Not released until 2013]
NO STRANGER TO HEARTACHE (Campbell / Hawkes)
[Not released until 2013]

During a visit to the UK, Len caught up with old friend William 'Junior' Campbell, to collaborate on a couple of songs in the style of both of their heroes.

Junior Campbell: "Len - 'Chip', but I always called him "Arry' - and I had been pals for years. First met when he was with Davy Sands and The Essex and we - The Gaylords morph Marmalade - around '66 when we were both with Peter Walsh's Starlite Artists and before he joined the Tremeloes. Much later, around '76-'78 we did some songwriting together and on one occasion he came to my then house at Wentworth and we knocked out two songs in the style of our beloved Everlys as a labour of love. We then recorded both at Gordon Mills' home studio in Weybridge. Mike Beaton whom we both knew from Starlite days as a promo man, was by then running Larry Utall's Private Stock Records in the UK and had had big success with David Soul and Frankie Valli, he also released 2 singles of my own. We played him the tracks and he loved them. We had come up with name 'Kentucky Rain' purely spontaneously whilst writing the songs. The record was all set for release when Larry suddenly pulled the plug on the label and Mike went off with a large settlement I believe. Mike said we should collect our tapes before he went so I suppose, in theory we could claim ownership of the masters as the record was certainly never listed or scheduled for release. That's the story."

The mid-tempo 'Dream Baby Dream' and the slower 'No Stranger To Heartache' are uncannily-accurate recreations of The Everly Brothers' classic sound. They only received a limited release on the download-only Junior Campbell 'The Very Best of... Back Then...' collection in 2013, but both songs - at time of writing - are also on Junior Campbell's YouTube channel.

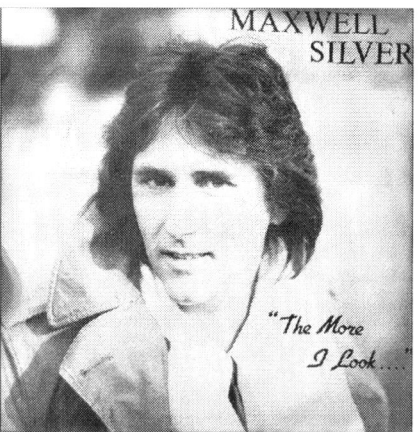

1985: SINGLE [BMR 001]

17 AND READY (Silver)
THE PAIN (Silver)

1985: SINGLE [BMR 002]

THE MORE I LOOK (Silver)
THE PAIN (Silver)

After rejoining/reforming The Tremeloes in 1979, Len's solo releases would be few and far between for the next 20-odd years. However, he did sneak out a couple of 1985 singles under the name 'Maxwell Silver'. '**17 and Ready**' is a Pop-rock song that's very much of its time - brittle over-loud drums, prominent keyboards, piercing guitars - but with enough of a melody to make it palatable. Better was the B-side, the minor-keyed and mid-tempo '**The Pain**', which was deemed good enough to be the B-side of the follow-up too, while the 2nd A-side was the pleasant '**The More I Look**'. Both singles were produced by Joe Gillingham - who would be a Tremelo himself within a few years.

THE MINSTREL SONG (Hawkes)

More obscure but vastly superior is the Country '**The Minstrel Song**'. It was released on the impossible to find 1988 charity record 'Show The Children We Care', but deserves far greater exposure.

After again leaving The Tremeloes in 1988, Len concentrated on promoting his son Chesney Hawkes' career, but by the late '90s he was tempted to return to live performances. He initially did this by forming a couple of versions of his own (fake) Tremeloes - much to the chagrin of the (real) Tremeloes - still at this point featuring both Dave Munden and Rick Westwood. Happily, everything was soon forgiven, and he would eventually be sharing stages with his old colleagues again.

'Chip Hawks Tremeloes': Bob Benham, Chip Hawkes, Rob Fisher, Jodie Hawkes.

'Chip Hawkes Trems': Ted Tomlin, Chip Hawes, Chris North, unknown.

2003: ALBUM [Store For Music SFMCD031]

THE HITS OF THE TREMELOES

HERE COMES MY BABY / SUDDENLY YOU LOVE ME / I LIKE IT THAT WAY / CALL ME NUMBER ONE / BY THE WAY / RIDE ON / LIGHTS OF PORT ROYAL / ME AND MY LIFE / MY LITTLE LADY / I SHALL BE RELEASED / THE FACE / EVEN THE BAD TIMES ARE GOOD / HELLO BUDDY / SILENCE IS GOLDEN

Following his late '90s 'comeback', Len's new releases become increasingly hard to follow, with re-cuts, re-compilations and re-issues galore - along with some new recordings. Higher profile than most was 2003's 'The Hits of The Tremeloes', and among the expected hits were a few surprises, including a Len-sung '**Ride On**' (sounding almost as good as the Bob-led single 30 years earlier), the mid-'70s solo era track '**The Face**', the 1980 flop single '**Lights Of Port Royal**', and a particularly poignant '**By The Way**'. Everything is well-recorded and mixed, with only the crisper production and more up-front drums betraying its New Millenium origins.

RUNAWAY TRAIN (Pirner)

2003 saw the release of a fascinating CD called 'Back To The Future', featuring '60s stars singing contemporary '90s songs - including Mike Pender with 'Weather With You', Dave Dee with 'Don't Look Back In Anger', Billy J. Kramer with 'Losing My Religion' and Mike D'Abo with 'Would I Lie To You'. The whole album was produced by Len and backed by The Chip Hawkes Band, with his own vocal contribution being a great cover of Soul Asylum's 1992 hit **'Runaway Train'**.

2004: ALBUM: [Private Pressing]

THE CLASS OF '64

THE CLASS OF '64

JUST ONE LOOK / TILL THE END OF THE DAY / HERE COMES MY BABY / LONG COOL WOMAN / TIRED OF WAITING / (CALL ME) NUMBER ONE / THE AIR THAT I BREATHE / SUDDENLY YOU LOVE ME / BUS STOP / WATERLOO SUNSET / SILENCE IS GOLDEN / LOLA / LOOK THROUGH ANY WINDOW / YOU REALLY GOT ME / EVEN THE BAD TIMES ARE GOOD

In 2004, Len put together a little Super-Group, along with members from a couple of other legendary '60s bands.

Len: "The Class of '64 was my idea. I got the drummer from The Kinks, the original drummer Mick Avory, the bass player from The Hollies and people like that, that I met in 1964. We came together and we called ourselves 'The Class of '64' and that's a great band because we can do Hollies hits, Kinks hits and Tremeloes hits. It's really good and we have a lot of fun."

The CD is a bit predictable, but it was on stage where the fun really happened. Eventually there were line-up changes, with The Swinging Blue Jeans' Alan Lovell being at least one later member.

Chip Hawkes with Alan Lovell in The Class of '64.

HOW COME (Lane / Westlake)

First released by Ronnie Lane and Slim Chance in December 1973, the rootsy '**How Come**' is a song that could've been tailor-made for Len. It first appeared on the German 'A Tribute to Rod Stewart & His Faces - Rhythm of My Heart' in 2004, and then became more widely available on 'Do Ya Think I'm Sexy - The Songs of Rod Stewart' four years later.

ON THE WIND (Hawkes)

As with the earlier 'The Minstrel Song', one of Len's best songs was released on a disc that is virtually impossible to find - this time the 2006 German charity disc 'Colours Of Life Vol. 1'. Beautifully but fragilely sung, the acoustic '**On The Wind**', with its touching lyrics about the death of a close friend, is rumoured to be about Alan Blakley. If so, Len did him very proud indeed.

IT'S ALL OVER NOW (Womack / Womack)

Another cover, and another tribute, '**It's All Over Now**' appeared on 2007's 'A Tribute To The Rolling Stones' collection.

June 2008: SINGLE [H2 Music]

NOT MY CHILD (Hawkes)
NOT MY CHILD (KARAOKE) (Hawkes)

Sounding like a smoother Chris Norman of Smokie, '**Not My Child**' is a modern Pop-Rock song, and with lyrics like "She's the daughter of a crazy one-night stand", the subject matter was perfect for a rather good Promo Video.

'Not My Child' Promo Video.

THE TREMELOES - EVEN THE BAD TIMES ARE GOOD!

2009: Album [H2 Music CD 409.103]

ME AND MY LIFE

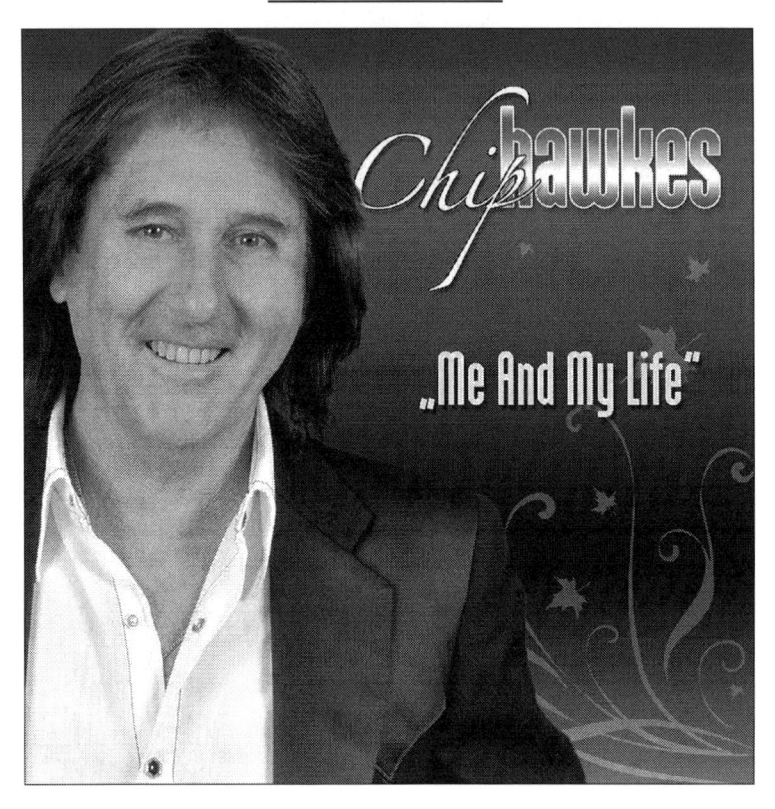

I'M A BELIEVER (Hochholzer / Kumpusch / Hawkes)
ALWAYS HAVE, ALWAYS WILL (Hawkes / Pitchford)
ME AND MY LIFE (Blakley / Hawkes)
THE MORE I LOOK (Hawkes)
TEN LOST (Hawkes)
USED TO BE THAT GIRL (Hawkes / Hawkes / Seebach / Seebach)
NOT MY CHILD (Hawkes)
IF YOU THINK YOU KNOW HOW TO LOVE ME (Chinn / Chapman)
SAD SUN (Hawkes / Dulake)
FATHER & SON (Stevens) *(with Chesney Hawkes)*
I'M NOT TO BLAME (Hawkes)
THIS LADY (Hawkes)
THAT'S WHAT FRIENDS ARE FOR (Schneider / Metz) *(with Olaf Berger)*

It had been 34 years since Chip Hawkes had last released an album of (mostly) new songs, and here - at last! - he finally did it again. Not all of it is great, but there's enough strong material to make this arguably the finest of all Tremeloes-spin-off albums.

Amongst the highlights, '**I'm A Believer**' is a fast, rootsy Pop-Rocker (and *not* The Monkees classic), in a similar style to The Traveling Wilburys' better songs; the 1970 hit '**Me and My Life**' is updated with a slightly dance-orientated beat and a bubbling synthesiser; '**The More I Look**' is a superior re-cut of the Maxwell Silver-era song; '**Ten Lost**' with its clever, more downbeat, nod to 'Even The Bad Times Are Good' is tough Pop Rocker about a broken relationship ('Even The Good Times Are Bad' perhaps?); and '**Father & Son**' is a suitably touching version of the 1970 Cat Stevens classic, with Len's more mature voice complimenting Chesney's youthful tenor. Not everything is great - the vocals on Smokie's '**If You Think You Know How To Love Me**' sound even more hoarse than Chris Norman's on the original, and the dual German/English language '**That's What Friends Are For (Dafür Sind Freunde Da)**' is a well-intentioned collaboration that doesn't really work - but, overall, it's an album well worth seeking out.

A Chip & Chesney duet, 'Father & Son' was belatedly issued as a single in 2012.

2011: ALBUM [HAWCD01]

UNPLUGGED

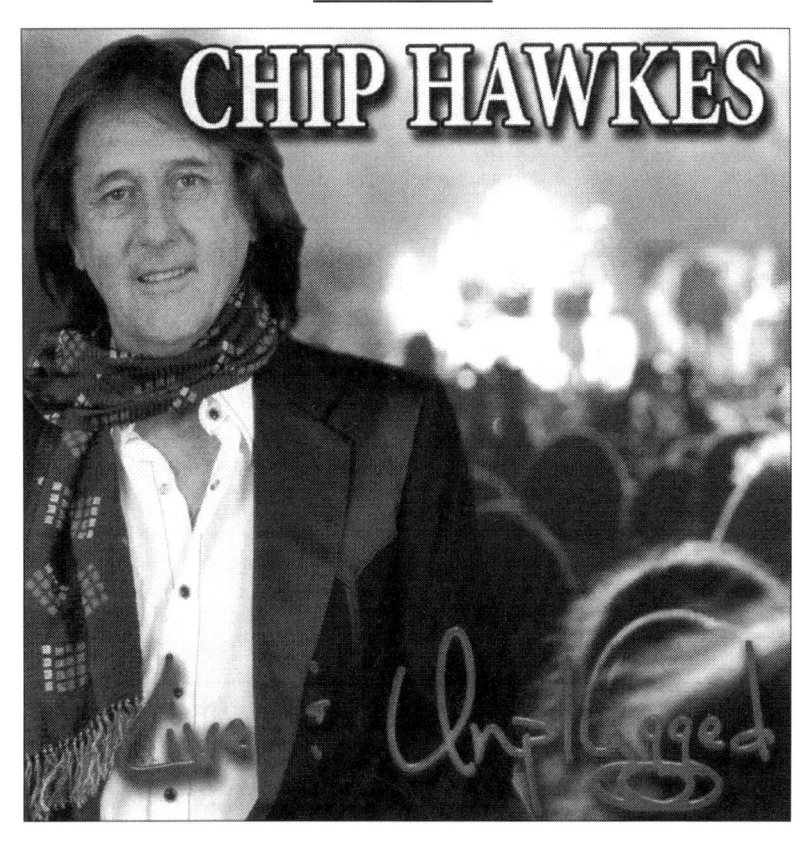

EVEN THE BAD TIMES ARE GOOD / SUDDENLY YOU LOVE ME / HERE COMES MY BABY / CALL ME NUMBER ONE-ME & MY LIFE-YELLOW RIVER / NOT MY CHILD / MY LITTLE LADY / SILENCE IS GOLDEN / SUNNY AFTERNOON / THE MORE I LOOK / FATHER & SON / THE SUN AIN'T GONNA SHINE ANYMORE

Although Len would continue to be very active, both on tour and in releasing compilations, his last *new* recordings to date appear to be this live concert from Nottingham in 2011. All the hits are present and correct, as are a few songs from his recent album, but surprises include great versions of The Kinks' **'Sunny Afternoon'** and Frankie Valli/The Walker Brothers' **'The Sun Ain't Gonna Shine Anymore'**.

PART 6:
THE TREMELOES
(1978 - 2023)

February 1978: SINGLE [Single: CBS S 6072] {Germany only}

German picture sleeve

GING GANG GOOLIE (Blakley / Munden)
LONELY ROBOT (Blakley / Munden / Stevens)

The return of The Tremeloes wasn't the result of one big, highly-publicised reunion. First of all, there were just the occasional singles, featuring various line-ups, and it wouldn't be until the end of 1982 that the classic line-up of Alan, Dave, Rick and Chip would share a concert stage again. The choice of song for this German-only single didn't exactly help matters, and is probably the worst A-side ever to be released under the Tremeloes name. Based on the old Boy Scouts sing-a-long, '**Ging Gang Goolie**' had already been a hit for The Scaffold in

1969. The Tremeloes' update features a comedic vocal from Dave, a Bo Diddley rhythm guitar, and a bleeping and wah-wah-ing keyboard. It was promoted on Germany's 'Pop '78' TV show, complete with a live vocal, featuring the unique line-up of Dave (vocals), Alan (guitar), Rick (keyboards) - and, *possibly*, The Rubettes' Tony Thorpe (drums).

One of Alan Blakley's more eccentric studio experiments, '**Lonely Robot**' is "sung" in what can only be described as a Stephen Hawking-esque voice.

Performing 'Ging Gang Goolie' on 'Pop '78', 1978.

Performing 'Lonely Nights' on 'Dolle Dinsdag', 1979.

November 1978: SINGLE [CBS S 6539] {Europe only}

Belgian picture sleeve

LONELY NIGHTS (Blakley / Carman)
GROOVER (Munden)

Only released in select European countries (though it did sneak out in the UK under the pseudonym 'Network' on the Private Stock label), and co-written with ex-Jumbo and ex-Tremelo Paul Carman, '**Lonely Nights**' is a Bee Gees-styled Disco song, with Dave sounding like a less squeaky Barry Gibb. Again, not what one would expect from The Tremeloes, though it's actually not bad at all. Despite featuring Dave, Alan and Rick on the Dutch picture sleeve (and a vintage circa 1974 pic featuring Dave, Alan, Chip and Bob on the German sleeve), when performed on Belgian TV's 'Dolle Dinsdag' the line-up was Dave (drums), Alan (guitar) and, on bass, a temporary band member whose identity currently remain a mystery.

'**Groover**' is a Bluesy Elvis Presley-styled number, similar to his song 'Trouble', with Dave doing a convincing vocal that manages to tread that fine line between tribute and parody.

Unknown, Alan Blakley and Dave Munden, February 1979.

So far, there had been one crucial member missing from The Tremeloes' 1978 semi-reunions - and that member was of course Len 'Chip' Hawkes.

Len: "In 1979 my family and I decided to return to England. I thought the time was right to reform The Tremeloes. I called Alan but unfortunately he was committed to producing The Rubettes, none the less Rick and Dave were more than happy to join me, and The Tremeloes were born again."

With Alan unable or unwilling to participate in a full reunion, Dave, Rick and Len initially got together with guitarist Ian Ellis, who was then replaced by former-Christie member Vic Elmes [Victor George Elmes, b. 10-5-47 – d. 20-4-2017]

Vic: "I went to live in Germany in 1980, when I joined the Tremeloes for a year, and then after that, teamed up with Mike Blakley again for a Christie revival tour."

THE TREMELOES - EVEN THE BAD TIMES ARE GOOD!

Rick Westwood, Dave Munden, Ian Ellis, Chip Hawkes.

Rick: "I took this picture (above) with the camera on and tripod and time delay in my back garden."

Rick Westwood, Chip Hawkes, Vic Elmes, Dave Munden.

January 1980: SINGLE [AMI AIS 100]

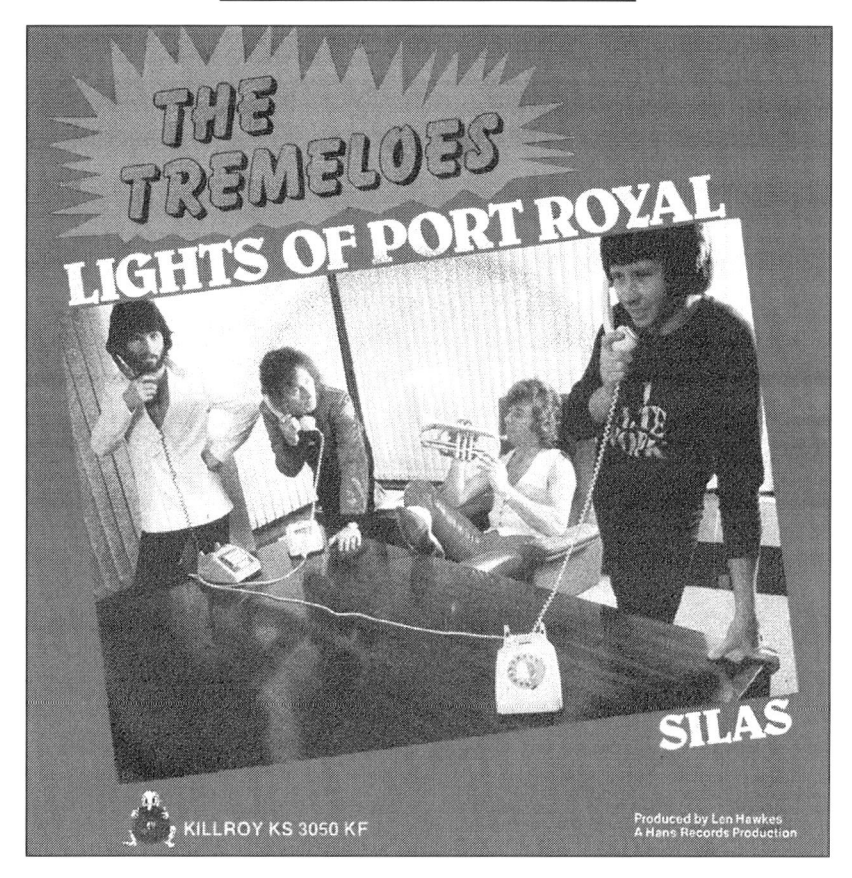

Dutch picture sleeve

THE LIGHTS OF PORT ROYAL (Jefferies)
SILAS (Hawkes)

The Tremeloes' first single since the return of Chip Hawkes, Len brought back with him a Country influence for the pleasant mid-tempo accordion-led '**The Lights Of Port Royal**'. As with the previous two singles, they promoted it on TV - this time Germany's 'Plattenküche' - with the unique one-off line-up of Len (guitar & vocals), Dave (accordion & vocals), Rick (drums) and Vic Elmes (bass).

The Len-composed '**Silas**' is a rootsy Country-tinged rocker, and definitely has the edge over the A-side.

By 1981, Dave, Rick and Chip were joined by the returning Bob Benham. Not that things were always easy.

Len: "When I came back from America and formed the band again with Dave and Rick, they were terrible times. They were really depressing times. 'Cause the 60s had 'had its day'. It was the end of the 70s, and Punk was all about, and it really ruined it for us. And then Al rejoined the band, and we started getting more popular again."

Dave Munden, Chip Hawkes, Bob Benham, Rick Westwood.

November 1981: SINGLE [Polydor POSP 381]

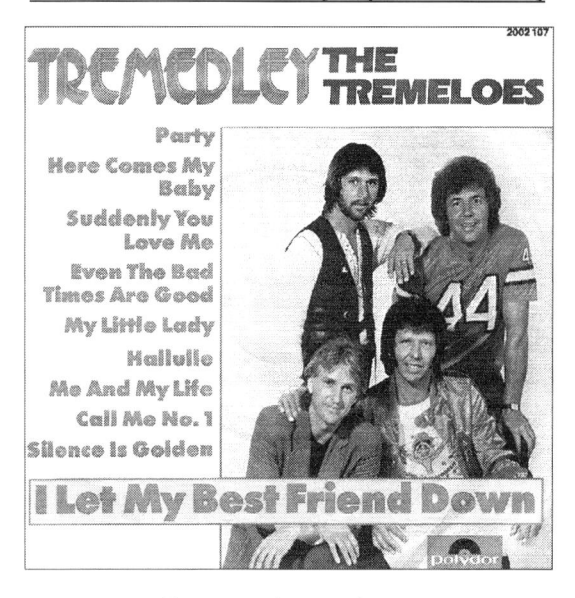

German picture sleeve

TREMEDLEY (Various)
I LET MY BEST FRIEND DOWN (Hawkes)

In 1981, there was a sudden craze for medleys of old '60s classics - something Brian Poole and The Tremeloes had pioneered on their first album! It was kicked-off by the hugely successful Stars on 45, Dutch sound-a-likes who specialised in recreations of The Beatles and others from the same era. Some vintage acts capitalised on this themselves, with The Hollies compiling their own medleys as 'Holliedaze' b/w 'Holliepops' (and reuniting with Graham Nash to appear on 'Top Of The Pops'), while The Tremeloes recorded their own '**Tremedley**'. Starting with the new song '**Party**', the medley then continues with eight of the band's biggest hits. Unfortunately, 'Tremedley' (sometimes called 'Tremelodies') wasn't the hit the band hoped for, despite promotion on top-rated German TV show 'Musikladen'.

An odd mixture of Glammy guitar riffs, Country music structure and falsetto chorus, '**I Let My Best Friend Down**' sounds like an unfinished demo, with just perfunctory backing and no harmonies.

THE TREMELOES - EVEN THE BAD TIMES ARE GOOD!

December 1981: ALBUM [Pickwick SHM 3097]

GREATEST HITS

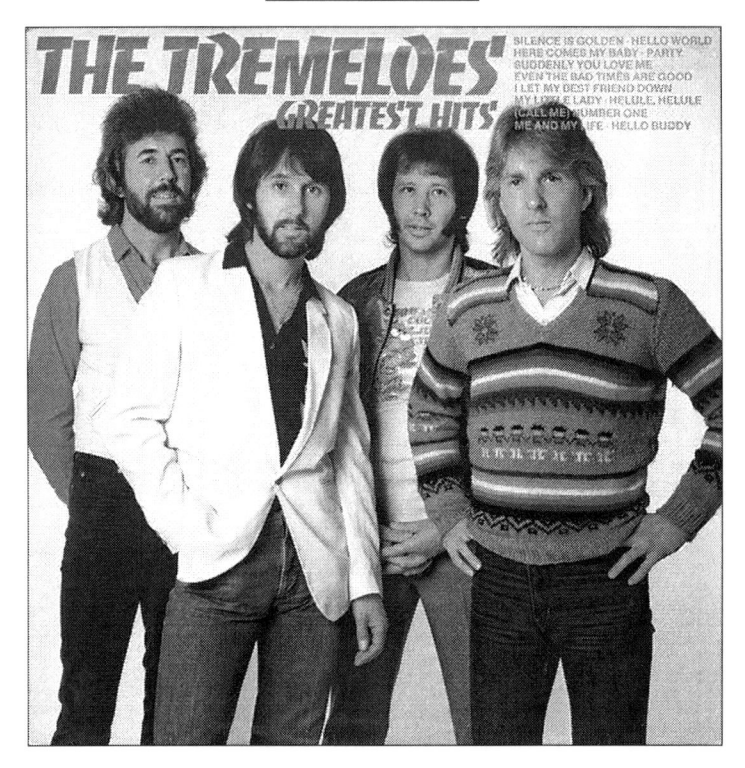

SILENCE IS GOLDEN (Crewe / Guadio)
HELLO WORLD (Hazzard)
HERE COMES MY BABY (Stevens)
PARTY (Hawkes)
HELLO BUDDY (Blakley / Hawkes)
EVEN THE BAD TIMES ARE GOOD (Murray / Callander)
(CALL ME) NUMBER ONE (Blakley / Hawkes)
MY LITTLE LADY (Pace / Panzeri / Pilat / Blakley / Hawkes)
HELULE HELULE (Kabaka / Blakley / Hawkes)
I LET MY BEST FRIEND DOWN (Hawkes)
ME AND MY LIFE (Blakley / Hawkes)
SUDDENLY YOU LOVE ME (Pace / Panzeri / Palat / Callander)
CANDY MAN (Ross / Neil) *[Not Released Until 1988]*
BY THE WAY (Blakley / Hawkes) *[Not Released Until 1988]*

Much as fans would've preferred new material, commercial needs required The Tremeloes to instead re-cut their hits, with the only "new" songs being the recent B-side '**I Let My Best Friend Down**' and the full version of the fun but unadventurous '**Party**'. Mostly sticking closely to the original templates, they don't embarrass themselves on the re-recordings, even if they add nothing to the originals. Probably recorded during these sessions - but not released until 1988's German 'Silence Is Golden' CD on the Laserlight label - are a thrilling Dave-sung '**Candy Man**' and a more mellow but equally good re-cut of '**By The Way**'.

By the end of the following year, the classic line-up of Alan, Dave, Rick and Chip would finally fully unite.

Dave: "Alan Blakley had been active as a producer, first as mentioned for our own album 'Don't Let The Music Die' by Space-Tremeloes, and then for The Rubettes, Mungo Jerry, and during the '80s for the hit manufacturers Stock-Aitken-Waterman, who also had our (later) keyboard player Joe Gillingham in their team."

Len: "Alan had fulfilled his contractual commitments, and rejoined the band in 1982. We then had six more great years happily touring the world."

March 1983: SINGLE [CBS A3133]

Dutch picture sleeve

WORDS (Fitoussle)
I WILL RETURN (Spence)

Their first full, classic line-up reunion release, the Synth-Pop '**Words**' had already been a huge continental hit for French musician F.R. David, but as far as the band new, he had no plans to release it in the UK. The Tremeloes do a nice job on it, particularly vocally, and it even entered the UK charts at No. 91. Then, the original version got a belated UK release, getting to No. 2 in the charts while The Tremeloes' single was quickly forgotten. So near, yet so far - though it did top the charts in Zimbabwe. A superb specially made video (despite Len's perm!) was broadcast on the UK's 'The Video Entertainers', but there was no other TV promotion.

A sort of 'Radio Ga Ga' meets calypso, the best thing about '**I Will Return**' is the return of The Tremeloes' trade-mark harmonies.

Performing 'Words' on 'The Video Entertainers', 1983.

October 1983: SINGLE [BR Music BR 56010] {Netherlands only}

Dutch picture sleeve

SOMEONE (Petty / Greines)
YOU CAN GET IT (Blakley / Hawkes)

As well as being a giant hit back in the Brian Poole era, The Tremeloes had already revived 'Someone, Someone' for single release in 1975 with a Dave Munden lead vocal. So the prospect of them recording it yet again for the Dutch BR label was, on paper at least, a disappointing one. Yet the slightly-re-titled '**Someone**' is unexpectedly excellent, with a flawless Len lead vocal. It was promoted live on Dutch TV's 'AVRO's Platengala' - complete with an orchestra - but didn't chart.

The biggest disappointment of the 1982-1988 reunion was the lack of new songs composed by the once highly prolific Alan Blakley and Chip Hawkes, with the release of just two B-sides by the duo during this period. '**You Can Get It**' is a very good Dave-sung Pop-Rocker, with a fine twin guitar solo. However, the main lyrics are a little *too* close to Jimmy Cliff's 1970 Reggae classic 'You Can Get It If You Really Want It' for it to be totally original.

Performing 'Someone' on 'AVRO's Platengala', 1983.

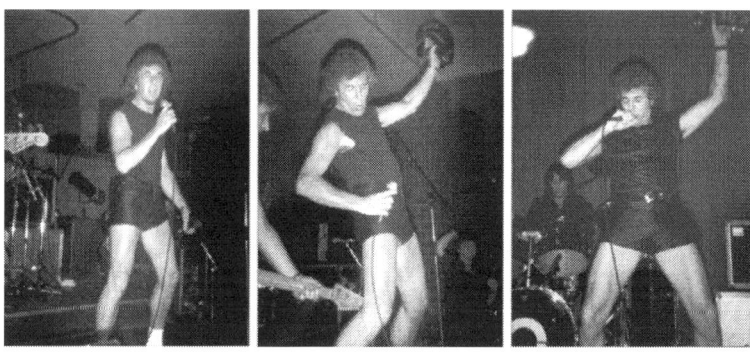

Chip drums while Dave dances! Somewhere in the UK, mid '80s.
(© Bren Goodwin)

October 1984: SINGLE [Meteor MTS 002]

SILENCE IS GOLDEN (Gaudio / Crewe)
THE LAST WORD (Blakley / Hawkes)

Harking back to their biggest hit, the 1984 remake of '**Silence Is Golden**' starts with an excerpt of 'God Save The Queen' played on the organ, before a largely acapella vocal performance, with the organ gradually sneaking in again towards the end. Few who heard it could fail to be moved by something so stunningly beautiful, even if it did not chart.

A Blakley-Hawkes original, the Synth-Pop '**The Last Word**' could almost be titled 'Words part 2' - a sound-a-like that was probably intended to be that way.

1984: ALBUM [Heartbreak Hotel Records - HH1] {Spain only}

THE HITS

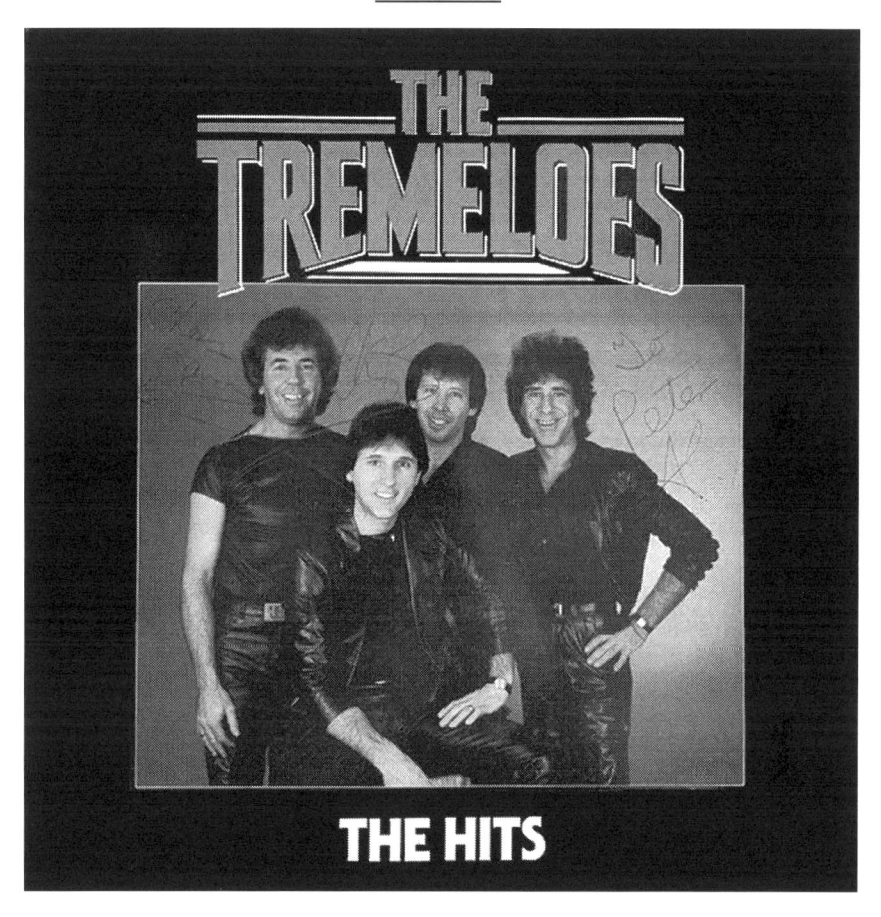

EVEN THE BAD TIMES ARE GOOD (Murray / Callander)
(CALL ME) NUMBER ONE (Blakley / Hawkes)
CANDY MAN (Ross / Neil)
HELULE HELULE (Kabaka / Blakley / Hawkes)
SILENCE IS GOLDEN (Crewe / Guadio)
SUDDENLY YOU LOVE ME (Pace / Panzeri / Palat / Callander)
ME AND MY LIFE (Blakley / Hawkes)
HERE COMES MY BABY (Stevens)
SOMEONE (Petty / Greines)
MY LITTLE LADY (Pace / Panzeri / Pilat / Blakley / Hawkes)

In March 1984, The Tremeloes got together in Chris Squire's studio in Surrey, where they again re-recorded their hits. Overall, they're very good versions, with a refreshing live-in-the-studio sound, but probably the highlight is a Reggae re-arrangement of 'My Little Lady'. The imaginatively-titled 'The Hits' got a very limited release in Spain, and doesn't appear to have ever been issued on CD, so remains unheard by the majority of fans. It would be the *only* album the full reunion line-up ever made.

CANDY MAN (Ross / Neil)
YELLOW RIVER (Christie)
MY LITTLE LADY (Pace / Panzeri / Pilat / Blakley / Hawkes)

As well as other previously issued '80s material, the 1985 Meteor LP 'Silence Is Golden' included exclusive live versions of '**Candy Man**', '**My Little Lady**', and, significantly, '**Yellow River**' - significant because this was the first ever official release of a Tremeloes version of the song, several years before the 1970 recordings were issued.

1987: SINGLE [Topflite TOPS 2]

ANGEL OF THE MORNING (Taylor)
AM I DREAMING (Hawkes)

'**Angel Of The Morning**' had been a stage favourite since 1968 - indeed, a live version was done for the BBC that year, and it was also on the following year's 'Live In Cabaret' album. So again, The Tremeloes re-recorded something they were very familiar with, though that said, Dave sings this keyboard-led version as well as he ever did.

With Funky guitar in the verses and more Country-ish guitars in the chorus, '**Am I Dreaming**' has an unusual structure, and with just minimal keyboards, it sounds far less dated than most material from this era.

Bren Goodwin and her mum with The Tremeloes, mid-'80s.
(© Bren Goodwin)

1988: SINGLE [Mojo MOJ 109 770]

German picture sleeve

SILENCE IS GOLDEN (NEW RECORDING '88) [1988]
(Crewe / Guadio)
SILENCE IS GOLDEN (DUB VERSION) [1988]
(Crewe / Guadio)

The Tremeloes had already re-cut the song at least three times so far during the '80s, and now they put out a single with two more versions of '**Silence Is Golden**'. The A-side in particular is dreadful - while perfectly sung, it features a loud and very inappropriate brittle-drummed dance beat, and keyboards that all but drown out the vocals.

Around April 1988, the quartet added a 5th member, with keyboardist Joe Gillingham.

Joe: "After two years of writing, recording and touring the band, Mojo Hannah (a Country-Rock outfit) split, and the original nucleus became the House band at Southern Music. Writing Library Music and Jingles followed and a chance to write songs and record them. It was during this period that lots of associations were made with other musicians, one being Alan Blakley. At that time The Tremeloes were not working so we spent time together writing songs and recording them on a Porta studio in a friend's house. Eventually The Tremeloes reformed and I was asked to play a session for Radio One. I filled in on piano for these sessions and soon after became a Tremelo myself."

Then, around three months later, Len decided to leave the band, to be replaced by bassist and singer Davey Fryer.

Len: "In 1988 I decided, after a lot of soul searching, to leave the band and manage my son Chesney."

Rick: "We added Joe in 1988 and Chip Hawkes left the same year, so Davey was brought into the band."

Dave: "Len left the band twice. The second time around, he was tired of playing the same set. When he left again in 1988, he said 'During the last Tremeloes year I hated 90 percent of our gigs.'"

1988: SINGLE [Qualitel Q7-S 1034] {Netherlands only}

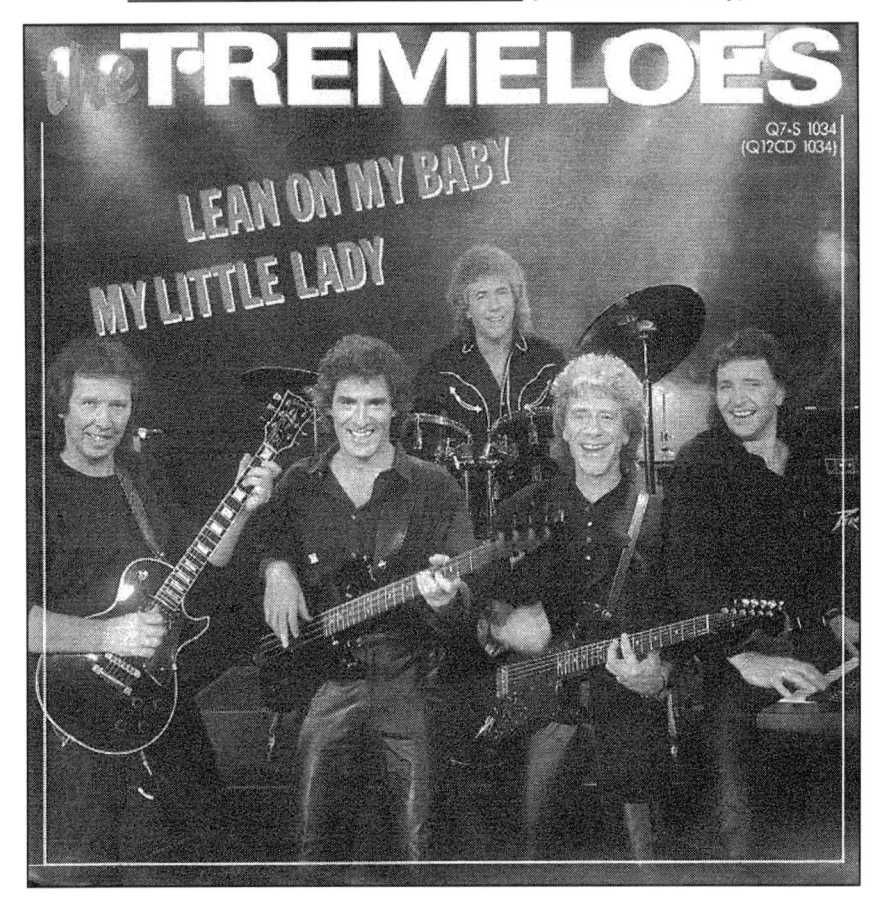

Dutch picture sleeve

LEAN ON ME BABY (Spence)
MY LITTLE LADY (Blakley / Hawkes / Pace / Panzeri / Pila)

Now a quintet comprising (above photo): Rick Westwood, Davey Fryer, Dave Munden, Alan Blakley and Joe Gillingham, The Tremeloes wasted no time in going into the studio, re-recording the hits (again), along with a handful of new songs. Backed by a re-cut of '**My Little Lady**', '**Lean On Me Baby**' (wrongly listed as 'Lean On *My* Baby' on the picture sleeve), was the preview single, and once you're past the 80s production with typically over-loud drums, it's a very good modern mid-tempo Pop song, with strong Dave vocals, impressive guitar and a nice catchy chorus.

1988: ALBUM [Qualitel Q-LP 263-1] {Europe & S. Africa only}

MILLION SELLERS

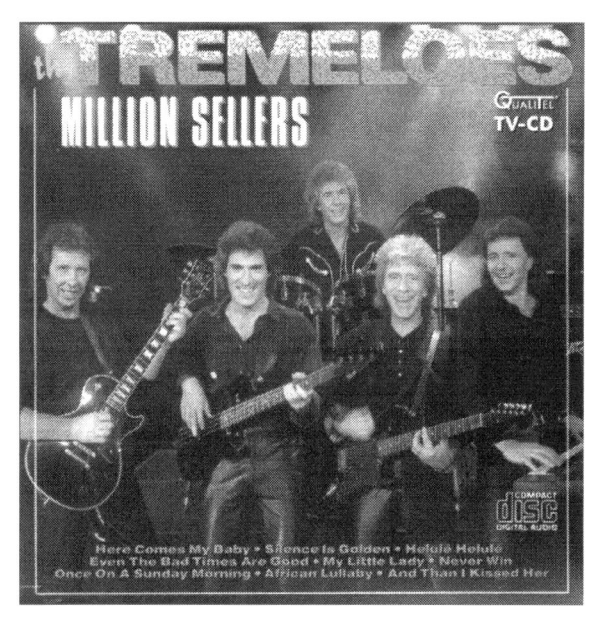

EVEN THE BAD TIMES ARE GOOD (Murray / Callander)
SILENCE IS GOLDEN (Crewe / Guadio)
HELULE HELULE (Kabaka / Blakley / Hawkes)
NEVER WIN (Gillingham / Roker)
ONCE ON A SUNDAY MORNING (Aguile / Kusik / Snyder / Blakley / Hawkes)
AFRICAN LULLABY (Blakley / Gillingham)
HELLO WORLD (Hazzard)
MY LITTLE LADY (Pace / Panzeri / Pilat / Blakley / Hawkes)
HERE COMES MY BABY (Stevens)
I LIKE IT THAT WAY (Blakley / Hawkes)
SOMEONE (Petty / Greines)
AND THEN I KISSED HER (Spector / Greenwich)
LEAN ON ME BABY (Spence)
ST. TROPEZ (Blakley / Gillingham)
ME AND MY LIFE (Blakley / Hawkes)
CALL ME NUMBER ONE (Blakley / Hawkes)

Instead of doing their best to recreate the sounds of the late '60s and early '70s, for these post-Chip remakes The Tremeloes went for a bang up-to-date production - which in 1988, meant booming reverb-heavy drums, plenty of keyboards and not enough guitars. Additionally, while a fine singer in his own right, Davey's voice lacks the distinction of Len's. The more interesting tracks are old songs with radically new arrangements: **'Once On A Sunday Morning'** is far more laid-back, almost middle-of-the-road, in comparison to the party-like original, while **'Hello World'** is sung by Dave as a slow ballad.

Of the new songs, as well as the new single **'Lean On Me Baby'**; **'Never Win'** is a dramatic modern ballad, with a great Dave lead vocal, and almost cinematic orchestrated-keyboard touches; album highlight **'African Lullaby'** has largely African lyrics with an English chorus; the Dave-sung **'And Then I Kissed Her'** is a nice update of The Crystals (1963) / The Beach Boys (1965) classic; and **'St. Tropez'** is a danceable Dave and Davey duet, pitched somewhere between The Four Tops and the then-emerging Boy Bands.

The Tremeloes in the UK, late '80s. (© Frank Connor)

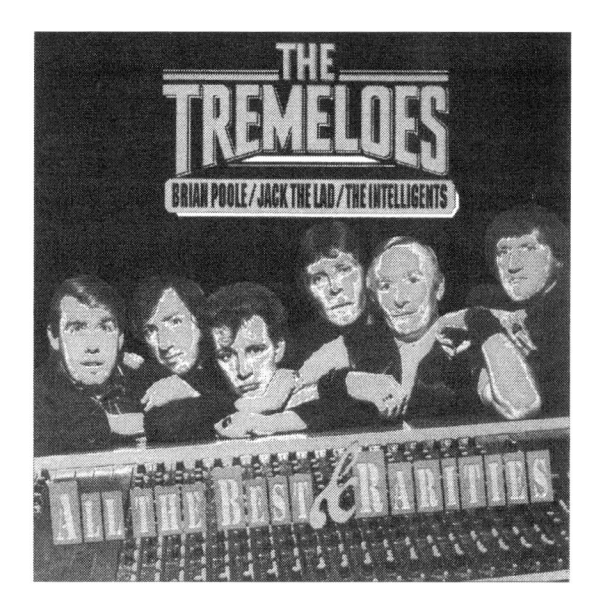

TWIST AND SHOUT (Russell / Medley)
HEY BABY (Channel / Cobb)
SILENCE IS GOLDEN (Gaudio / Crewe)
DO YOU WANNA DANCE (Freeman)
IT'S ALL OVER NOW (Womack / Womack)
DO IT AGAIN (Blakley / Gillingham)
KEEP ON YOUR FEET (Blakley / Gillingham)

The 1989 CD 'The Tremeloes - All The Best & Rarities' was mentioned earlier in the Alan Blakley solo section - and, also featured are seven songs with the mysterious credit "By various members of The Tremeloes" - though you can be pretty sure that neither Len, Dave or Rick are involved. They're far more likely to be Alan Blakley solo experiments, with some of them just plain weird: '**Twist and Shout**' (featured on the CD in complete form and as a brief reprise) is given a Ska arrangement, while '**Hey Baby**' is Reggae; '**Silence Is Golden**' is laid-back but mid-tempo, with country-picked guitar and no falsetto; Bobby Freeman's (via Cliff Richard and The Shadows) '**Do You Wanna Dance**' and '**Do It Again**' are New Wave-ish, and both '**It's All Over Now**' and '**Keep On Your Feet**' are slightly-Disco-fied. Nothing on here is essential, but it's an intriguing release nevertheless.

Several of The Tremeloes' children have gone on to have successful music careers, including Len's son Chesney (who had a world-wide smash with 'The One and Only') and daughter Keely, and Brian's daughters Shelly and Karen (who had hits as Alisha's Attic before becoming highly successful songwriters). In addition, Alan's daughter Claudie Blakley has become one of the country's leading actresses.

Chesney Hawkes and Keely Hawkes.

Karen & Shelly Poole in Alisha's Attic and Claudie Blakley.

Brian: "Karen has written three No. 1 records, and Shellie a hit film 'My Old School' and many top 10s. Between them they've written for Westlife, Will Young, Kylie Minogue, Danni Minogue, Jamelia, Becky Hill, K-Pop, Janet Jackson, Mae Muller, Rita Ora, Lily Allen. Both are award winners for their writing. Very proud of both!"

1992: SINGLE [LadyLand Records - LL 5007-8] {Germany only}

German picture sleeve

FAREWELL & GOODBYE (Rochel / Blakley / Fryer / Gillingham)
[Radio Version]
FAREWELL & GOODBYE (Rochel / Blakley / Fryer / Gillingham)
[Extended Version]
THE RISING SUN (Fryer / Gillingham)
FAREWELL & GOODBYE (Rochel / Blakley / Fryer / Gillingham)
[Karaoke Version]

Still featuring the same 5-piece line-up as in 1988, the 3/4 'waltz' time **'Farewell & Goodbye'** is pleasantly sung by Davey, enhanced by some superb Beach Boys-esque harmonies that are allowed to shine, thanks to the nicely understated instrumentation.

'The Rising Sun' has military styled drumming, keyboards, and an anthemic football crowd chorus.

THE TREMELOES - EVEN THE BAD TIMES ARE GOOD!

1992: ALBUM [Line LICD 9.01206 O]

ALL FOR ONE AND ONE FOR ALL {Germany only}

AFRICAN LULLABY (Blakley / Gillingham)
THE CRIME OF LIFE (Blakley / Gillingham)
I SHALL BE RELEASED (Dylan)
JODIE (Gillingham)
ST. TROPEZ (Blakley / Gillingham)
SO MUCH TO SAY (Blakley / Gillingham)
ALL FOR ONE AND ONE FOR ALL (Blakley / Gillingham)
AFRICAN LULLABY [Acapella] (Blakley / Gillingham)
LEAN ON ME BABY (Spence)
NEVER WIN (Gillingham / Roker)
ANGEL OF THE MORNING (Taylor)
ANITA (Fryer)
PRAYER FOR PEACE (Fryer)
ROCK 'N' ROLL (LIVE): JOHNNY B. GOODE - BONEY MORONIE
(Berry / Williams)

In 1992, The Tremeloes finally released their first album of (mostly) new material in 17 years. It would also be their *last* proper album, excluding compilations and live releases. While not everything on it is a classic, it's better than anyone could've expected from a band that had been around for 30 years.

Four of the tracks had previously been issued on 1988's 'Million Sellers' album: '**African Lullaby**' - included here in both original form and as a near-acapella remix, '**St. Tropez**', '**Lean On Me Baby**' and '**Never Win**'. It also includes a couple of re-makes; a lovely version of '**Angel Of The Morning**' that is less bombastic than the 1987 single version, and a dreadful dance version of '**I Shall Be Released**'.

Most of the rest are new compositions by Davey Fryer and/or Joe Gillingham, proving themselves to be far more than just side-men. '**The Crime Of Life**' and '**So Much To Say**' are no more than mediocre, but Joe's '**Jodie**' is a beautiful ballad, '**All For One and One For All**' is a power ballad with prominent guitar, Davey's '**Anita**' is a calypso-rhythm Pop song, with an intro not unlike 'Here Comes My Baby', and '**Prayer For Peace**' is a touching anti-war sound. The closing '**Rock 'N 'Roll (Live): Johnny B. Goode - Boney Moronie**' is exciting stuff, though the fade-in suggests it was part of a longer medley.

It is no surprise that the band by this time were often in Germany.

Rick: "We have never stopped playing on the road, we've played in Germany, we play all over the world all the time. Just because we don't have a record doesn't mean to say that we've stopped working, because we work all the time."

Dave: "German fans tend to get more excited, and we are happy that they still like us after all these years. And the percentage of young people is higher, back in the United Kingdom we tend to play more holiday camps."

Davey: "We do such a lot of work here, we spend a lot of time here, and we do get on well with the Germans, we've worked with them for years. The band is over here virtually every weekend, and it is like second home."

It wasn't *all* fun though... far from it!

Rick: "On 15th June 1991, we were playing at The Waldbühne in Berlin. A British soldier who got upset about being asked to leave the backstage area came across me heading towards the stage with my guitar around my neck. He came up behind me and without warning, turned me round and smashed me in the face. It was a massive punch and I went down on the floor in a heap - He had broken my nose into bits and knocked a front tooth out. I eventually got up and walked back to the dressing room, the rest of the boys were still there and wondered what had happened.

Our good friend Ricky Gee drove me immediately to hospital to get checked out in case I had concussion or something. I had to have my nose reset but it was too late at night to get an anaesthetist so the surgeon squirted pain killing juice up my nose and set about resetting the broken bones. The pain was unbelievable and I went into a shaking spasm and was screaming in agony. It was the worst pain I have ever had in my entire life... but my nose was straight. Ricky had to leave because the sound of me screaming was really upsetting for him.

Alan Williams from The Rubettes took my place on stage that night. We had a TV show the next day so Alan covered for me with that as I flew back home with my face in a plaster cast. I was waiting for my luggage at Heathrow Airport when I got back and Henry Cooper came over and asked if I had been fighting and asked if the other bloke came off worse. How brilliant to meet up with Henry while I was looking like that!

The consequences of that episode cost me a lot of money over a long time. I did a few shows in Germany with the plaster cast across my face, much to the amusement of the German audiences. The guitar I had around my neck was covered in blood and I left it there for many years until my mate Richard Marsh bought it from me fairly recently."

It was around this time that Alan Blakley started getting ill - prompting some publicity photos featuring The Tremeloes as a 4-piece.

Rick Westwood, Davey Fryer, Dave Munden, Joe Gillingham.

In late 1993, Davey Fryer left the band for around three months, to be replaced by John Berry - someone who'd had previous experience working with both The Tremeloes and Brian Poole.

John: "In around 1984 I answered an Ad in the Melody Maker to become the Lead Singer/Bass Player in London Rock and Roll Band - 'Blackcat'. It turned out that they also backed Screaming Lord Sutch and Brian Poole, and we soon became Brian's full time backing band for around two years. When I joined Love Affair in late 1985 I found myself on a tour with The Tremeloes and Marmalade and struck up a friendship with what was then the full original line-up. On joining Les Gray's Mud in 1987 our paths continually crossed, as we had the same management - Steve Colyer. Sometime in the late 80s I stood in for Len Hawkes who was ill, for a show in London, with no rehearsal!

When Davey Friar left in 1993 I auditioned and joined Dave, Alan, Rick and Joe. I played with them until January 1994. It was for a relatively short period of time because I did stand out as being much younger. At the photo session I suggested that the three originals should be in the front- but they insisted that they wanted a new look. There had been some comments from agents that they no longer looked like the original line up and they became aware that Davey wanted to come back, I therefore returned to Mud, who had not found anyone to replace me that fitted in."

Dave Munden, Rick Westwood, John Berry, Joe Gillingham, Alan Blakley.

John: "In 2003 I joined Slade (with whom I am with to this day - 20 years plus) as Les Gray had retired due to ill health. As a footnote, in 2004 when Davey Fryer left for the second time, I got a call from Rick Westwood asking me if I would be interested in re-joining. We continued to meet over the years both on tour and socially and have always remained great friends."

JERUSALEM (Parry / Gillingham / Blakley)
BEFORE YOU KNOW IT WILL BE CHRISTMAS
(Blakley / Fryer / Gillingham)

With Davey Fryer back in the band, The Tremeloes contributed two new recordings to the various artists 'Thommy's Christmas Party' album in 1994 - "Thommy" being Thomas Gottschalk, a well-known presenter of music TV shows in Germany.

Based on original lyrics by William Blake, the patriotic anthem '**Jerusalem**' was first published in 1916 by Sir Hubert Parry. A wonderful Classical-meets-Rock arrangement, with sweeping strings, male backing vocals and pounding drums, it's topped by a dramatic and passionately-sung Dave Munden lead vocal.

A group original, '**Before You Know It Will Be Christmas**' is a more typical Christmas song, with jangling "bell" sounds, jolly lyrics, and some very nice harmonies.

THE TREMELOES - EVEN THE BAD TIMES ARE GOOD!

The Tremeloes in the UK, with Anthony Connor, early '90s. (© Frank Connor)

Dave Munden, Rick Westwood, Alan Blakley, Joe Gillingham, Davey Fryer.

ALAN DAVID BLAKLEY

[7-4-42 - 1-6-96]

Alan started missing some tours during 1993 and 1994, but he was seen on stage for a few UK dates as late as March 1995. By the end of that year though, he was forced to retire, and sadly passed away on the 1st June 1996. The Tremeloes' driving force was gone.

Brian: "When Alan got ill we spent a lot of time on the phone together talking, trying to cheer him up. He was having a pretty bad time. Sometimes I feel he's still here. We're not going to make a big thing about it, he'd hate that. He was a happy man."

Dave: "He was a lovely guy, and a great friend for more than 40 years."

Len: "My late friend and mentor Alan Blakley taught me so many valuable things. Without his enormous energy and strength of character, the name Tremeloes would never have been heard."

BACK HOME FOR CHRISTMAS (Gillingham / Fryer)

With Dave, Rick, Joe and Davey now carrying on as a 4-piece, in 1998 they contributed to another German Christmas CD, this time entitled 'The Best of Christmas Pop'. Featuring Dave on lead vocals, **'Back Home For Christmas'** is a reasonable enough Pop-Rocker with suitably seasonal-themed lyrics.

In 2002, there was a fascinating UK tour under the banner 'Call Up The Groups', where the various members of the bands collaborated on stage - i.e., all of the guitarists got together, then all of the drummers, etc. Within a couple of years, The Barron Knights' Peter Langford would be instrumental in getting Brian Poole and The Tremeloes to reunite, for the first time in nearly four decades.

Dave with Rod Allen from The Fortunes, backed by The Barron Knights.

The singing drummers from The Tremeloes, The Barron Knights,
The Fortunes and Marmalade.
(© John Truman)

In December 2004, Davey Fryer left The Tremeloes for the 2nd time - this time permanently. Replacing him was Jeff Brown, previously a singer and bassist in several other famous bands.

Jeff: "I knew The Tremeloes because we'd done a lot of work with Sweet and Slade and Smokie and Suzi Quatro all around Germany, and The Tremeloes were always on the bill, and they were a great bunch of guys, they really were. I just got a phone call from Dave Munden, and he said their bass player had just basically left, he went to Germany for Christmas and never came home again. So he said 'Are you interested?', I said 'Yeah, why not?!' He said 'One thing, can you sing 'Silence Is Golden'', I said 'Yes, I can', so he said 'Oh good, you're in!'"

A couple of months later - 21st February 2005 to be precise - Brian Poole and The Tremeloes reunited, with a line-up of Brian Poole, Dave Munden, Rick Westwood, Mick Clarke and Joe Gillingham.

Brian "Boxing Day 2004. When we watched the news it was hard to believe that we were seeing an earthquake, and a Tsunami devastating the Indian Ocean shorelines and many people losing their lives and homes. The initial shock went on for months and many people were looking at ways to help restore some normality to the devastated areas, from setting up charities to arranging concerts where the proceeds would go to these charities.

Now over the years, much has been written and said about The Tremeloes, Chip Hawkes and me. Much of it straight from the donkey's arse. We were at this time 2005 often talking to each other on the phone (our wives said that the aforementioned donkey had lost its hind legs to us) many times over, after all we had more than most to talk about.

So, when my good friend and near-neighbour Pete Langford of the Barron Knights called and asked if I would like to take part in a concert to raise money for the Tsunami appeal to be held at the Stables, near Milton Keynes, I said definitely yes. During this conversation he said that the Tremeloes would also be on the show, to which I replied jokingly 'OK they can call us Brian Poole and the Tremeloes like old times, you might sell a few more tickets'. He said 'Well that's OK because you are doing it together'. 'Oh are we?', 'Yes you are.' So we all agreed that we would be appearing together.

Now here is a bit of Tremeloes history. When Alan Howard left the Tremeloes in the mid '60s we asked Mick Clarke, who had been in The Symbols, another 'Dagenham Motown' band to join us. He was a Tremelo for a few months and eventually left and formed The Rubettes, who had many hits in the '70s. Mick is a great musician and harmony singer who had stayed close friends with all of us although we didn't see much of him over the years. Probably because Chip Hawkes could not appear on the concert date due to prior engagement with his Class of '64 show, the Tremeloes asked Mick if he would join us for this occasion and the said yes, which was really great for us all because Mick was the only other (still playing) Tremeloes bass player from the original days, the other was of course Chip. Also joining us was Joe Gillingham, the present keyboard player with the Tremeloes who I have known as a friend and worked with over many years. This was a great event and an enjoyable night for all concerned. They even say that history was made by the Tremeloes and me by performing together for the first time in 38yrs."

The following year, in the autumn of 2006, Brian Poole and The Tremeloes did a full UK 40th Anniversary Reunion Tour.

Dexex Franks Presents

Brian Poole & The Tremeloes

Original members Brian Poole, Chip Hawkes, Dave Munden & Rick Westwood

together for the first time in over 40 years

Twist and Shout   Do You Love Me   Candy Man   Someone Someone
Here Come's My Baby   Even The Bad Times Are Good   Suddenly You Love Me   My Little Lady
and the classic hit: Silence Is Golden

Friday 8 September 7.30pm
£14.50 (reductions available)

St David's Hall   029 2087 8444
Neuadd Dewi Sant   www.stdavidshallcardiff.co.uk

CARDIFF
CAERDYDD

Brian Poole and The Tremeloes: Chip, Rick, Jeff, Brian, Joe and Dave.

2008: ALBUM [Private Pressing]

LIVE! IN EUROPE

SUDDENLY YOU LOVE ME / HERE COMES MY BABY / (CALL ME) NUMBER ONE / I SHALL BE RELEASED / HELULE HELULE / ME AND MY LIFE / YELLOW RIVER / SOMEONE SOMEONE / CANDY MAN / DO YOU LOVE ME / ANGEL OF THE MORNING / GOOD LOVIN' / TWIST AND SHOUT / MY LITTLE LADY / SILENCE IS GOLDEN / EVEN THE BAD TIMES ARE GOOD

Despite their long deserved reputation as a great live band, to date there had only been one live Tremeloes album - 1969's 'Live In Cabaret'. Nearly forty years later and with only two of the same members, this doesn't *quite* match up to that, but it comes far closer than one could've expected. Vocally and instrumentally tight, this limited release, only available from merchandise stalls at gigs, is highly entertaining, with Jeff Brown proving himself a highly capable co-front man.

THE TREMELOES - EVEN THE BAD TIMES ARE GOOD!

2010: ALGUM [Private Pressing]
THE ONES THAT GOT AWAY

SLOWDOWN (Gillingham)
OPEN UP (Gillingham / Munden)
THE THREE BELLS (Gilles / Reisfeld)
I STILL BELIEVE IN ANGELS (Gillingham)
EN TU MUNDO (Bell / Casal)
THE BIRTH OF SPRING (Gillingham)
BABY I'VE LOST YOU NOW (Westwood)
CIRCLE OF STONE (Fryer / Gillingham / Vanderbuildt)
YOU DON'T HAVE TO SAY YOU LOVE ME
(Donaggio / Pallavicini / Wickham / Napier-Bell)
I'M YOURS (Munden)
CAN'T SEE THE WOOD FROM THE TREES (Gillingham)
LEAN ON ME BABY (Spence)
NOTHING WOULD PLEASE ME MORE (Gillingham)
JERUSALEM (Parry / Gillingham / Blakley)

Another tour-only release, as the name implies, this CD consists of (largely) unreleased material, with at least some of it dating back as far as the early '90s. While not a "proper" album as such, there's some very interesting stuff on it.

Two of the songs are re-mixes of previously released tracks, with '**Lean On Me Baby**' sounding far more sparkling, and '**Jerusalem**' featuring a Rock guitar instead of a male vocal chorus. There are also a couple of re-makes: a stunning version of the Brian Poole-era hit '**The Three Bells**', with gorgeous harmonies and suitably subtle instrumentation, and a piano-and-orchestra (with a touch of guitar) '**En Tu Mondo**'.

Of the rest, '**Slowdown**', '**Can't See The Woods For The Trees**', and particularly, '**I'm Yours**' and '**Nothing Would Please Me More**' are Country, with some particularly good fast pickin' on the last song; '**Open Up**' is a Dave-sung mid-tempo song with mildly suggestive lyrics; '**I Still Believe In Angels**' and '**Circle Of Stone**' are Pop-Rock (it is easy to imagine Chesney Hawkes recording the latter); '**The Birth Of Spring**' is an instrumental, allowing Rick to do his best Hank Marvin impersonation; '**You Don't Have To Say You Love Me**' is a predictably good Dave-sung take on the 1966 Dusty Springfield classic; and, perhaps the biggest surprise of all, '**Baby I've Lost You Now**', a lovely song written by Rick and sung by Joe Gillingham.

Dave Munden, Joe Gillingham, Rick Westwood, Jeff Brown.

In December 2012, Rick Westwood retired from the band, to be replaced by Eddie Jones - who was in turn replaced by Syd Twynham (also in 'Mud 2'), from June 2014 onwards. Joe Gillingham also toured occasionally during this period as 'Wellington' in The Wombles!

(© Rebecca Xibalba - Shootin' Starz Photography)

During 2012-2015, Brian Poole and Chip Hawkes did several tours together.

Brian Poole and The Tremeloes toured the UK again in the Spring of 2014, with a line-up of Brian Poole (vocals), Dave Munden (vocals), Joe Gillingham (keyboards & vocals), Jeff Brown (lead vocals & bass), Eddie Jones (lead guitar & vocals) and Philip Wright (drums & vocals).

Brian Poole and The Tremeloes in 2014.
(© Rebecca Xibalba - Shootin' Starz Photography)

Dave Munden, Joe Gillingham, Syd Twynham, Jeff Brown.
(© Rebecca Xibalba - Shootin' Starz Photography)

Syd and Dave.
(© Rebecca Xibalba - Shootin' Starz Photography)

During the early weeks of 2014, Dave Munden missed some shows due to knee surgery. Initially recruited just as a stand-in was another talented singing drummer, namely Philip Wright of Paper Lace - a band who topped both the UK and US charts in 1974.

Philip: "I first met Dave at a TOTPs reunion and book launch in 2014. During our conversations he mentioned that he was having a double knee replacement operation, because of mobility problems. I jokingly said, 'If you need a stand in for any period, give me a call.' The Tremeloes at that point comprised Dave Munden, Joe Gillingham, Jeff Brown and Syd Twynham, who joined a couple of years before me. The long and short of it was that Dave did call me and asked if I would stand in for the operation period, we must have done three or four gigs without him, then he came back but was still unable to play, so he took a turn as the front man leader vocalist and decided that's how he wanted to continue, and he asked me to become a permanent member. I joined and completed a 'Silver Sixties' tour and then toured Germany extensively."

Philip Wright, Jeff Brown, Syd Twynham, Joe Gillingham, Dave Munden.
(© Rebecca Xibalba - Shootin' Starz Photography)

Up until late 2016, the line-up of Dave Munden, Joe Gillingham, Jeff Brown, Philip Wright and Syd Twynham remained fairly stable. And then, Dave Munden left The Tremeloes - to concentrate on touring with Brian and Len as 'Brian Poole and The Tremeloes'.

The remaining members of the former Tremeloes - Joe, Jeff, Philip and Syd - continued as 'The Trems'. There have been some accusations of them only being a tribute band - whatever, but they remain a fun live act, and with a pedigree of The Tremeloes, The Sweet, Mud and Paper Lace, how could they be anything but?

From around January 2018 up until November 2018, there was the nearest thing possible to a full classic The Tremeloes reunion, with Dave Munden (vocals), Rick Westwood (lead guitar) and Len 'Chip' Hawkes (vocals), augmented by Mick Clarke (bass & vocals) and Len's son Jodie Hawkes (drums & vocals). They only gigged occasionally, but thrilled wherever they went. The ever affable Rick Westwood actually guested occasionally with both The Tremeloes *and* The Trems during this period (as more than one ex-Tremelo told the author, "Everyone loves Rick!").

The Trems: Syd Twynham, Joe Gillingham, Jeff Brown, Philip Wright.
(© Rebecca Xibalba - Shootin' Starz Photography)

SUDDENLY YOU LOVE ME / HERE COMES MY BABY / (CALL ME) NUMBER ONE / I SHALL BE RELEASED / HELULE HELULE / ME AND MY LIFE / YELLOW RIVER / SOMEONE / HELLO BUDDY / DO YOU LOVE ME / TWIST AND SHOUT / MY LITTLE LADY / EVEN THE BAD TIMES ARE GOOD / SILENCE IS GOLDEN / ROCK AND ROLL

As well as touring, The Trems issued a hard-to-find live CD that was only available from concert merchandise stalls. Highlights include a stunning 'I Shall Be Released' and a nice version of the seldom-heard 'Hello Buddy'.

At time of writing in late 2023, the line-up of The Trems is Jeff Brown (lead vocals and bass), Chris Kirby-Williams (drums and vocals), Mark Wright (guitar and vocals) and Scott Thomas (keyboard and vocals). Joe Gillingham is recovering from health problems, while Syd Twynham and Philip Wright are busy touring with their other bands.

Photo taken by Rick Westwood at Len's house.

From 2015 to 2017, Brian, Len and Dave did several tours together as 'Brian Poole and The Tremeloes'. On the 2017 'Sixties Gold' Tour, Mick Clarke was added as a stand-in for whenever anyone who got ill, replacing each of them at various dates, and all performing together as a 4-piece at least once.

Throughout 2018, Dave's health deteriorated, and he became increasingly frail. His final ever show was at The Indoor Bowls Club in Hornchurch, East London, on 24th November 2018, where by accounts he remained in great voice. After almost six decades with The Tremeloes, and the *only* constant member throughout the band's many changes, it really was the end of an era.

Rick: "I played on stage with Dave at his last performance at The Bowls Club in Hornchurch, Essex. He was in good form and got the audience going despite his illness."

Chip, Mick and Dave, 2018.
(© Carol & Len Hawkes)

Dave's last show - Hornchurch, 24th November 2018.
(©Linda Knight)

Rick, Len and Dave, watching Brian Poole in High Wycombe, 16th March 2019.
It was the last time they were all seen together.
(© Noreen Rolph)

Richard Marsh, Mick Clarke, Chip Hawkes, Rick Westwood, Jodie Hawkes.
(© Carol & Len Hawkes)

Vienna, Austria, 19th March 2019: Len 'Chip' Hawkes, Mick Clarke, Richard Marsh.
It was this line-up's only performance.
(©Paul Trondl - www.trondl.com)

After Dave retired, the band continued with a line up of Len (vocals), Rick (lead guitar), Mick (vocals & bass), Jodie Hawkes (drums & vocals) and Richard Marsh (rhythm guitar & vocals). Then, following an upbeat and happy show in Bexhill, East Sussex, on 13th July 2019, Rick Westwood took the decision to finally fully retire: he'd first retired in 2012, and had only agreed to return as long as the concerts remained just occasional events, but at this point it looked likely that The Tremeloes would have an increasingly busy schedule in the near future.

Rick's last stand: '60s Revolution', Bexhill, 13th July 2019.
(© Cathy Saxon & Simon Newbury)

Rick's replacement was Vanity Fare's Eddie Wheeler, so from August 2019 until February 2020, The Tremeloes were Len (vocals), Mick Clarke (vocals & bass), Jodie Hawkes (drums & vocals), Richard Marsh (rhythm guitar & vocals) and Eddie Wheeler (lead guitar & vocals). Any further shows though, were put paid by the global covid pandemic.

Mick Clarke, Eddie Wheeler, Len 'Chip' Hawkes, Richard Marsh, Jodie Hawkes.
(© Carol & Len Hawkes)

Less than two years after his enforced retirement, Dave Munden died on the 15th October 2020. His surviving bandmates put out a statement.

Brian: "When talking together today about the death of our friend and band mate Dave Munden, Chip Hawkes and me thought we, on behalf of all of us, will remember him as we knew him. A fun person who had many talents which we all saw come out over the 60 odd years that we knew him. There are many real memories that abound and will only be remembered by us. Dave Munden joined Al and me to become the first Tremilos when he was about 15 years old. The rest is history. Chip remembers also his Tremeloes years with Alan, Rick and Dave with such fondness and affection. If every story about the talented Dave Munden were told it would never end, so goodbye old friend and keep a place for us in the band.

Much Love,

Chip and Brian, reminiscing with Rick"

THE TREMELOES - EVEN THE BAD TIMES ARE GOOD!

DAVID CHARLES MUNDEN

[2-12-43 – 15-10-20]

(© Rebecca Xibalba - Shootin' Starz Photography)

With the same late 2019/early 2020 line-up of Len, Mick, Jodie, Richard and Eddie, The Tremeloes were booked for the 'Sixties Gold' tour during September - November 2021. On the opening night at the Congress Theatre in Eastbourne on 11th September 2021, Len gave it his very best, but he struggled to complete the show, and it was very clear to everyone that he was not at all well. It was Len's final show to date. His son Chesney had been relaxing on a beach in Portugal, but he flew in to save the tour, heroically and impressively, fronting The Tremeloes for the first time in his life. Keeping it in the family, Chesney was occasionally joined by his 15 year old son Indiana Hawkes.

A year later, the October - November 2022 'Sixties Gold' tour, featured a new line-up, consisting of Chesney Hawkes (vocals & guitar), Jodie Hawkes (drums & vocals), Martin Kennedy (lead guitar & vocals) and Alan Vosper (bass & vocals).

Alan Vosper, Chesney Hawkes, Jodie Hawkes, Martin Kennedy.
(© Carol & Len Hawkes)

Chesney: "I always wanted to be a musician. I wasn't bothered about being a 'pop star' - I just wanted to play guitar for a living. My dad was a member of The Tremeloes and one of my earliest memories is watching him at a gig... leather trousers, open-neck shirt, hair flowing in the breeze! That was the life for me."

Chesney Hawkes, fronting The Tremeloes in 2022.
(© Rebecca Xibalba - Shootin' Starz Photography)

The future Tremeloes?
Brian Spence, Colin Chisholm, Alan Vosper, Jodie Hawkes, Martin Kennedy.
(© Carol & Len Hawkes)

Following the late 2022 UK tour, and with reports that Chesney (probably wisely) wanted to concentrate on his own solo career rather than become a full-time Tremelo, it was thought to be the end of The Tremeloes as a touring band. Then, in October 2023, yet another line-up was announced, this time featuring Jodie Hawkes (drums & vocals), Martin Kennedy (lead guitar & vocals), Alan Vosper (now switching to guitar & vocals), Colin Chisholm (lead vocals) and Brian Spence (bass & vocals). Colin and Brian have a long connection with The Tremeloes, having both been in '70s band Bilbo Baggins (later Bilbo) who were produced by Alan Blakley, while Brian later wrote the songs 'I Will Return' in 1983 and 'Lean On Me Baby' in 1988 for The Tremeloes. At time of writing in November 2023 though, all they've done is have some photos taken together, and don't have any gigs booked until late 2024 - so it remains to be seen if they still have the same line-up by then.

Regardless of what happens in the future under The Tremeloes name, the members from the band's heyday have had few regrets.

Brian: "What would I do differently? Absolutely nothing!"

Dave: "Yes, I would do it all again. Maybe differently, maybe not. But I do know that I have been very lucky to have had a life like mine."

Len: "I consider my career with The Trems a life-long privilege and would not change one single day!"

THE TREMELOES BAND MEMBERS

By **Dick Stoll**

(edited by Peter Checksfield)

<u>1956</u> (no name)

Brian Poole [Brian Edwin Poole, b. 2-11-41] (vocals & acoustic guitar), **Alan Blakley** [Alan David Blakley, b. 7-4-42 - d. 1-6-96] (vocals & acoustic guitar / keyboards)

<u>1956 - 1957: (sometimes) The Rhythm Revellers</u>

Brian Poole (lead vocals & lead guitar), **Alan Blakley** (vocals, guitar & occasional drums), **Alan Howard** [Alan Henry Howard, b. 17-10-41] (tenor saxophone, then bass guitar)

<u>1958 - Late 1962: The Tremilos / Brian Poole and The Tremeloes</u>

Brian Poole (lead vocals), **Alan Blakley** (vocals & rhythm guitar), **Alan Howard** (bass), **Graham Scott** [b. 1940] (lead guitar), **Dave Munden** [b. 2-12-43 - d. 5-10-20] (vocals & drums)

<u>Late 1962 - May 1966: Brian Poole and The Tremeloes</u>

Brian Poole (lead vocals), **Alan Blakley** (vocals, rhythm guitar & keyboard), **Alan Howard** (bass), **Dave Munden** (vocals & drums), **Rick Westwood (aka Ricky West)** [Richard Charles Westwood, b. 7-5-43] (vocals & lead guitar)

<u>May 1966 - August 1966: Brian Poole and The Tremeloes</u>

Brian Poole (lead vocals), **Alan Blakley** (vocals, rhythm guitar & keyboards), **Dave Munden** (vocals & drums), **Rick Westwood** (vocals & lead guitar), **Mick(y) Clarke** [Michael William Clarke, b. 10-8-46] (vocals & bass)

<u>August 1966 - January 1967: Brian Poole and The Tremeloes</u>

Brian Poole (lead vocals), **Alan Blakley** (vocals, rhythm guitar & keyboards), **Dave Munden** (vocals & drums), **Rick Westwood** (vocals & lead guitar), **Len 'Chip' Hawkes** [Leonard Donald Stanley Hawkes, b. 2-11-45] (lead vocals & bass guitar)

January 1967 - September 1972: The Tremeloes

Alan Blakley (vocals, rhythm guitar & keyboards), **Dave Munden** (lead vocals & drums), **Rick Westwood** (vocals & lead guitar), **Len 'Chip' Hawkes** (lead vocals & bass guitar)

October 1972 - December 1974: The Tremeloes / The Trems

Alan Blakley (vocals, rhythm guitar & keyboards), **Dave Munden** (lead vocals & drums), **Len 'Chip' Hawkes** (lead vocals & bass), **Bob Benham** [Robert Benham, 28-4-1949 or 1951] (vocals, lead guitar & piano)

1975: The Tremeloes / Space

Dave Munden (lead vocals & drums), **Rick Westwood** (bass), **Bob Benham** (vocals & guitar), **Aaron Woolley** [Aaron John Woolley] (vocals & guitar)

Early 1976: The Tremeloes

Dave Munden (lead vocals & drums), **Bob Benham** (vocals & guitar), **Paul Isaacs** (lead guitar), **Paul Carman** [d. 14-5-21] (bass guitar)

Late 1976: The Tremeloes

Dave Munden (lead vocals, drums), **Rick Westwood** (lead guitar), **Paul Isaacs** (vocals & guitar), **Joe Breen** (vocals & bass)

THE TREMELOES TEMPORARILY DISBANDED DURING 1976 - 1978

March 1978: The Tremeloes

Alan Blakley (rhythm guitar), **Dave Munden** (lead vocals), **Rick Westwood** (keyboard), *possibly* **Tony Thorpe** [b. 20-7-45] (drums = temporary substitute) [This was for a one-off performance for German TV]

February 1979: The Tremeloes

Dave Munden (lead vocals, drums), **Alan Blakley** (guitar), unknown (bass) [This was for a one-off performance for Belgian TV]

May 1979 - December 1979: The Tremeloes

Dave Munden (lead vocals & drums), **Rick Westwood** (lead guitar), **Len 'Chip' Hawkes** (lead vocals & bass guitar), **Ian Ellis** (guitar & vocals)

December 1979 - 1980: The Tremeloes

Dave Munden (lead vocals & drums), **Rick Westwood** (lead guitar), **Len 'Chip' Hawkes** (lead vocals & bass guitar), **Vic Elmes** (guitar & vocals)

1981 - 1982: The Tremeloes

Dave Munden (lead vocals & drums), **Rick Westwood** (guitar & bass), **Len 'Chip' Hawkes** (lead vocals, bass & guitar), **Bob Benham** (vocals & guitar)

January 1983 - April 1988: The Tremeloes

Alan Blakley (rhythm guitar, keyboards & vocals), **Dave Munden** (lead vocals & drums), **Rick Westwood** (lead guitar), **Len 'Chip' Hawkes** (lead vocals & bass)

April 1988 - July 1988: The Tremeloes

Alan Blakley (rhythm guitar, keyboards & vocals), **Dave Munden** (lead vocals & drums), **Rick Westwood** (lead guitar), **Len 'Chip' Hawkes** (lead vocals & bass), **Joe Gillingham** [Michael Gillingham, b. 14-2-46] (keyboards & vocals)

July 1988 - December 1993: The Tremeloes

Alan Blakley (rhythm guitar, keyboards & vocals), **Dave Munden** (lead vocals & drums), **Rick Westwood** (lead guitar), **Joe Gillingham** (keyboards & vocals), **Davey Fryer** [David Anthony Fryer, b. 31-10-51] (lead vocals & bass)

December 1993 - February 1994: The Tremeloes

Alan Blakley (rhythm guitar, keyboards & vocals) [selective dates only], **Dave Munden** (lead vocals & drums), **Rick Westwood** (lead guitar), **Joe Gillingham** (keyboards & vocals), **John Berry** (vocals & bass)

February 1994 - December 1995: The Tremeloes

Alan Blakley (rhythm guitar, keyboards & vocals) [selective dates only], **Dave Munden** (lead vocals & drums), **Rick Westwood** (lead guitar), **Joe Gillingham** (keyboards & vocals), **Davey Fryer** (lead vocals & bass)

December 1995 - December 2004: The Tremeloes

Dave Munden (lead vocals & drums), **Rick Westwood** (lead guitar), **Joe Gillingham** (keyboards & vocals), **Davey Fryer** (lead vocals & bass)

January 2005 - December 2012: The Tremeloes

Dave Munden (lead vocals & drums), **Rick Westwood** (lead guitar), **Joe Gillingham** (keyboards & vocals), **Jeff Brown** (lead vocals & bass)

21st February 2005 (one-off performance): Brian Poole & The Tremeloes

Brian Poole (lead vocals), **Dave Munden** (lead vocals & drums), **Rick Westwood** (lead guitar), **Mick Clarke** (bass & vocals), **Joe Gillingham** (vocals & keyboards)

September 2006 - October 2006: Brian Poole & The Tremeloes

Brian Poole (lead vocals), **Dave Munden** (lead vocals & drums), **Rick Westwood** (lead guitar), **Len 'Chip' Hawkes** (lead vocals & guitar), **Joe Gillingham** (vocals & keyboards), **Jeff Brown** [b. 14-7-60] (bass & vocals)

January 2013 - January 2014: The Tremeloes

Dave Munden (lead vocals & drums), **Joe Gillingham** (keyboards & vocals), **Jeff Brown** (lead vocals & bass), **Eddie Jones** [Edwin Jones, b. 1950] (vocals & lead guitar)

January 2014 - March 2014: The Tremeloes

Dave Munden (lead vocals) [Dave missed some shows due to knee-surgery; after he returned, he gave up playing the drums, becoming the front-man instead], **Joe Gillingham** (keyboards & vocals), **Jeff Brown** (lead vocals & bass), **Eddie Jones** (vocals & lead guitar), **Philip Wright** [b. 9-4-48] (drums & vocals)

March 2014 - May 2014: Brian Poole & The Tremeloes

Dave Munden (lead vocals), **Joe Gillingham** (keyboards & vocals), **Jeff Brown** (lead vocals & bass), **Eddie Jones** (lead guitar & vocals), **Philip Wright** (drums & vocals)

June 2014 - December 2016: The Tremeloes

Dave Munden (lead vocals), **Joe Gillingham** (keyboards& vocals), **Jeff Brown** (lead vocals & bass), **Philip Wright** (drums & vocals), **Syd Twynham** [Ian Twynham, 19-3-55] (lead guitar & vocals) [Eddie Jones would occasionally return when other members were absent]

March 2015 - April 2015: Brian Poole & The Tremeloes

Brian Poole (vocals), **Dave Munden** (vocals), **Len 'Chip' Hawkes** (vocals) - occasionally joined by **Rick Westwood** (lead guitar)

October 2015 - November 2015: Brian Poole & The Tremeloes

Brian Poole (vocals), **Dave Munden** (vocals), **Len 'Chip' Hawkes** (vocals)

December 2016 - December 2023+: The Trems

Joe Gillingham (keyboards& vocals), **Jeff Brown** (lead vocals & bass), **Philip Wright** (drums & vocals), **Syd Twynham** (lead guitar & vocals) [In December 2016, Dave Munden quit The Tremeloes to concentrate on touring with Brian Poole and Len 'Chip' Hawkes as "Brian Poole & The Tremeloes. The remaining members would carry on as 'The Trems', though at time of writing Jeff Brown is the only consistent member, with the others coming and going as other commitments or health dictate. Occasionally up until 2018 they were joined by **Rick Westwood** (lead guitar)]

September 2016 - December 2017: Brian Poole & The Tremeloes

Brian Poole (vocals), **Dave Munden** (vocals), **Len 'Chip' Hawkes** (vocals), **Mick Clarke** [occasional stand-in for other members] (vocals)

January 2018 - November 2018: The Tremeloes

Dave Munden (vocals), **Rick Westwood** (lead guitar), **Len 'Chip' Hawkes** (vocals), **Mick Clarke** (bass & vocals), **Jodie Hawkes** [b. 1973] (drums & vocals)

January 2019 - March 2019: The Tremeloes

Rick Westwood (lead guitar), **Len 'Chip' Hawkes** (vocals) & **Mick Clarke** (vocals)

March 2019: The Tremeloes

Len 'Chip' Hawkes (vocals), **Richard Marsh** (vocals) & **Mick Clarke** (vocals)

July 2019: The Tremeloes

Len 'Chip' Hawkes (vocals), **Rick Westwood** (lead guitar), **Mick Clarke** (vocals & bass guitar), **Jodie Hawkes** (drums & vocals) and **Richard Marsh** (rhythm guitar & vocals)

August 2019 - February 2020: The Tremeloes

Len 'Chip' Hawkes (vocals), **Mick Clarke** (vocals & bass), **Jodie Hawkes** (drums & vocals), **Richard Marsh** (rhythm guitar & vocals), **Eddie Wheeler** [b. 27-12-44] (lead guitar & vocals)

September 2021 - November 2021: The Tremeloes

Len 'Chip' Hawkes (vocals) [one show only], **Chesney Hawkes** [b. 22-9-71] (vocals & rhythm guitar) [all remaining shows], **Mick Clarke** (vocals & bass), **Jodie Hawkes** (drums & vocals), **Richard Marsh** (vocals and rhythm guitar), **Eddie Wheeler** (vocals & lead guitar) - occasionally joined by and/or **Indiana Hawkes** [b. 21-11-2005] (vocals & guitar)

October 2022 - November 2022: The Tremeloes

Chesney Hawkes (vocals & rhythm guitar), **Jodie Hawkes** (drums & vocals), **Martin Kennedy** (lead guitar & vocals), **Alan Vosper** (bass & vocals)

October 2023+: The Tremeloes?

Jodie Hawkes (drums & vocals), **Martin Kennedy** (lead guitar & vocals), **Alan Vosper** (guitar & vocals), **Colin Chisholm** [b. 1-5-53] (lead vocals) and **Brian Spence** [b. 7-2-53] (bass & vocals)

THE TREMELOES' TV & FILM APPEARANCES

This is an updated version of a list which first appeared in the book 'Channelling The Beat!'. All performances listed in **BOLD** are known to still survive, either in TV vaults or private collections. Dates, unless specified otherwise, refer to broadcast dates; taping dates for pre-recorded shows have been added when known. Occasionally, shows were broadcast on more than one date, in different regions of the UK; in these cases, the earliest known date is listed. For concert footage, the dates of the actual concerts are shown, with broadcast dates added where known. Generally, only actual performances are listed, not interviews, documentaries or news report. If anyone has any additional info, no matter how trivial, then please get in touch!

BRIAN POOLE AND THE TREMELOES

19-05-62 - 'Thank Your Lucky Stars' (ABC - UK): Twist Little Sister

00-02-63 - **'Just For Fun'** movie (Columbia Pictures): Keep On Dancing *(The group are introduced as "The Tremeloes"!)*

11-05-63 - 'Thank Your Lucky Stars' (ABC - UK): Keep On Dancing

01-06-63 - 'Thank Your Lucky Stars' (ABC - UK): Twist and Shout

09-08-63 - 'Ready Steady Go!' (Rediffusion - UK): Twist and Shout / Do You Love Me *(Brian Poole and The Tremeloes were the very first act on the very first episode of this ground-breaking TV show)*

09-08-63 - 'Joe and The Music' (Grampian - UK): ?

10-08-63 - 'Lucky Stars - Summer Spin' (ABC - UK): Twist and Shout *('Lucky Stars (Summer Spin)' was the seasonal title for 'Thank Your Lucky Stars')*

14-09-63 - 'Lucky Stars - Summer Spin' (ABC - UK): Do You Love Me

11-10-63 - 'Ready Steady Go!' (Rediffusion - UK): Do You Love Me

15-11-63 - 'Ready Steady Go!' (Rediffusion - UK): I Can Dance

22-11-63 - 'Scene at 6.30' (Granada - UK): I Can Dance

26-11-63 - 'The Five O'clock Club' (Rediffusion - UK): I Can Dance

05-12-63 - 'Crackerjack' (BBC - UK): I Can Dance

07-12-63 - 'Thank Your Lucky Stars' (ABC - UK): I Can Dance

18-01-64 - 'Thank Your Lucky Stars' (ABC - UK): Candy Man / I Wish I Could Dance

29-01-64 - 'Top Of The Pops' (BBC - UK): Candy Man (Video)

31-01-64 - 'Ready Steady Go!' (Rediffusion - UK): Candy Man

05-02-64 - 'Top Of The Pops' (BBC - UK): Candy Man (Video)

12-02-64 - 'Top Of The Pops' (BBC - UK): Candy Man

19-02-64 - 'Top Of The Pops' (BBC - UK): Candy Man *(This is a repeat of the 12-02-64 performance)*

25-02-64 - 'Hi There! It's Rolf Harris' (BBC - UK): We Know / Candy Man

04-03-64 - 'Top Of The Pops' (BBC - UK): Candy Man *(This is a repeat of the 12-02-64 performance)*

03-05-64 - **'Big Beat '64 Part 1'** (UK): Candy Man / Do You Love Me *(This was taped at 'The New Musical Express Poll Winners Concert' on 26-04-64)*

08-05-64 - 'Ready Steady Go!' (Rediffusion - UK): Someone, Someone

12-05-64 - 'Scene at 6.30' (Granada - UK): Someone, Someone

16-05-64 - 'Open House' (BBC2 - UK): Someone, Someone

19-05-64 - 'The Five O'Clock Club' (Rediffusion - UK): Someone, Someone

20-05-64 - 'Top Of The Pops' (BBC1 - UK): Someone, Someone

21-05-64 - 'A Swingin' Time' (BBC, UK): Someone, Someone

23-05-64 - 'Thank Your Lucky Stars' (ABC - UK): Someone, Someone

25-05-64 - 'Top Beat' (BBC2 - UK): Swinging On A Star / Someone,

Someone / Twist and Shout *(This was taped on 22-05-64)*

27-05-64 - **'The Liverpool Sound'** (Seven Network - Australia): Twist and Shout / Candy Man / Swinging On A Star / Three Bells / Do You Love Me / When The Saints Go Marching In [with Gerry and The Pacemakers, Dusty Springfield, Gene Pitney and Johnny O'Keefe] *(This was taped in Melbourne in April 1964)*

00-05-64 - **'Bandstand'** (Nine Network - Australia): Do You Love Me + probably other songs *('Do You Love Me' was repeated in a programme of highlights on 17-09-66 and still survives. The original transmission date is unknown, and all other songs are lost)*

03-06-64 - 'Top Of The Pops' (BBC1 - UK): Someone, Someone *(This is a repeat of the 20-05-64 performance)*

05-06-64 - 'Ready Steady Go!' (Rediffusion - UK): Someone, Someone

10-06-64 - 'Top Of The Pops' (BBC1 - UK): Someone, Someone

17-06-64 - 'Top Of The Pops' (BBC1 - UK): Someone, Someone

24-06-64 - 'The Tich and Quackers Show' (BBC1 - UK): Someone, Someone

26-06-64 - 'Top Of The Pops' (BBC1 - UK): Someone, Someone *(This is a repeat of an earlier performance)*

00-07-64 - **'Swinging UK'** movie short (Harold Baim Productions - UK): Do You Love Me

00-07-64 - **'UK Swings Again'** movie short (Harold Baim Productions - UK): Someone, Someone

01-07-64 - 'Top Of The Pops' (BBC1 - UK): Someone, Someone

08-07-64 - 'Top Of The Pops' (BBC1 - UK): Someone, Someone (Video)

14-07-64 - 'The Cool Spot' (BBC1 - UK): Someone, Someone / Do You Love Me *(This was taped on 12-07-64)*

07-08-64 - 'Ready Steady Go!' (Rediffusion - UK): Twist and Shout / Do You Love Me / Twelve Steps To Love

15-08-64 - 'Lucky Stars - Summer Spin' (ABC - UK): Twelve Steps To Love

11-09-64 - 'The Five O'Clock Club' (Rediffusion - UK): Twelve Steps To Love

12-09-64 - 'Open House' (BBC2 - UK): Twelve Steps To Love

12-10-64 - 'The Beat Room' (BBC2 - UK): Twelve Steps To Love / Twist and Shout *(This was taped on 05-07-64)*

07-11-64 - 'Pop Spot' (ABC - UK): Three Bells

09-12-64 - 'Top Beat' (BBC2 - UK): Twelve Steps To Love / It's All Right *(This was taped on 07-12-64)*

18-12-64 - 'Ready Steady Go!' (Rediffusion - UK): Three Bells

21-12-64 - 'Discs-A-Gogo' (TWW - UK): Three Bells

25-12-64 - 'The Five O'Clock Club' (Rediffusion - UK): Three Bells

26-12-64 - 'Thank Your Lucky Stars' (ABC - UK): Three Bells

00-12-64 - 'A Touch of Blarney' movie (Republic of Ireland): Don't Cry *(This obscure movie was filmed in Ireland in December 1964. It has yet to re-surface, and probably no longer survives)*

01-01-65 - 'Crackerjack' (BBC1 - UK): Three Bells

21-01-65 - **'Top Of The Pops'** (BBC1 - UK): Three Bells

04-02-65 - 'Top Of The Pops' (BBC1 - UK): Three Bells

31-07-65 - 'Lucky Stars - Summer Spin' (ABC - UK): I Want Candy

02-08-65 - 'Gadzooocks!' (BBC2 - UK): Love Me Baby / I Want Candy

05-08-65 - 'Top Of The Pops' (BBC1 - UK): I Want Candy

06-08-65 - 'Ready Steady Go!' (Rediffusion - UK): I Want Candy

30-09-65 - **'Blue Peter'** (BBC1 - UK): The Uncle Willie / I Want Candy

04-11-65 - 'Top Of The Pops' (BBC1 - UK): Good Lovin'

11-11-65 - 'Five O'clock Funfair' (Rediffusion - UK): Good Lovin'

13-11-65 - 'Thank Your Lucky Stars' (ABC - UK): Good Lovin'

29-12-65 - 'Now!' (TWW - UK): Good Lovin'

00-07-66 - **'Africa Shakes'** movie (South African Film Studios - South Africa): Come On In *(Although not released until 1966, this was filmed around April-May 1964 during Brian Poole and The Tremeloes' world tour. It definitely survives too, though this author has so far failed to locate a copy)*

THE TREMELOES

19-01-67 - 'Top Of The Pops' (BBC1 - UK): Here Comes My Baby

09-02-67 - 'Top Of The Pops' (BBC1 - UK): Here Comes My Baby

10-02-67 - 'Crackerjack' (BBC1 - UK): Here Comes My Baby

16-02-67 - 'Top Of The Pops' (BBC1 - UK): Here Comes My Baby *(This is a repeat of an earlier performance)*

02-03-67 - 'Top Of The Pops' (BBC1 - UK): Here Comes My Baby *(This is a repeat of an earlier performance)*

20-04-67 - 'Top Of The Pops' (BBC1 - UK): Silence Is Golden

22-04-67 - 'The Clay Cole Show' (WPIX - USA): ?

25-04-67 - 'Dee Time' (BBC1 - UK): Silence Is Golden

26-04-67 - 'The Record Star Show' (BBC1 - UK): Here Comes My Baby

In April 1967, The Tremeloes taped a pilot for an unreleased series called 'Presenting The Tremeloes'. The first (and only) episode was called 'Seven League Boots', and was taped on location in Brighton and Scotland, but despite plans for a possible 26-part series, no more were made, and this pilot was never broadcast.

04-05-67 - 'Top Of The Pops' (BBC1 - UK): Silence Is Golden *(This is a repeat of the 20-04-67 performance)*

08-05-67 - **'Beat! Beat! Beat!'** (HR - Germany): Loving You Is Sweeter Than Ever / Silence Is Golden / Here Comes My Baby

09-05-67 - **'Die Drehscheibe'** (ZDF - Germany): Here Comes My Baby

11-05-67 - 'Top Of The Pops' (BBC1 - UK): Silence Is Golden *(This is a repeat of the 20-04-67 performance)*

14-05-67 - 'Vibrato' (RTB - Belgium): ?

16-05-67 - 'As You Like It' (Southern - UK): Silence Is Golden

18-05-67 - 'Top Of The Pops' (BBC1 - UK): Silence Is Golden

19-05-67 - 'Joe and Co.' (BBC1 - UK): Silence Is Golden

20-05-67 - 'Moef Ga Ga' (Netherlands): Here Comes My Baby / Silence Is Golden

25-05-67 - 'Top Of The Pops' (BBC1 - UK): Silence Is Golden

01-06-67 - 'Top Of The Pops' (BBC1 - UK): Silence Is Golden *(This is a repeat of an earlier performance)*

11-06-67 - 'The London Palladium Show' (UK): Here Comes My Baby / Silence Is Golden

15-06-67 - 'Moef Ga Ga' (AVRO - Netherlands): Silence Is Golden

17-06-67 - 'The Clay Cole Show' (WPIX - USA): ?

08-07-67 - 'Upbeat' (Syndicated - USA): ?

27-07-67 - 'Top Of The Pops' (BBC1 - UK): Even The Bad Times Are Good

01-08-67 - 'Dee Time' (BBC1 - UK): Even The Bad Times Are Good

10-08-67 - 'Top Of The Pops' (BBC1 - UK): Even The Bad Times Are Good *(This is a repeat of the 27-07-67 performance)*

12-08-67 - 'Piccadilly Palace' (ABC - USA): Silence Is Golden / Here Comes My Baby *(Taped in the UK, this was later broadcast on 'Two Of A Kind' the only difference being this earlier broadcast was in colour instead of black and white)*

12-08-67 - 'The Clay Cole Show' (WPIX - USA): ?

17-08-67 - 'Top Of The Pops' (BBC1 - UK): Even The Bad Times Are Good *(This is a repeat of the 27-07-67 performance)*

19-08-67 - 'The Hy Lit Show' (WKBS - USA):

31-08-67 - 'Top Of The Pops' (BBC1 - UK): Even The Bad Times Are Good

09-09-67 - 'Billy Cotton's Music Hall' (BBC1 - UK): Medley: Here Comes My Baby - Silence Is Golden / Even The Bad Times Are Good

15-09-67 - 'As You Like It' (Southern - UK): Even The Bad Times Are Good

02-10-67 - **'Blue Peter'** (BBC1 - UK): Here Comes My Baby *(This features the band demonstrating Stylophones!)*

26-10-67 - 'Top Of The Pops' (BBC1 - UK): Be Mine

03-11-67 - 'Crackerjack' (BBC1 - UK): Be Mine

25-11-67 - 'Dee Time' (BBC1 - UK): Be Mine

25-12-67 - 'Top Of The Pops' (BBC1 - UK): Silence Is Golden

00-00-68 - **'Gogo-Scope'** (ORTF - Austria): Even The Bad Times Are Good / Silence Is Golden

05-01-68 - 'New Release' (Southern - UK): Suddenly You Love Me

11-01-68 - 'Top Of The Pops' (BBC1 - UK): Suddenly You Love Me

17-01-68 - **'Tomorrow's World'** (BBC1 - UK): Silence Is Golden *(This is a rehearsal for the 25-12-67 'Top Of The Pops' episode)*

20-01-68 - 'Doddy's Music Box' (ABC - UK): Suddenly You Love Me

25-01-68 - 'Top Of The Pops' (BBC1 - UK): Suddenly You Love Me

26-01-68 - 'Crackerjack' (BBC1 - UK): Suddenly You Love Me

27-01-68 - 'Dee Time' (BBC1 - UK): Suddenly You Love Me

01-02-68 - 'Top Of The Pops' (BBC1 - UK): Suddenly You Love Me *(This is a repeat of the 25-01-68 performance)*

02-02-68 - **'Popside'** (SVT - Sweden): Suddenly You Love Me / Running Out

04-02-68 - 'Two Of A Kind' [a.k.a. 'The Morcambe and Wise Show'] (ATV

- UK): Silence Is Golden / Here Comes My Baby *(This was previously broadcast in the USA as 'Piccadilly Palace')*

11-02-68 - 'The Golden Shot' (ATV - UK): Suddenly You Love Me

02-05-68 - 'Top Of The Pops' (BBC1 - UK): Helule Helule

04-05-68 - 'Time For Blackburn!' (Southern - UK): Helule Helule

16-05-68 - 'Top Of The Pops' (BBC1 - UK): Helule Helule

17-05-68 - 'Whistle Stop' (BBC1 - UK): Helule Helule

25-05-68 - 'Billy Cotton's Music Hall' (BBC1 - UK): Helule Helule

30-05-68 - 'Top Of The Pops' (BBC1 - UK): Helule Helule

01-06-68 - 'Dee Time' (BBC1 - UK): Helule Helule

01-06-68 - 'Time For Blackburn!' (Southern - UK) Helule Helule

13-08-68 - **'Liberace in London'** (Thames - UK): Show Me / The 59th Street Bridge Song (Feelin' Groovy) [with Liberace]

16-08-68 - 'Colour Me Pop' (BBC2 - UK): Medley: Here Comes My Baby - Silence Is Golden - Helule Helule - Run Baby Run - Shake Hands / (If You Think You're) Groovy / Medley: Loving You Is Sweeter Than Ever - Reach Out, I'll Be There - Walk Away Renee / Even The Bad Times Are Good (film clips) / Angel Of The Morning / Mountain Dew / Too Many Fish In The Sea / Suddenly You Love Me

12-09-68 - 'Top Of The Pops' (BBC1 - UK): My Little Lady

14-09-68 - 'Time For Blackburn!' (Southern - UK): My Little Lady

20-09-68 - 'Crackerjack' (BBC1 - UK): My Little Lady

21-09-68 - 'Dee Time' (BBC1 - UK): My Little Lady

03-10-68 - 'Top Of The Pops' (BBC1 - UK): My Little Lady

10-10-68 - 'Top Of The Pops' (BBC1 - UK): My Little Lady *(This is a repeat of an earlier performance)*

24-10-68 - 'Top Of The Pops' (BBC1 - UK): My Little Lady *(This is a repeat of an earlier performance)*

01-11-68 - 'Time For Blackburn!' (Southern - UK): My Little Lady

28-11-68 - 'Top Of The Pops' (BBC1 - UK): I Shall Be Released

06-12-68 - 'Crackerjack' (BBC1 - UK): I Shall Be Released

25-12-68 - 'All Kinds Of Music' (ATV - UK): ?

28-12-68 - 'Happening For Lulu' (BBC1 - UK): Ain't Nothing But A House Party [with Lulu] + probably 1 other song

25-01-69 - **'Beat Club'** (Radio Bremen - Germany): My Little Lady

27-01-69 - 'Jam' (TROS - Netherlands): I Shall Be Released

22-02-69 - **'Beat Club'** (Radio Bremen - Germany): I Shall Be Released

00-02-69 - **'Beat Club'** outtake (Radio Bremen - Germany): Hello World *(This performance wasn't broadcast until the 00's)*

09-03-69 - 'The Golden Shot' (ATV - UK): Hello World

20-03-69 - 'Top Of The Pops' (BBC1 - UK): Hello World

21-03-69 - 'The Basil Brush Show' (BBC1 - UK): Hello World

10-04-69 - 'Top Of The Pops' (BBC1 - UK): Hello World *(This is a repeat of the 20-03-69 performance)*

25-04-69 - **'Die Drehscheibe'** (ZDF - Germany): I Shall Be Released

28-04-69 - 'Jam' (TROS - Netherlands): Hello World

29-04-69 - 'Pop Scotch' (Grampian - UK): Hello World

13-06-69 - 'The Basil Brush Show' (BBC1 - UK): Once On A Sunday Morning

19-06-69 - 'Top Of The Pops' (BBC1 - UK): Once On A Sunday Morning

09-08-69 - 'The Frankie Howerd Show' (ATV - UK): ?

17-10-69 - 'Crackerjack' (BBC1 - UK): (Call Me) Number One

23-10-69 - 'Top Of The Pops' (BBC1 - UK): (Call Me) Number One

06-11-69 - 'Top Of The Pops' (BBC1 - UK): (Call Me) Number One *(This is *a repeat of the 23-10-69 performance)*

07-11-69 - 'Crackerjack' (BBC1 - UK): (Call Me) Number One

12-11-69 - **'Vera Lynn'** (BBC2 - UK): Silence Is Golden / Suddenly You Love Me [with Vera Lynn]

13-11-69 - 'Top Of The Pops' (BBC1 - UK): (Call Me) Number One

22-11-69 - **'4-3-2-1, Musik Fur Junge Leute'** [aka '4-3-2-1, Hot and Sweet'] (ZDF - Germany): (Call Me) Number One *(This was filmed in London's Trafalgar Square)*

31-12-69 - **'Pop Go The Sixties'** (BBC1-ZDF - UK): Silence Is Golden

07-03-70 - 'Disco 2' (BBC2 - UK): ?

12-03-70 - **'The Basil Brush Show'** (BBC1 - UK): By The Way / Yellow River

12-03-70 - 'Top Of The Pops' (BBC1 - UK): By The Way

27-04-70 - 'Mike and Bernie's Scene' (Thames - UK): ?

On 04-06-70, The Tremeloes taped an unbroadcast pilot for a show provisionally titled 'Kitch's Club'.

10-07-70 - **'Doing Their Thing'** (Granada - UK): Good Times / No Comprendes (Yellow River) / Medley: Games People Play - Proud Mary / Medley: Hello World - My Little Lady - Here Comes My Baby - Helule Helule / Medley: I Shall Be Released - Once On A Sunday Morning - Silence Is Golden - Even The Bad Times Are Good - Suddenly You Love Me / Mountain Dew / Medley: Hound Dog - Rip It Up - Johnny B. Goode - Whole Lotta Shakin' Goin' On

03-09-70 - **'Top Of The Pops'** (BBC1 - UK): Me and My Life

17-09-70 - **'Top Of The Pops'** (BBC1 - UK): Me and My Life *(This is a repeat of the 03-09-69 performance)*

19-09-70 - 'Stewpot' (LWT - UK): Me and My Life

07-10-70 - 'Lift Off' (Granada - UK): Me and My Life

08-10-70 - 'Top Of The Pops' (BBC1 - UK): Me and My Life

09-10-70 - 'The Basil Brush Show' (BBC1 - UK): Me and My Life

18-10-70 - 'The Golden Shot' (ATV - UK): Me and My Life

29-10-70 - 'Top Of The Pops' (BBC1 - UK): Me and My Life *(This is a repeat of an earlier performance)*

21-11-70 - 'Ev' (LWT - UK): Me and My Life

04-02-71 - 'Top Of The Pops' (BBC1 - UK): Right Wheel, Left Hammer, Sham

23-02-71 - 'TopPop' (AVRO - Netherlands): Right Wheel, Left Hammer, Sham

27-02-71 - **'Stewpot'** (LWT - UK): Me and My Life / Right Wheel, Left Hammer, Sham *(This was taped on 02-02-71)*

03-03-71 - **'Hits A Go Go'** (NDR - Switzerland): Right Wheel, Left Hammer, Sham

26-06-71 - **'Whittaker's World Of Music'** (LWT - UK): Hello Buddy

04-07-71 - 'The Basil Brush Show' (BBC1 - UK): Hello Buddy

08-07-71 - 'Top Of The Pops' (BBC1 - UK): Hello Buddy

07-08-71 - 'Lift Off' (Granada - UK): Hello Buddy

08-08-71 - 'The Golden Shot' (ATV - UK): Hello Buddy

11-09-71 - **'Disco'** (ZDF - Germany): Hello Buddy

04-11-71 - **'Top Of The Pops'** (BBC1 - UK): Too Late (To Be Saved)

13-11-71 - **'Disco'** (ZDF - Germany): Silence Is Golden

15-12-71 - 'Lift Off' (Granada - UK): Too Late (To Be Saved)

12-02-72 - **'Disco'** (ZDF - Germany): Too Late (To Be Saved)

17-02-72 - **'Hits A Go Go'** (NDR - Switzerland): Too Late (To Be Saved)

12-04-72 - 'Lift Off With Ayshea' (Granada - UK): I Like It That Way

13-05-72 - **'The Basil Brush Show'** (BBC1 - UK): I Like It That Way

24-05-72 - 'The Dave Cash Radio Programme' (HTV - UK): ?

28-05-72 - 'The Golden Shot' (ATV - UK): I Like It That Way

31-05-72 - 'Lift Off With Ayshea' (Granada - UK): I Like It That Way

24-06-72 - **'Disco'** (ZDF - Germany): I Like It That Way

05-07-72 - 'The Dave Cash Radio Programme' (HTV - UK): Me and My Life

02-08-72 - 'Eddy Ready Go' (NCRV - Netherlands): I Like It That Way

20-11-72 - **'Night Club'** (BBC2 - UK): My Little Lady

13-12-72 - **'Lift Off With Ayshea'** (Granada - UK): Blue Suede Tie

07-01-73 - 'The Golden Shot' (ATV - UK): Blue Suede Tie

22-01-73 - **'TopPop'** (AVRO - Netherlands): Blue Suede Tie

29-01-73 - **'TopPop'** (AVRO - Netherlands): Blue Suede Tie *(This is a repeat of the 22-01-73 performance)*

03-03-73 - **'Disco'** (ZDF - Germany): Blue Suede Tie

14-03-73 - 'Frankie Howerd In Ulster' (BBC1 - UK): Blue Suede Tie

18-05-73 - 'Lift Off With Ayshea' (Granada - UK): Ride On

28-05-73 - 'TopPop' (AVRO - Netherlands): Ride On

21-07-73 - **'Disco'** (ZDF - Germany): Ride On

07-10-73 - **'Hits A Go Go'** (NDR - Switzerland): Ride On

25-11-73 - **'Spotlight'** (ORF - Austria): Ride On / You Can't Touch Sue

27-12-73 - **'Top Of The Pops'** [10th Anniversary Show] (BBC1 - UK): Silence Is Golden

17-02-74 - 'The Golden Shot' (ATV - UK): Do I Love You

31-08-74 - **'Disco'** (ZDF - Germany): Say O.K. (Say Ole You Love Me)

31-03-78 - **'Pop '78'** (SWR/ARD - Germany): Ging Gang Goolie

00-02-79 - **'Dolle Dinsdag'** (BRT - Belgium): Silence Is Golden / Lonely Nights

13-05-80 - **'Plattenküche'** (WDR - Germany): Lights Of Port Royal

23-10-81 - **'Hear Here'** (STV - UK): Yellow River / Angel Of The Morning / Even The Bad Times Are Good / Here Comes My Baby / Good Hearted Woman / Helule Helule / Silence Is Golden *(There are unconfirmed reports of a shorter edit, featuring Twist and Shout / Good Hearted Woman / Helule Helule / Hello Buddy, with Chip supposedly playing the drums on 'Twist and Shout'. The author has been unable to verify this)*

17-12-81 - **'Musikladen'** (Radio Bremen - Germany): Tremedley

28-08-82 - **'Ein Kessel Buntes'** (ARD - Germany): ?

03-03-83 - **'Unforgettable'** (C4 - UK): (Call Me) Number One / Silence Is Golden

12-07-83 - **'The Video Entertainers'** (Granada - UK): Words

13-10-83 - **'AVRO's Platengala 1983'** (AVRO - Netherlands): Medley: My Little Lady - Even The Bad Times Are Good / Someone, Someone

13-11-84 - **'Des O'Connor Tonight'** (Thames - UK): ?

03-03-85 - **'Heroes and Villains'** (C4 - UK): Here Comes My Baby / Even The Bad Times Are Good *(This was broadcast on 28-02-89 and repeated on 02-10-90. For this one show Dave Munden was replaced by substitute drummer John Dymond, also known as 'Beaky' from Dave Dee, Dozy, Beaky, Mick and Tich)*

23-04-88 - **'Goud van Oud'** (Veronica - Netherlands): Medley: Silence Is Golden - Even The Bad Times Are Good - My Little Lady

29-05-88 - **'ITV Telethon '88'** (ITV - UK): Here Comes My Baby / (Call Me) Number One

24-07-88 - **'Fernsehgarten'** (ZDF - Germany): Medley: Here Comes My Baby - Suddenly You Love Me - Even The Bad Times Are Good - My Little Lady - Helule Helule - Me and My Life - Silence Is Golden

31-12-88 - **'Top Of The Pops'** [25th Anniversary Show] (BBC1 - UK): Silence Is Golden

01-01-89 - **'ZDF Silvester-Tanzparty'** (ZDF - Germany): Silence Is Golden *(This was rebroadcast as 'Die Grosse Internationale Oldie-Party' in 2003)*

30-01-89 - **'Daytime Live'** (BBC1 - UK): ?

00-00-89 - **'Oldie Party'** (ZDF - Germany): Here Comes My Baby / Silence Is Golden / Even The Bad Times Are Good / Suddenly You Love Me / Helule Helule

18-05-91 - **'RSH Oldie Night'** (Germany): ?

00-00-92 - **Unknown TV show** (German TV): All For One and One For All

00-00-92 - **'Oldie Night'** (N3 - Germany): Yellow River / Candy Man / Do You Love Me / My Little Lady / African Lullaby / Angel Of The Morning [with Peter Sarstedt]

29-08-92 - **'Let's Have A Party'** (ZDF - Germany): Silence Is Golden

00-00-93 - **'Golden Schlagerparade'** (Germany): Silence Is Golden

00-00-93 - **'OPA Oldie Parade'** (Germany): (Call Me) Number One / Silence Is Golden

21-05-95 - **'Musik Liegt In Der Luft'** (ZDF - Germany): ?

14-03-97 - **'A Night Out With Money'** (UK): ?

15-03-97 - **'Golden Years In Concert'** (Belgium): Suddenly You Love Me / Here Comes My Baby / My Little Lady / Even The Bad Times Are Good / Silence Is Golden

00-00-97 - **'Elmis Witzige Oldie-Show'** (SAT3 - Germany): Here Comes My Baby / My Little Lady / Silence Is Golden

00-03-07 - **'The British Beat Live'** (USA): Here Comes My Baby / Silence Is Golden *(Filmed in the UK for USA TV & DVD release)*

00-00-11 - **'Oldies But Goldies'** (NDR - Germany): Here Comes My Baby / Silence Is Golden

08-12-16 - **'Weihnachtsfeier Unterm Baum'** (WDR - Germany): Here Comes My Baby / Silence Is Golden

BRIAN POOLE

28-05-66 - 'Thank Your Lucky Stars' (ABC - UK): Hey Girl

17-06-66 - 'The Five O'Clock Club' (Rediffusion - UK): Hey Girl

12-04-69 - 'Doebidoe' (Netherlands): Send Her To Me [with THE SEYCHELLES]

28-06-69 - **'Beat-Club'** (Radio Bremen - Germany): Send Her To Me [with THE SEYCHELLES] *(a performance without Dave Lee Travis' introduction and with inferior camera angles also circulates)*

22-07-83 - **'Unforgettable'** (C4 - UK) Someone, Someone / Do You Love Me [with TRAMLINE]

03-03-85 - **'Heroes and Villains'** (C4 - UK): Do You Love Me / Candy Man [with BLACK CAT] *(As with The Tremeloes' performance, this was broadcast on 28-02-89 and repeated on 02-10-90)*

05-05-85 - **'A Royal Celebration Of Peace'** (LWT - UK): Twist and Shout

00-05-89 - **Promo Video** (UK): Ain't Nothing But A House Party [The Corporation]

00-05-89 - **'This Morning'** (ITV - UK): Ain't Nothing But A House Party (Promo excerpt) / Ain't Nothing But A House Party (live acoustic) [The Corporation]

CHIP HAWKES

00-00-02 - **Unknown TV show** (Germany): Silence Is Golden

00-00-08 - **Promo Video** (UK): She's Not My Child

29-06-08 - **'Fernsehgarten'** (ZDF - Germany): Father and Son (with Chesney Hawkes)

00-00-09 - **Unknown TV show** (ZDF - Germany): That's What Friends Are For (Dafür Sind Freunde Da) (with Olaf Berger)

THE TREMELOES' BBC RADIO PERFORMANCES

The Tremeloes taped many sessions for BBC radio during the '60s & early '70s. Below are all known broadcast dates, though this list is very likely incomplete. Songs from the 'Live At The BBC 1964-67' and 'BBC Sessions' official CDs are in **bold**!

27-05-61 - 'Saturday Club': unknown titles - *credited as 'The Tremilos'*

30-09-61 - 'Saturday Club': unknown titles - *credited as 'Brian Poole and The Tremilos'*

16-06-62 - 'Saturday Club': unknown titles

11-08-62 - 'Saturday Club': unknown titles

18-08-62 - 'Saturday Club': unknown titles

22-12-62 - 'Saturday Club': unknown titles

13-04-63 - 'Saturday Club': unknown titles

29-06-63 - 'Saturday Club': unknown titles

31-08-63 - 'Saturday Club': unknown titles

09-11-63 - 'Saturday Club': unknown titles

28-12-63 - 'Saturday Club': unknown titles

01-02-64 - 'Saturday Club': unknown titles

14-03-64 - 'Saturday Club': unknown titles

09-05-64 - 'Saturday Club': unknown titles

11-07-64 - 'Saturday Club': **Walk Right In / Baby Blue / Someone, Someone**

05-09-64 - 'Saturday Club': unknown titles

02-01-65 - 'Saturday Club': unknown titles

00-01-65 - unknown show: **Well, Who's That / Three Bells / Twelve**

Steps To Heaven

00-02-65 - 'Delaney's Delight': **Well, Who's That / Three Bells / Time Is On My Side**

13-03-65 - 'Saturday Club': **Uncle Willie / Sho' Miss You Baby / Hands Off**

08-05-65 - 'Saturday Club': unknown titles

00-05-65 - unknown show: **After Awhile / My Baby Left Me / Well Alright**

14-08-65 - 'Saturday Club': **Love Me Baby / I Go Crazy / I Want Candy**

00-10-65 - 'This Must Be The Place': **She Said Yeah / It's All Over Now Baby Blue / Twist and Shout**

00-11-65 - 'This Must Be The Place': **Baby It's You / Good Lovin' / She Said Yeah**

28-05-66 - 'Saturday Club': **Like A Rolling Stone / Hey Girl / Walkin' My Cat Named Dog**

03-09-66 - 'Saturday Club': **Loving You Is Sweeter Than Ever / Good Day Sunshine / What A State I'm In** - *1st song is Brian Poole and The Tremeloes, 2nd & 3rd songs are The Tremeloes only*

29-10-66 - 'Saturday Club': **Everything I Touch Turns To Tears / Hey Girl / Everything's Wrong** - *Brian Poole solo*

21-01-67 - 'Saturday Club': **Here Comes My Baby / Run Baby Run**

00-04-67 - unknown show: **That Reminds Me Baby / Loving You Is Sweeter Than Ever** - *Brian Poole solo*

12-04-67 - 'Saturday Club': **Too Many Fish In The Sea / Silence Is Golden**

29-04-67 - 'Saturday Club': **I'll Take You Where The Music's Playing / It Takes Two**

29-07-67 - 'Saturday Club': **Even The Bad Times Are Good / Running Out**

23-10-67 - 'Happening Sunday': **Be Mine / Come On Home / Medley: Reach Out I'll Be There - Loving You Is Sweeter Than Ever / Norman Stanley James St. Clare**

18-11-67 - 'Saturday Club': unknown titles

27-01-68 - 'Saturday Club': **Gimme Little Sign / Suddenly You Love Me / Walk Away Renee**

04-05-68 - 'Saturday Club': **Ain't Nothing But A Houseparty / Helule Helule / My Baby Left Me / Sing Sorta Swingle**

12-08-68 - 'David Symonds Show': - **I'll See You There / Angel Of The Morning / (If You Think You're) Groovy**

14-09-68 - 'Saturday Club': unknown titles

28-09-68 - 'Dave Cash': **My Little Lady**

21-12-68 - 'Saturday Club': unknown titles

29-12-68 - 'Pete's Sunday People': **I Miss My Baby / I Shall Be Released / Good Times**

18-01-69 - 'Saturday Club': unknown titles

23-03-69 - 'Symonds On Sunday': **Hello World / En Tu Mondo**

27-05-69 - 'Jimmy Young': **Once On A Sunday Morning / Proud Mary / Can't Turn You Loose / Blessed**

10-09-69 - 'Radio 1 Club': **(Call Me) Number One / You**

30-09-69 - 'Saturday People': **What Can I Do**

00-01-70 - unknown show: Anything / Yellow River

00-08-70 - unknown show: Try Me / Me and My Life / Long Road

00-08-70 - unknown show: Before I Sleep / Me and My Life

00-11-70 - unknown show: I Swear / But Then I

00-02-71 - unknown show: Right Wheel, Left Hammer, Sham / Wait For Me

00-07-71 - unknown show: Hello Buddy

00-10-71 - unknown show: Too Late (To Be Saved) / If You Ever

00-02-72 - unknown show: How Can You Say Goodbye / Do I Love You

00-04-72 - unknown show: I Like It That Way / Hands Off / Gotta Get Away

00-04-72 - unknown show: Blue Suede Tie / Lauree Lee

00-00-75 - unknown show: Silence Is Golden *(acoustic version)*

SELECTED DISCOGRAPHY

(* = not released in the UK)

SINGLES

BRIAN POOLE AND THE TREMELOES

04-62: Twist Little Sister / Lost Love

09-62: Blue / That Ain't Right

01-63: A Very Good Year For Girls / Meet Me Where We Used To Meet

03-63: Keep On Dancing / Run Back Home

06-63: Twist and Shout / We Know

09-63: Do You Love Me / Why Can't You Love Me

11-63: I Can Dance / Are You Loving Me At All

01-64: Candy Man / I Wish I Could Dance

05-64: Someone, Someone / Till The End Of Time

05-64: Twenty Miles / Come On In / Swinging On A Star / Yakety Yak (EP)

08-64: Twelve Steps To Love / Don't Cry

11-64: Three Bells / Tell Me How You Care

03-65: Time Is On My Side / Sho' Miss You Baby / It's All Right / You Don't Own Me (EP)

04-65: After Awhile / You Know

07-65: I Want Candy / Love Me Baby

07-65: I Go Crazy / Love Me Baby *

11-65: Good Lovin' / Could It Be You?

BRIAN POOLE

05-66: Hey Girl / Please Be Mine - B-side is Brian Poole and The Tremeloes

09-66: Everything I Touch Turns To Tears / I Need Her Tonight

03-67: That Reminds Me Baby / Tomorrow Never Comes

10-67: Just How Loud / The Other Side Of The Sky

03-69: Send Her To Me / Pretty In The City - with The Seychelles

07-69: What Do Women Most Desire / Treat Her Like A Woman - with The Seychelles

08-75: Satisfied / Red Leather - with Carousel

04-83: Do You Love Me - Twist and Shout / Time and Tide - with Tramline

11-83: Someone, Someone / Bye Bye Baby - with Black Cat

THE TREMELOES (unless stated otherwise)

06-66: Blessed / The Right Time

08-66: Good Day Sunshine / What A State I'm In

01-67: Here Comes My Baby / Gentleman Of Pleasure

04-67: Silence Is Golden / Let Your Hair Hang Down

07-67: Even The Bad Times Are Good / Jenny's Alright

10-67: Be Mine (Mi Seguirai) / Suddenly Winter

01-68: Suddenly You Love Me / As You Are

02-68: E In Silenzio (Silence Is Golden) / Even The Bad Times Are Good *

05-68: Helule Helule / Girl From Nowhere

09-68: My Little Lady / All The World To Me

10-68: I'm Gonna Try / Girl From Nowhere *

11-68: I Shall Be Released / I Miss My Baby

11-68: My Little Lady / Helule Helule / Suddenly You Love Me / Even The Bad Times Are Good (EP)

03-69: Hello World / Up, Down, All Around

05-69: Jacqueline / Up, Down, All Around *

06-69: Once On A Sunday Morning (Cuando Sali De Cuba) / Fa La La, La La, La Le

10-69: (Call Me) Number One / Instant Whip

02-70: By The Way / Breakheart Motel

08-70: Me and My Life / Try Me

01-71: Right Wheel, Left Hammer, Sham / Take It Easy

02-71: Wake Me I Am Dreaming (Mi Ritorni In Menti) / Wait A Minute - *Dave Munden*

06-71: Hello Buddy / My Woman

10-71: Too Late (To Be Saved) / If You Ever

04-72: Hello Sailor / Taurus - *Gone West [Rick Westwood]*

05-72: I Like It That Way / Wakamaker

11-72: Blue Suede Tie / Yodel Ay

04-73: Ride On / Hands Off - *as 'Tremeloes'*

07-73: Make Or Break / Movin' On - *as 'The Trems'*

10-73: You Can't Touch Sue / Story For The Boys - *as 'The Trems'*

01-74: Do I Love You / Witchcraft - as 'Tremeloes'

07-74: Say O.K. (Say Ole You Love Me) / Pinky *

10-74: Good Time Band / Hard Woman

02-75: Someone Someone / My Friend Delaney

04-75: Rocking Circus / Don't Let The Music Die - Space

05-75: Sorry (Lyn's Song) / Windows Are Nice - *Alan Blakley*

08-75: Be Boppin' Boogie / Ascot Cowboys - *as 'Tremeloes'*

08-75: Friend Of A Friend / Times Are Changing - *Chip Hawkes*

00-76: Lost Without You / Gimme Rock 'n' Roll * - *Alan Blakley*

01-77: One More Dusty Road / She Couldn't Figure My Reason - *Chip Hawkes*

06-77: Eleanor Rigby / Save Your Pity - *Chip Hawkes*

02-78: Ging Gang Goolie / Lonely Robot *

12-78: Lonely Nights / Groover

01-80: Lights Of Port Royal / Silas

11-81: Tremelodies / I Let My Best Friend Down

03-83: Words / I Will Return

10-83: Someone / You Can Get It

10-84: Silence Is Golden / The Last Word

00-87: Angel Of The Morning / Am I Dreaming

00-88: Silence Is Golden (New Recording '88) / Silence Is Golden (Dub Version)

00-88: Lean On Me Baby / My Little Lady *

00-92: Farewell & Goodbye / The Rising Sun *

06-08: Not My Child / Not My Child (Karaoke) - *Chip Hawkes*

ALBUMS

BRIAN POOLE AND THE TREMELOES

05-63: Big Big Hits Of '62

09-63: Twist and Shout

02-65: It's About Time

THE TREMELOES (unless stated otherwise)

05-67: Here Come the Tremeloes

12-67: Alan, Dave, Rick and Chip

07-68: World Explosion! *

10-69: Live in Cabaret

00-70: May Morning *(Not released until 2000)*

11-70: Master

11-74: Shiner

06-75: Don't Let the Music Die *(initially released as 'Space')*

00-76: Nashville Album - *Chip Hawkes*

12-81: Greatest Hits

00-84: The Hits *

00-88: Million Sellers

00-92: All For One and One For All *

00-03: The Hits Of The Tremeloes - *Chip Hawkes*

00-09: Me and My Life * - *Chip Hawkes*

00-08: Live! In Europe

00-10: The Ones That Got Away

00-11: Unplugged - *Chip Hawkes*

SELECTED COLLECTORS COMPILATIONS

00-00 - Boxed [4xCD] - *The Tremeloes*

00-04 - BBC Sessions [2xCD] - *The Tremeloes*

00-13 - Live At The BBC 1964-67 [2xCD] - *Brian Poole and The Tremeloes*

SONG INDEX

17 and Ready [CH] - *219*
A Very Good Year For Girls - *14*
African Lullaby - *251, 256*
After Awhile - *55, 56*
Ain't Nothin' But A House Party - *127*
Ain't Nothing But A House Party [BP] - *86*
All For One and One For All - *256*
All I Wanna Do In Life [CH] - *216*
All Pull Together - *156*
All The World To Me - *133*
Alley Oop - *28, 127*
Always Have, Always Will [CH] - *226*
Am I Dreaming - *247*
And Then I Kissed Her - *251*
Angel Of The Morning - *147, 247, 256, 269*
Anita - *256*
Anything - *156*
Are You Loving Me At All - *34*
As You Are - *118*
Ascot Cowboys - *203*
Baby - *163*
Baby Blue - *47*
Baby I've Lost You Now - *270*
Baby It's You - *65*
Baby Workout - *28*
Back Home For Christmas - *264*
Barefootin' [BP] - *208*
Be Boppin' Boogie - 203
Be Mine (Mi Seguirai) - *111*
Beer Duel - *156*
Before I Sleep - *163*
Before You Know It Will Be

Christmas - *261*
Big Bad Boogie - *191*
Blessed - *91, 147*
Blue - *12*
Blue Suede Tie - *176*
Boola Boola - *163*
Breakheart Motel - *150*
Breaking Up Is Hard To Do - *18*
Bring It On Home To Me [BP] - *84*
Buddy Holly Medley [BP] - *87*
Bunch Of Rapes - *156*
Bus Stop [CH] - *223*
But Then I... - *163*
By The Way - *150, 163, 238*
By The Way [CH] - *221*
Bye Bye Baby [BP] - *81*
(Call Me) Number One - *144, 238, 245, 251, 269, 279*
(Call Me) Number One [CH] - *221, 223, 228*
Can We Hold On [BP] - *84*
Can't See The Wood From The Trees - *270*
Can't Turn You Loose - *141*
Candy Man - *36, 238, 245, 246, 269*
Candy Man [BP] - *83, 84*
Celebration - *199*
Chevrolet [BP] - *83, 84*
Chills - *56*
Circle Of Stone - *270*
Come On Home - *113*
Come On In - *45*
Cool Jerk - *113*
Could It Be You [BP] - *84*
Could It Be You - *66*
Da Doo Ron Ron - *28*

(Dance With The) Guitar Man - *18*
Devil Woman - *18*
Do I Love You - *186*
Do It Again - *253*
Do You Love Me - *24, 269, 279*
Do You Love Me [BP] - *81, 83, 84, 87*
Do You Wanna Dance - *253*
Dole Q [AB] - *212*
Don't Be Afraid Little Darlin' - *28*
Don't Cry - *48*
Don't Ever Change - *18*
Don't Let The Music Die - *198*
Dream Baby (How Long Must I Dream) - *18*
Dream Baby Dream [CH] - *218*
E In Silenzio - *121*
Eleanor Rigby [CH] - *216*
En Tu Mondo - *131*
Even The Bad Times Are Good - *104, 108, 147, 238, 245, 251, 269, 279*
Even The Bad Times Are Good [CH] - *221, 223, 228*
Everly Brothers Medley [BP] - *87*
Every Little Bit Hurts - *116*
Everyday - *127*
Everything I Touch Turns To Tears [BP] - *75*
Everything's Wrong [BP] - *75*
F.B.I. - *147*
Fa La La, La La, La Le - *142*
Farewell & Goodbye - *255*
Father & Son [CH] - *226*
Feel So Lonely [BP] - *83, 84*
Friend Of A Friend [CH] - *215*
Funky Feeling [AB] - *210*
Games People Play - *147*

Gentleman Of Pleasure - *94*
Ghost Riders [BP] - *83, 84*
Gimme Good Lovin' [BP] - *83, 84*
Gimme Little Sign - *121*
Gimme Rock'n'Roll [AB] - *211*
Ging Gang Goolie - *230*
Ginny Come Lately - *18*
Girl From Nowhere - *124, 127*
Good Day Sunshine - *92, 104*
Good Lovin' - *66, 269*
Good Lovin' [BP] - *83, 84*
Good Old Rock 'N' Roll [BP] - *83, 84*
Good Time Band - *190*
Good Times - *147*
Groover - *232*
Halfway To Paradise - *18*
Hands Off (1) - *56*
Hands Off (2) - *180*
Happy Song - *113*
Hard Time - *156*
Hard Woman - *190, 191*
Heard It All Before - *56*
Heaven Knows Why - *174*
Hello Buddy - *169, 238, 279*
Hello Buddy [CH] - *221*
Hello Sailor [RW] - *208*
Hello World - *138, 147, 238, 251*
Help - *191*
Helule Helule - *124, 127, 238, 245, 251, 269, 279*
Here Comes My Baby - *94, 104, 147, 238, 245, 251, 269, 279*
Here Comes My Baby [CH] - *216, 221, 223, 228*
Hey Baby - *18, 253*
Hey Girl - *68*
Hey Girl [BP] - *74*
Hey Little Girl [BP] - *83, 84*

How Can You Say Goodbye - *172*
How Come [CH] - *224*
I Can Dance - *34*
I Can't Even Breathe Down Here - *156*
I Can't Stop Loving You - *18*
I Could Make You Love Me - *56*
I Go Crazy - *64*
I Let My Best Friend Down - *237, 238*
I Like It That Way - *174*
I Like It That Way [CH] - *221, 251*
I Miss My Baby - *136*
I Need Her Tonight [BP] - *75*
I Shall Be Released - *136, 147, 256, 269, 279*
I Shall Be Released [CH] - *221*
I Still Believe In Angels - *270*
I Swear - *163*
I Take What I Want - *122*
I Want Candy - *62*
I Want Candy [BP] - *83, 84*
I Want It Easy - *191*
I Will Return - *240*
I Wish I Could Dance - *36*
I You Know - *156*
I'll See You There - *127*
I'll Take You Home - *156*
I'll Take You Where The Music's Playing - *103*
I'm A Believer [CH] - *226*
I'm A Loner [CH] - *214*
I'm Gonna Try - *131*
I'm Not To Blame [CH] - *226*
I'm Sorry - *199*
I'm With You All The Way - *113*
I'm Your Hero - *189*
I'm Yours - *270*

If You Ever - *172*
If You Gotta Make A Fool Of Somebody - *28*
If You Think You Know How To Love Me [CH] - *226*
(If You Think You're) Groovy - *130*
Instant Whip - *144*
It Might As Well Rain Until September - *18*
It Takes Two - *103*
It's All Over Now - *253*
It's All Over Now [CH] - *224*
It's All Over Now Baby Blue - *64*
It's All Right - *53*
It's So Easy Telling Lies [CH] - *216*
Jacqueline - *140*
Jenny's Alright - *108*
Jerusalem - *261, 270*
Jodie - *256*
Just How Loud [BP] - *75*
Just One Look [CH] - *223*
Keep On Dancing - *15, 28*
Keep On Your Feet - *253*
Lauree Lee - *179*
Lean On Me Baby - *250, 251, 256, 270*
Let Your Hair Hang Down - *97, 104*
Let's Dance - *18*
Let's Turkey Trot - *31*
Let's Twist Again - *18*
Like A Rolling Stone - *68*
Loco-Motion - *18*
Lola [CH] - *223*
Lonely Dolly - *191*
Lonely Nights - *232*
Lonely Robot - *230*
Long Cool Woman [CH] - *223*
Long Road - *163*

Look Through Any Window [CH] - *223*
Lost and Found - *199*
Lost Love - *11*
Lost Without You [AB] - *211*
Love Is A Guessing Game [CH] - *216*
(Love Left Me) Bleeding [AB] - *212*
Love Me Baby - *62*
Love Me Baby [BP] - *83*
Love Song - *191*
Loving You Is Sweeter Than Ever - *70*
Loving You Is Sweeter Than Ever [BP] - *75, 104*
Make Or Break - *182*
Mandy Downs - *199*
May Morning - *156*
Me and My Life - *161, 163, 238, 245, 251, 269, 279*
Me and My Life [CH] - *221, 226*
Meet Me Where We Used To Meet - *14, 28*
Michael Row The Boat Ashore - *56*
Mountain Dew - *147*
Movin' On - *182*
Moving On [BP] - *84*
Mr. Bass Man - *31*
My Baby Left Me - *61, 126*
My Friend Delaney - *191, 195*
My Little Lady - *133, 147, 238, 245, 246, 250, 251, 269, 279*
My Little Lady [CH] - *221, 228*
My Town - *104*
My Woman - *169*
Negotiations In Soho Square - *113*
Never Win - *251, 256*
No Comprendes (Yellow River) - *154*

No More Sad Songs - *171*
No Stranger To Heartache [CH] - *218*
No, No, No - *116, 170*
Norman Stanley James St. Clare - *113*
Not My Child [CH] - *225, 226, 228*
Nothing Would Please Me More - *270*
Now's The Time - *163*
On Love - *116*
On The Wind [CH] - *224*
Once On A Sunday Morning - *142, 251*
One Broken Heart For Sale - *31*
One More Dusty Road [CH] - *216, 217*
One Of The Boys - *191*
Open Up - *270*
Out Of My Mind - *31*
Out Of Time [BP] - *87*
Over The Mountain, Across The Sea - *28*
Party - *237, 238*
Peanuts - *28*
Peggy Sue - *127*
Pinky - *187*
Play The Oldies [BP] - *84*
Please Be Mine - *67*
Prayer For Peace - *256*
Pretty In The City [BP] - *77*
Proud Mary - *147*
Rag Doll - *56, 127*
Reach Out I'll Be There - *122*
Ready For The Times To Get Better [CH] - *216*
Red Leather [BP] - *79*
Reggae Music [AB] - *213*

Remember Looking Back - *162*
Return To Sender - *18*
Ride On - *180*
Ride On [CH] - *221*
Riders In The Sky [CH] - *216*
Right Wheel, Left Hammer, Sham - *167*
Rock 'N' Roll (Live): Johnny B. Goode - Boney Moronie - *256*
Rock 'N' Roll Medley [BP] - *83*
Rock and Roll - *279*
Rockin' Band [AB] - *212*
Rocking Circus - *198, 199*
Roses Are Red (My Love) - *18*
Round and Round - *104*
Run Baby Run (Back Into My Arms) - *104, 147*
Run Back Home - *15*
Runaway Train [CH] - *222*
Running Out - *113*
Sad Goodbye - *191*
Sad Sun [CH] - *226*
Sadie - *185*
Sadness Of Tomorrow - *143*
Sandy - *31*
Satisfied [BP] - *79*
Save Your Pity [CH] - *217*
Say O.K. (Say Ole You Love Me) - *187*
Send Her To Me [BP] - *77*
September, November, December - *191*
Shake A Tail Feather [BP] - *84*
Shake Hands (and Come Out Crying) - *104, 147*
She Couldn't Figure My Reason [CH] - *217*
She Said Yeah - *64*

Sheila - *18*
Sherry - *18*
Sho' Miss You Baby - *53*
Show Me - *122*
Silas - *235*
Silence Is Golden - *97, 113, 147, 238, 244, 245, 248, 251, 253, 269, 279*
Silence Is Golden [BP] - *84*
Silence Is Golden [CH] - *221, 223, 228*
Sing Sorta Swingle - *113*
Slowdown - *270*
So Much To Say - *256*
Someone, Someone - *42, 56, 195, 242, 245, 251, 269, 279*
Someone, Someone [BP] - *81, 83, 84, 87*
Sometimes When We Touch [BP] - *84*
Song For Andre - *199*
Song Of A Broken Heart - *56*
Sorry (Lyn's Song) [AB] - *209*
South Street - *28*
Speedy Gonzales - *18*
St. Tropez - *251, 256*
St. Tropez [BP] - *84*
Star In A Rock 'N' Roll Band - *84*
Story For The Boys - *184*
Stranger On The Shore - *18*
Suddenly Winter - *111, 113*
Suddenly You Love Me - *118, 147, 238, 245, 269, 279*
Suddenly You Love Me [CH] - *221, 223*
Sunday Monday Tuesday [CH] - *214*
Sunny Afternoon [CH] - *228*

Sunshine Games - *113*
Superdrain [AB] - *212*
Swinging On A Star - *45*
Take It Easy - *167*
Take It From The Top [AB] - *212*
Tango Torromolinus [AB] - *213*
Taurus [RW] - *208*
Tell Me How You Care - *50*
Ten Lost [CH] - *226*
That Ain't Right - *12*
That Reminds Me Baby [BP] - *75*
That's What Friends Are For [CH] - *226*
The Air That I Breathe [CH] - *223*
The Birth Of Spring - *270*
The Crime Of Life - *256*
The Face [CH] - *216, 221*
The Lady's Got Style - *184*
The Last Word - *244*
The Lights Of Port Royal - *235*
The Lights Of Port Royal [CH] - *221*
The Lion Sleeps Tonight - *127*
The Minstrel Song [CH] - *219*
The More I Look [CH] - *219, 226*
The Other Side Of The Sky [BP] - *75*
The Pain [CH] - *219*
The Right Time - *91*
The Rising Sun - *255*
The Sun Ain't Gonna Shine Anymore [CH] - *228*
The Swiss Maid - *18*
The Uncle Willie - *56*
The Uncle Willie [BP] - *84*
These Days - *181*
Things - *18*
Think Of What You Said - *156*
This Lady [CH] - *226*
Three Bells - *50, 270*

Three Bells [BP] - *83, 84*
Till The End Of The Day [CH] - *223*
Till The End Of Time - *42*
Till The Sun Goes Down - *156*
Time Is On My Side - *53, 56*
Time Is On My Side [BP] - *83*
Times Are Changing [CH] - *215*
Times Have Changed - *56*
Tired Of Waiting [CH] - *223*
To Love Somebody [BP] - *84*
Tomorrow Never Comes [BP] - *75*
Too Late (To Be Saved) - *172*
Too Many Fish In The Sea - *113*
Travelling Circus - *127*
Treat Her Like A Woman [BP] - *77*
Tremedley - *237*
Trifle Tower - *199*
Try Me - *161*
Turn On With Thee - *156*
Twelve Steps To Love - *48*
Twenty Miles - *28*
Twist and Shout - *22, 28, 253, 269, 279*
Twist and Shout [BP] - *81, 83, 84, 87*
Twist Little Sister - *11, 28*
Twistin' The Night Away - *18*
Up, Down, All Around - *138*
Used To Be That Girl [CH] - *226*
Victoria Boots - *199*
Wait A Minute [DM] - *207*
Wait For Me - *163*
Wakamaker - *174*
Wake Me I Am Dreaming [DM] - *207*
Walk Away Renee - *121*
Walk Right Back [CH] - *216*
Walk Right In - *47*

Walkin' My Cat Named Dog - *68*
Want Your Love [BP] - *83*
Wardance [AB] - *212*
Waterloo Sunset [CH] - *223*
We Know - *22, 28*
Well Alright - *61*
Well, Who's That - *56*
What A State I'm In - *92, 104*
What Can I Do - *151*
What Do Women Most Desire [BP] - *77*
What Do You Want With My Baby - *56*
When I'm With Her - *104*
When We Dance [AB] - *212*
Why Can't You Love Me - *24*
Willow Tree - *163*
Willy and The Hand Jive - *127*
Wilma Lou [CH] - *216*
Windows Are Nice - *199*
Windows Are Nice [AB] - *209*
Witchcraft - *186*
Words - *240*
Yakety Yak - *45*

Yellow River - *152, 154, 246, 269, 279*
Yellow River [CH] - *228*
Yodel Ay - *176*
You - *104*
You Can Get It - *242*
You Can't Sit Down - *56*
You Can't Sit Down [BP] - *84*
You Can't Touch Sue - *184*
You Don't Have To Say You Love Me - *270*
You Don't Know Like I Know - *122*
You Don't Love Me Any More (And I Can Tell) - *28*
You Don't Own Me - *53*
You Gotta Know - *189*
You Know - *55*
You Really Got Me [CH] - *223*

[AB] = Alan Blakley solo
[BP] = Brian Poole solo
[CH] = Chip Hawkes solo
[DM] = Dave Munden solo
[RW] = Rick Westwood solo

SOURCES & BIBLIOGRAPHY

'50 Years of Reminiscing with Len 'Chip' Hawkes & Brian Poole' (DVD, 2013)

'BBC Sessions' sleeve notes and audio interviews, 2004

'Boxed' booklet, 2000

'Christie: The history of Yellow River' (Dutch TV documentary), 2001

'Even The Bad Times Are Good' by Heinz Dietz, 2008

'Live At The BBC 1964-67' sleeve notes and audio interviews, 2013

'Melody Maker' interview, 1970

'Rave' magazine, 1967

'Record Collector' Brian Poole interview with Alan Clayson, 1996

'The Complete CBS Recordings 1966-72' booklet, 2020

www.45cat.com

www.beat-magazine.co.uk

www.brianpoole.com

www.but-my-eyes-still-see.tumblr.com

www.carmenyatescelebrityinterviews.jimdofree.com

www.celebrityradio.biz

www.chiphawkes.net

www.chiphawkes.org

www.discogs.com

www.essexlive.news

www.express.co.uk

www.facebook.com/groups/TheTremeloes

www.facebook.com/LenChipHawkes

www.jeffchristie.com

www.jpost.com

www.missingepisodes.proboards.com

www.phoenixfm.com

www.secondhandsongs.com

www.somethingelsereviews.com

www.southwalesargus.co.uk

www.theguardian.com

www.the-searchers.co.uk

www.the-shortlisted.co.uk

www.thetremeloes.co.uk

www.tremeloes.co.uk

www.tremeloes.oldiemusic.de

www.tvpopdiaries.co.uk

OTHER BOOKS BY PETER CHECKSFIELD

'Channelling The Beat! The Ultimate Guide to UK '60s Pop on TV' (2018)

'Look Wot They Dun! The Ultimate Guide to UK Glam Rock on TV in The '70s' (2019)

'The Beatles - Tell Me What You See: The Ultimate Guide to John, Paul, George & Ringo on TV and Video' (2019)

'Let's Stomp! American Music that made The British Beat 1954 - 1967' (2020)

'Untamed Youth! The Ultimate Visual Guide to 50s & 60s Rock & Pop at The Movies' (2020)

'Having A Rave Up! The Definitive Guide to British Beat Albums in The Sixties' (2021)

'Shindig! America's Flat-Out Ass-Kickin' Rock 'n' Roll TV Show' (2021)

'Top of the Pops: The Lost Years Rediscovered 1964-1975' (2021)

'Top of the Pops: The Punk & New Romantic Years 1976-1986' (2022)

'Christmas Everyday! Glam Rock Albums 1970-1976' (2022)

'Undercover: 500 Rolling Stones Cover Versions That You Must Hear!' (2022)

'Jerry Lee Lewis - Breathless! Every Song From Every Session, 1952-2022' (2023)

'The Searchers - Crazy Dreams! Every Song From Every Session, 1963-2023' (2023)

www.peterchecksfield.com

ABOUT THE AUTHOR

Peter Checksfield is the author of more than a dozen critically-acclaimed books on music, including publications on 'Top of the Pops', 'Shindig!', The Beatles, The Rolling Stones, The Searchers and Jerry Lee Lewis. His books have been positively reviewed by 'Record Collector', 'Shindig!', 'Now Dig This!', 'Mojo', 'Ugly Things', 'Wired Up!', 'Rock 'n' Reel', 'The Beat', 'Folkrocks' and many more, and he's been interviewed on radio shows in the UK, USA and Australia.

email: peterchecksfieldauthor@gmail.com